T0334542

FICTIONALITY

Does fiction enhance reality, or threaten our sense of what is real? What, if anything, is special about experiencing fictional works and worlds? Today we speak casually of parallel universes and virtual reality; how much do we really know about what these phenomena involve?

In *Fictionality*, Karen Petroski explains how philosophers and literary theorists have approached these questions in the Western literary tradition, from Greek antiquity to the present day. The book introduces readers to both long-running and contemporary debates about:

- The value and dangers of engagement with fiction;
- The origins of fictional artworks, especially literary works, in Western literature;
- The role played by imagination in engaging with fiction;
- The peculiarities of fictional "worlds";
- The structure of linguistic reference within fictional artworks;
- The functions of fictionality in non-linguistic artworks such as film and television;
- The role played by fictionality outside artworks, for example, in philosophy, law, and politics.

Fictionality offers an accessible and comprehensive introduction to this field of increasing critical and theoretical interest. Bringing together theoretical insights from a variety of perspectives, it will be an essential resource for anyone studying fictionality.

Karen Petroski is Professor at the Saint Louis University School of Law, USA. She earned a Ph.D. in Literature before attending law school, practicing law, and then teaching. She has published a number of works on fictionality, including *Fiction and the Languages of Law* (Routledge, 2018).

THE NEW CRITICAL IDIOM

SERIES EDITOR: JOHN DRAKAKIS, UNIVERSITY OF STIRLING

The New Critical Idiom is an invaluable series of introductory guides to today's critical terminology. Each book:

- provides a handy, explanatory guide to the use (and abuse) of the term;
- offers an original and distinctive overview by a leading literary and cultural critic;
- relates the term to the larger field of cultural representation.

With a strong emphasis on clarity, lively debate and the widest possible breadth of examples, *The New Critical Idiom* is an indispensable approach to key topics in literary studies.

Pastoral
Second edition
Terry Gifford

Fantasy
Lucie Armitt

Intertextuality
Third edition
Graham Allen

Literary Geography
Sheila Hones

Metafiction
Yaël Schlick

Ecocriticism
Third edition
Greg Garrard

Fictionality
Karen Petroski

For more information about this series, please visit: www.routledge.com/The-New-Critical-Idiom/book-series/SE0155

FICTIONALITY

Karen Petroski

Routledge
Taylor & Francis Group
LONDON AND NEW YORK

Designed cover image: MirageC, Getty

First published 2023
by Routledge
4 Park Square, Milton Park, Abingdon, Oxon OX14 4RN

and by Routledge
605 Third Avenue, New York, NY 10158

Routledge is an imprint of the Taylor & Francis Group, an informa business

British Library Cataloguing-in-Publication Data
A catalogue record for this book is available from the British Library

Library of Congress Cataloging-in-Publication Data
Names: Petroski, Karen, author.
Title: Fictionality / Karen Petroski.
Description: Abingdon, Oxon ; New York, NY : Routledge, 2023. |
Series: The new critical idiom |
Includes bibliographical references and index. |
Identifiers: LCCN 2022046539 (print) | LCCN 2022046540 (ebook) |
ISBN 9780367752316 (hardback) | ISBN 9780367752293 (paperback) |
ISBN 9781003161585 (ebook)
Subjects: LCSH: Fiction—History and criticism—Theory, etc. |
Fictions, Theory of. | LCGFT: Literary criticism.
Classification: LCC PN3331 .P47 2023 (print) |
LCC PN3331 (ebook) | DDC 808.3–dc23/eng/20230131
LC record available at https://lccn.loc.gov/2022046539
LC ebook record available at https://lccn.loc.gov/2022046540

ISBN: 978-0-367-75231-6 (hbk)
ISBN: 978-0-367-75229-3 (pbk)
ISBN: 978-1-003-16158-5 (ebk)

DOI: 10.4324/9781003161585

Typeset in Times New Roman
by Newgen Publishing UK

CONTENTS

SERIES EDITOR'S PREFACE

The New Critical Idiom is a series of introductory books that seeks to extend the lexicon of literary terms, in order to address the radical changes which have taken place in the study of literature during the last decades of the twentieth century. The aim is to provide clear, well-illustrated accounts of the full range of terminology currently in use, and to evolve histories of its changing usage.

The current state of the discipline of literary studies is one where there is considerable debate concerning basic questions of terminology. This involves, among other things, the boundaries which distinguish the literary from the non-literary; the position of literature within the larger sphere of culture; the relationship between literatures of different cultures; and questions concerning the relation of literary to other cultural forms within the context of interdisciplinary studies.

It is clear that the field of literary criticism and theory is dynamic and heterogeneous. The present need is for individual volumes on terms which combine clarity of exposition with an adventurousness of perspective and a breadth of application. Each volume will contain as part of its apparatus some indication of the direction in which the definition of particular terms is likely to move, as well as expanding the disciplinary boundaries within which some of these terms have been traditionally contained. This will involve some re-situation of terms within the larger field of cultural representation and will introduce examples from the area of film and the modern media in addition to examples from a variety of literary texts.

ACKNOWLEDGMENTS

Sincere thanks to the team at Routledge who have helped to make this book possible: John Drakakis and Zoe Meyer for their support for the project at the proposal stage; Polly Dodson, Chris Ratcliffe, Karen Raith, Fiona Hudson Gabuya, and Aishwarya M for their patience and assistance throughout the writing, submission, and editing process; and John Drakakis again for his editorial feedback and suggestions, which have helped to improve the content of the book immensely. Thanks also to TJ Bross for his support throughout the writing and editing process.

INTRODUCTION

Everyone knows what fiction is. It is what is made up, make-believe, pretend. Fiction is the opposite of fact. Assumptions like these have been common in English-language literary and cultural criticism for most of the past few centuries. Critics assume that readers know what kinds of literary work count as fictional and that readers are not interested in examining the characteristic of fictionality as such. Instead, critics have focused mainly on other aspects of literary form and on how fictional works represent (or do not represent) the real world.

Public attitudes toward fiction have been similar. In much public and popular discourse, the term "fiction" functions as a synonym for "falsehood." In articles promising to separate fact from fiction, journalists use the term to announce the unmasking of deception. These usages presuppose an incompatibility between fiction and truth, as well as between fiction and fact, but seldom examine the concepts being contrasted. "Fiction" seems to be one of those terms—others might include "rights" and "identity"—that are central to modern discourse precisely because their meaning is rarely examined closely.

DOI: 10.4324/9781003161585-1

As this introduction will shortly explain, these assumptions about fiction have in one form or another been part of European culture since antiquity. Over the past half-century, however, scholars in several fields have questioned the view that there is little to say about fictionality. The work of these scholars has generated an increasingly interconnected body of theoretical arguments. This refocusing of critical attention has fostered a scholarly literature mostly created by humanists but valuable as well to research in other fields such as psychology (see, e.g., Starr 2015).

Many of these theorists have been driven not just by curiosity about a comparatively neglected topic but also by a sense that the topic might be growing more important in practical terms. Publications in English have been using the term "fiction" more often. A frequency search in Google's digital library shows that usage of the word remained fairly stable from 1800 to 1960 and then began a gradual increase to a rate of usage, as of 2022, of twice that of the earlier norm. Popular cultural products of the past half-century or so in the West have also increasingly addressed questions of representation and existence similar to those that many scholars of fictionality examine. From *The French Lieutenant's Woman* (1969) to *The Matrix* (1999) and *Watchmen* (2020), any number of popular narratives have thematized the relationship between narrative or experiential artifacts and the realm of represented existence that such artifacts can disclose. This popular-culture preoccupation does not necessarily indicate comfort with fictionality. If anything, the endurance of these themes in popular culture might be a sign of the continued difficulty of articulating the contours of the phenomena in question, coupled with a persistent sense that they might, for some reason, be growing increasingly important.

The practical stakes involved in understanding what counts as fictional are also becoming more and more evident. Contemporary public discourse is full of denunciations of alternative facts and fake news. Public figures routinely label opponents' positions "fiction." But it has remained challenging for commentators to explain exactly when and why it matters whether a politician is lying, mistaken, or engaging in fictionalizing when that politician accuses a news outlet of peddling fictions or a hoax. It can seem that the closer one looks at fictionality, the more elusive the concept becomes.

AMBIVALENCE ABOUT FICTIONALITY

Anxiety about deception and representational art is as old as Western civilization. Such concerns have been especially acute with regard to representational art that does not aspire to represent real-world events or people. So it would be inaccurate to say that concern over fiction is a modern development. What is relatively new is a more focused scholarly interest in understanding the characteristics of fictionality itself.

Early theorists of aesthetic representation often considered the relative harmfulness or utility of various kinds of representation. These discussions tended to address the potential effects of contact with imagined narratives rather than the features characteristic of such narratives. As Chapter 1 will explore in more detail, Plato's concern with the effects of representations on viewers and readers played an important role in his critical approach to mimesis, or representation, which has cast a long shadow over subsequent Western approaches to representational art. (I will treat the term "mimesis" as a synonym for "representation," even though this treatment simplifies the concept slightly. For key discussions of mimesis, see Potolsky 2006, Auerbach 1953, and Walton 1990.) Aristotle's *Poetics*, in contrast to Plato's dialogues, approached representational verbal art, especially theater, as valuable in its own right, at least if executed appropriately. Saint Augustine (354–430 CE), too, complicated Plato's account. In his *Soliloquies*, for example, Augustine distinguished between the fallacious (*fallax*) and the fabulous (*mendax*): the former "intends to deceive, while the latter does not," and thus the former is less defensible than the latter (Nelson 1973: 14; Eden 1986: 119–21). This familiar distinction between the intentionally deceptive and the overtly made-up, as well as Augustine's focus on the speaker's intent as a basis for the distinction, are echoed in most subsequent theoretical discussions of fiction.

A fictional narrative usually represents people and events; this representation might be more or less vivid or true to life, and the people and events it represents might be more or less worthy of imitation or admiration. Plato, Aristotle, and their followers were concerned mainly with the liveliness and exemplary value of fiction. Medieval poetics, in contrast, did not tend to address such issues, or indeed to examine representation more generally from a theoretical perspective

(Nelson 1973: 28). But authors of medieval romance were quite self-conscious about these issues, as Chapter 2 will explain. And medieval theologians and logicians were keenly interested in another facet of fictionality: its peculiar relationship with *existence* (Greene 2014), rather than its departure from lived experience. This kind of puzzle has retained the interest of philosophers down to the present day: if a fictional narrative mentions a man, does that man exist? In one sense, yes: the represented man exists as a representation of a man. In another sense, no: the represented man is not a real, flesh-and-blood man. The existence of non-tangible entities was of great interest to medieval scholars exploring questions of divinity and incarnation and their relationship to belief and truth. Their interests led these thinkers to frame discussions of imaginary beings in new ways. For example, in his *Glosses on Porphyry*, Peter Abelard (1079–1142) wrote, "Neither does the conception of a nonexistent thing make us 'deceived,' but rather the belief added to it. For even if I think of a rational crow, yet if I do not believe in it I am not deceived" (quoted in Greene 2014: 24).

Debates over the value and dangers of fictions grew especially heated in the sixteenth and seventeenth centuries (see, e.g., Nelson 1973: 38–115; Doody 1996: 258–73). Perhaps the best-known defense of aesthetic invention and representation from this period is Sir Philip Sidney's *Defence of Poetry* (ca. 1580), containing the famous apothegm that the "poet... nothing affirmeth and therefore never lieth" (1966: 52). In his treatise, Sidney was defending and praising not just what we would now think of as poetry but more generally all invented narrative, including antique prose novels, plays, and Aesop's fables (24, 33, 34, 51–53). Throughout the *Defence*, Sidney "openly acknowledge[s]" his debt to Aristotle's *Poetics* and also clearly harks back to Augustine's distinction between *fallax* and *mendax* (Eden 1986: 4, 159, 173). Like Aristotle and Augustine, Sidney stresses the practical and exemplary value of poetry, claiming for it "the... task of feigning images designed to inspire the will to virtuous action" (Eden 1986: 153). Sidney argued against the view that poetry—or fiction—was inherently dangerous.

But not all writers shared Sidney's view. William Nelson has suggested that the early seventeenth century saw the beginning of a growing "consciousness of fiction as frivolous and vain," a kind of backlash against what had been, in the sixteenth century, a much more adventurous attitude toward fiction (1973: 92). Works exemplifying this earlier adventurousness include Thomas More's *Utopia* (1516), Rabelais's *Gargantua and Pantagruel* (1532–64), and any number of increasingly self-referential romance narratives, culminating in Miguel de Cervantes's *Don Quixote* (1605–15), to name only examples in prose. In his work on the "fictive," Wolfgang Iser also presupposed a seventeenth- and early eighteenth-century cultural hostility to fiction in European letters (1993: 164).

There is no historical or theoretical consensus about when fiction first appeared in Western culture, but it is clear that the eighteenth century was a key period for the development of the kind of artifact that the term "fiction" now most readily calls to mind: the realistic novel in prose, heralded by works such as Daniel Defoe's *Robinson Crusoe* (1719), Samuel Richardson's *Pamela* (1740), and Henry Fielding's *Joseph Andrews* (1742; see generally Watt 1957; Gallagher 1994). Eighteenth-century critics sometimes moralized about the dangers of fiction in this form, especially in the hands of female readers. Samuel Johnson (1709–84) exemplified this moralizing attitude toward the new realistic novel alongside an awareness that such novels belong, in some sense, in the same category as more fantastic narratives. In one of his early *Rambler* essays, Johnson contrasts contemporary novels, which "exhibit life in its true state," with "works of fiction" of an earlier age, filled with "incredibilities" (1750: 174). Johnson notes that these earlier works—chiefly romances—placed readers "in very little danger of making any application" of the represented people and events to the readers' own lives (175). Contemporary novels, in contrast, "are the entertainment of minds unfurnished with ideas," that is, young people (175), and, because of the novels' realism and readers' naïveté, apt to be likened by these readers to their own circumstances. For this reason, Johnson urges novelists to represent virtuous characters and actions. His argument echoes Plato's grudging acceptance of some mimetic art while reversing the hierarchy of representational value suggested by Plato, through acknowledgment of some potential merit in incredible, unrealistic representations.

Johnson's Preface to his edition of Shakespeare's plays (1765) also contained a subtly different critical perspective on fiction. Part of Johnson's purpose in this preface was to refute critics who faulted Shakespeare's plays for failing to observe two of the three classic theatrical unities (of action, place, and time). According to classicist theorists, good dramatic art had to observe these unities on pain of losing audience engagement. Audiences would not, these critics argued, *believe* a dramatic representation of action that asked viewers to imagine they were watching first a scene set in Cairo and then one set in France, on the very same stage, just minutes later. In his Preface, Johnson proposed that the unities, at least of space and time, were in fact not necessary for audience engagement or great drama:

> The reflection that strikes at the heart [of the audience of a Shakespeare play] is not that the evils before us are real evils, but that they are evils to which we ourselves may be exposed. If there be any fallacy [in the audience's attitude], it is not that we fancy the players [unhappy] but that we fancy ourselves unhappy for a moment; but we rather lament the possibility than suppose the presence of misery, as a mother weeps over her babe when she remembers that death may take it from her. The delight of tragedy proceeds from our consciousness of fiction; if we thought murders and treasons real, they would please us no more.
>
> (432)

Later chapters of this book will show how Johnson's focus on audience experience and self-awareness anticipates observations by many later theorists of fiction and fictionality.

Johnson's commentary on fiction was insightful and influential but limited. Not until the end of the eighteenth century would any English-language theorist focus explicitly on fiction in its own right and under that name. One harbinger of a more sweeping and intensive concern with fiction appears in the work of Friedrich Schiller (1759–1805), whose *Aesthetic Letters* (1801)—to be discussed more fully in Chapter 1—praised the creation of semblance and the activity of play as the highest expressions of human freedom.

Writing around the same time as Schiller but from a very different perspective, Jeremy Bentham (1748–1832) developed a theory of fictions that also anticipated much subsequent thought on the subject, if only indirectly. Bentham's posthumously assembled notes on fiction began as a work preparatory to his planned treatises on legal reform. The notes had been published in Bentham's collected works during the nineteenth century, but only in scattered form. The linguist C.K.

Ogden reassembled the notes into a *Theory of Fictions*, first published in 1912. Bentham regarded fiction as a pervasive phenomenon; he maintained that a great deal of language dealt in fictions, even when describing real events. More specifically, Bentham argued that any noun referring to an abstraction, such as "motion" or "duty," referred to what he called a "fictitious entity," or "an entity to which, though by the grammatical form of the discourse employed in speaking of it, existence be ascribed, yet in truth and reality existence is not meant to be ascribed" (Ogden 1932: 12). Fictitious entities—the referents of nouns appearing to name abstractions—"owe their existence" to "language alone" (15). Bentham distinguished this kind of fiction from the fictions of "poets, priests, and lawyers" (18). What Bentham called "logical fictions," he considered "indispensable," if logically troubling (15). The "fictions of the poet," only loosely related to these logical-linguistic fictions, were, according to Bentham, "pure of insincerity" but not of significant further interest (18). He was, in contrast, highly critical of legal and religious fictions, which he described as having been used "to deceive, and by deception, to govern" (18).

Bentham's concern with identifying a dimension of fiction in practical and scientific discourse has been shared by many subsequent theorists of fictionality. At the end of the nineteenth century, for example, Hans Vaihinger (1911) examined the philosophical and scientific uses of fiction, and more specifically, the "as-if" attitude characteristic of fiction. (Not coincidentally, C.K. Ogden also translated Vaihinger's *Philosophy of As-If* into English in 1924.) As Chapter 7 in particular will explain, throughout the twentieth century, scholars in a variety of disciplines—not just criticism and theory—followed in Bentham's and Vaihinger's footsteps by explicitly training their attention on fiction and fictionality as topics of interest in their own right with implications beyond aesthetics.

Some of this more recent work lacks the evaluative and moralizing concerns characteristic of nearly all earlier writing on representation and make-believe. But some philosophical work has remained critical of fiction, for example, by characterizing fictional discourse in a Benthamite way as logically defective and linguistically aberrant. Although his focus was not mainly on fiction, the mid-twentieth-century philosopher of language J.L. Austin echoed this criticism in diluted form. Austin's discussion of performative utterances is fairly well known. Performative utterances are uses of language that do not simply communicate information but also and at the same time accomplish some act. Classic examples cited by Austin are a ship christening and the pronouncement of marriage vows. He defined a performative utterance as "a kind of utterance which looks like a statement and grammatically, I suppose, would be classed as a statement, which is not nonsensical, and yet is not true or false" either (1961: 235). Instead of being true or false, such utterances are according to Austin either successful or unsuccessful, either achieving the act in question or failing to do so. One of the ways that a performative utterance might be unsuccessful or infelicitous would be for the person making the utterance not to do so seriously:

> [W]e can issue an utterance of any kind whatsoever, in the course, for example, of acting a play or making a joke or writing a poem—in which case it would not be seriously meant and we shall not be able to say that we seriously performed the act concerned. If the poet says "Go and catch a falling star" or whatever it may be, he doesn't seriously issue an order. Considerations of this kind apply to any utterance at all, not only performatives.
>
> (241)

Austin made the implication of this observation for fiction even clearer in his book *How to Do Things With Words* (1962), where he observed:

> [A] performative utterance will... be *in a peculiar way* hollow or void if said by an actor on the stage, or if introduced in a poem, or spoken in soliloquy. This applies in a similar manner to any... utterance—a sea change in... circumstances [affects the force of the utterance]. Language in such circumstances is in special ways—intelligibly—used not seriously, but in a way *parasitic* on its normal use—ways which fall under the doctrine of the *etiolation* of language. All this we are *excluding* from consideration.
>
> (22; emphases in original)

As this passage makes clear, Austin's main concern in these papers was not to analyze fictional discourse. Like many other philosophers of language to be discussed in the following pages, he used literary examples mainly to illustrate points relating to more core philosophical concerns: in Austin's case, the ways in which language use can fall short of its intended goals, as well as the connection between truth and the meaningfulness or effectiveness of language. For Austin, one of the chief ingredients of any successful speech act was the proper context, and in particular, the proper kind of intention on the part of the speaker of the speech act. John Searle, a student of Austin, did offer a philosophical account of fictional discourse in a highly influential paper, "The Logical Status of Fictional Discourse" (1975). Searle began the paper by noting the "paradox" that "words... in a fictional story have their ordinary meanings and yet the rules that attach to those words... and define their meanings are not complied with" (319). One of these normal rules of language is that the words in a descriptive sentence refer to real-world entities. In a fictional narrative, this normal referential function of nouns is "not complied with." Searle resolved the paradox by concluding that the author of a passage of fictional discourse "is pretending... to make an assertion, or acting as if she were making an assertion" (324). Alternatively, he observed, one could say that the author of a fictional narrative is "engaging in a nondeceptive pseudo-performance which constitutes pretending to recount to us a series of events" (325). Like Austin, but much more directly, Searle analyzes fictional discourse as a derivative practice, a repurposing of ordinary language that renders fictional discourse unable to function according to the normal rules of language. Although Searle did not explicitly conclude that fictional discourse is inferior to ordinary language, his account does suggest that fictional discourse is impoverished in comparison with ordinary language use.

During the early and mid-1970s, the French poststructuralist theorist Jacques Derrida delivered and then published an essay, "Signature Event Context," that criticized some of the premises of Austin's speech-act theory and its implications (1981: 309–30). This essay, like much of Derrida's work, is a critique of Western philosophical approaches to language, here discussed as "communication." Derrida repeatedly points out how these theories identify spoken language as the paradigmatic form of linguistic communication and written language as secondary to, and derivative of, spoken language (310–13).

He argues that we might fruitfully regard writing as a more basic and exemplary use of language than speech because writing makes most obvious the potential independence of linguistic meaning from the intentions of a speaker or the attention of a particular listener:

> My "written communication" must... remain legible despite the absolute disappearance of every determined addressee in general in order for it to function as writing, that is, for it to be legible. It must be repeatable—iterable—in the absolute absence of the addressee... A writing that was not structurally legible—iterable—beyond the death of the addressee would not be writing... All writing..., for it to be what it is, must be able to function in the radical absence of every empirically determined addressee in general... What holds for the addressee holds also, for the same reasons, for the sender or the producer.
>
> (315–16)

Derrida seeks to show in this essay that we can justifiably view spoken language as a special case of language in general, including written language, and not vice versa. He praises Austin for breaking, in some ways, with the main stream of Western philosophical writing about language. As noted earlier, Austin defined performative utterances as examples of meaningful and effective speech acts that are not classifiable as true or false (Derrida 1981: 322). To this extent, Austin was resisting conventional philosophical views of the relationship between language and truth. But Derrida criticized Austin's reliance on the speaker's intentions as determining the effectiveness of linguistic acts (323). He also suggested that Austin's arguments depended more profoundly than Austin acknowledged on ostensibly parasitic forms of language use, both written language and fictional or non-serious discourse. Derrida asks readers,

> [I]s not what Austin excludes as anomalous, exceptional, "non-serious," that is, *citation* (on the stage, in a poem, or in a soliloquy), the determined modification of a general citationality—or, rather, a general iterability—without which there would not be even a "successful" performance? Such that... a successful performative is necessarily an "impure" performative.
>
> (1981: 325; see also Moati 2014: 4)

Derrida invited readers of his essay to question Austin's and Searle's implicit denigration of parasitic uses. He did not quite contend that "there is no difference between fictional and nonfictional language" (Alfino 1991: 147). Rather, he argued that "if we simply put off fictional discourse until later, as parasitic discourse, our account of nonfictional discourse might be impoverished and in error" (Farrell 1988: 63).

John Searle published a response to Derrida, "Reiterating the Differences," in which he argued that Derrida had misunderstood Austin, and Derrida in turn responded to Searle's criticism with a further essay later published as part of the book *Limited Inc.* (1988; see Moati 2014: 4–5). Most commentators on the Searle-Derrida debate seem to consider it a draw (see, e.g., Farrell 1988: 59; Halliwell 2002: 374). And indeed the question of how fictional discourse is related to normal or natural uses of language remains a topic of active debate among literary theorists, linguists, and philosophers. Some of the more recent accounts of fiction and fictionality that later chapters will consider deny any meaningful difference between fictional discourse and ordinary discourse (see Pratt 1977; Pavel 1986; Ronen 1994; Kintsch 1998; Everett 2013). Others take a more Austinian view, without necessarily arguing that parasitic uses of language are also inferior to ordinary language use (see Genette 1991; Rancière 2017).

Some commentators have suggested, like Derrida, that fictional discourse is in some ways logically and/or developmentally prior to ordinary discourse. In *Why Fiction?* (1999), for example, Jean-Marie Schaeffer explains,

> the birth of the fictional competence is... a very important factor in the process of mastering reality... [F]ar from being a parasitical outgrowth of a connection to the real that would be an originary given, the imaginary activity [and]... access to fictional competence [are]... important factor[s] in the establishment of a stable epistemic structure, that is, in the distinction between the self and reality.
>
> (140)

Schaeffer suggests that the

> deficit of fiction's social legitimacy [from Plato on] seems often to be linked to the fact that it rests on a competence shared by everyone

> and that it activates a mode of representation also shared by everyone, hence the difficulty of making it a mark of social "distinction."
>
> (209–10)

Like Schaeffer, John Gibson presents a quasi-anthropological explanation of the value of fiction. Gibson argues that "literature's relation to the world is… foundational rather than representational, consisting in literature's ability to bring before us narratives that hold in place and give structure to our understanding of large expanses of cultural reality" (2007: 10). He does not argue that fictional and "standard… descriptive speech" are continuous or based on a single "logic" or set of rules (2007: 159 and n.17) but that fictional discourse and, in particular, extended fictional narratives play an essential role in contemporary Western culture.

A distinct kind of recent scholarly defense of fictional discourse has developed within academic philosophy, starting in the 1970s but reminiscent of the positions of Bentham and Vaihinger. Known as "fictionalism," this type of philosophical theory originated with an attempt to revive the thought of Hans Vaihinger (Fine 1993). More recent fictionalist theories do not always acknowledge Vaihinger's model. The theories are united by their characterization of particular areas of thought and/or speech, such as our languages of mathematics and moral judgment, as being "riddled with myths" (Sainsbury 2009: 21) but not therefore invalid or inappropriate. R.M. Sainsbury describes fictionalism in relation to a particular area of theoretical discourse as the view that the concepts and terms used in that discourse "do not have to be true to be good" or valuable (2). Fictionalist accounts of particular topics are as hotly debated as any other philosophical topics. The existence of these philosophical debates is evidence that the perennial disagreement about whether "fictional" is a pejorative term, and whether fictionality is a troubling quality, shows no signs of abating. Indeed, these disagreements are migrating to new areas of intellectual activity.

SOME KEY TERMS

Some recent treatments of fiction and fictionality have been concerned with terminology: for example, with questions about when it is appropriate to use the term "fiction" rather than "fictionality," or what the difference is between the fictional and the fictive (see, e.g., Fludernik 2018). While the following chapters will sometimes note such issues, terminological clarification is not the main aim of this book. That said, some discussion of terminology will help to suggest the scope of the following chapters.

The title of this book is *Fictionality*. According to the *Oxford English Dictionary* (OED), this term refers to the "state or quality of being fictional" and was first used in this sense in 1883. The noun **fiction**, of course, was used well before this time and in a number of different senses dating back to Francis Bacon and Thomas Hobbes. Michael Wood has traced the use of the term "fiction" to the late fourteenth century and notes that "Caxton in 1483 uses 'fyction and fayning' together, perhaps thinking of their common Latin root," *fingere*, meaning "to devise or fabricate" (Wood 1993: xiii–xiv). The OED records that the noun "fiction" was used as long ago as the sixteenth century to designate the "species of literature which is concerned with the narration of imaginary events and the portraiture of imaginary characters," although this use became more common after 1750.

The following chapters will address mainly the category of literary fiction identified by the OED—aesthetic artifacts, particularly linguistic artifacts, that contain narrations of imaginary events—as well as the quality or qualities of fictionality exhibited by such artifacts. Chapter 7, however, will consider another sense of "fiction" noted by the OED: the "action of 'feigning' or inventing imaginary incidents, existences, states things, etc., whether for the purpose of deception or otherwise." This sense of the term is not limited to literary activity or even artistic activity generally: as Bentham and Vaihinger explained, we generate and rely on fictions in other areas of activity too.

Some recent scholarship has urged scholars to turn their attention to *fictionality* as such, rather than to fiction: to the quality or characteristic, rather than the category (e.g., Dawson 2015; Nielsen, Phelan, & Walsh 2015; Fludernik 2018; Nielsen 2019). One positive result of such a shift in focus might be to redirect scholarly attention away from the classification of texts (see, e.g., Roberts 1972) and toward investigating the different ways fictionality might work within a variety of artifacts we might otherwise place into different categories. This book follows these scholars' suggestions, focusing mainly on how the quality of fictionality functions, rather than on what works belong in the category fiction.

The OED lists and defines a number of other terms related to "fiction," including the adjectives **fictive** (first use 1493), **fictitious** (first use 1615), and **fictional** (first use 1843), and also the verb **fictionalize** (first use 1831). The older adjectival terms have been used in several broader and narrower senses. Instead of adopting different definitions for all the adjectival terms, this book will in general use the adjective **fictional** and will seek to distinguish more precise senses through context.

As noted previously, the Latin root of the English word "fiction" is *fingere*, and a number of scholars have investigated the implications of this etymology. Käte Hamburger noted that *fingere* has "radically differing meanings extending from that of shaping or inventing to that of deceitful fabrication" (1973: 55). Hamburger also observed that "the Latin verb [*fingere*], as it was carried over into... modern languages, has exclusively preserved the meaning of falsely alleging, simulating, imitating, and the like," as in the English "feign" and "feint" (56). In contrast, "the [Latin] substantive *fictio*" has "retained both the pejorative and the meliorative meanings of *fingere*..., but in such a way that the latter meaning, which denotes the function of creative forming, does... dominate over the pejorative meaning" (56). One of Hamburger's points is that the association of fiction with deception is not a modern phenomenon but rather an integral part of the development of the term and concept.

Another common way to approach definition of the term "fiction" is through contrast or opposition. Most often, the opposition is between "fiction" and one or both of two groups of associated terms. The first group has to do with **deception**, misrepresentation, and lying; the second relates to matters of **truth**, fact, and reality. A classic definition of "fiction," for example, explains it along Augustinian and Sidneyan lines as involving untrue statements not intended to deceive. The statements in question are untrue in that they do not describe any facts about the world, but they are not intended to mislead the audience and do not do so because the audience is aware of their falsity. Barbara Herrnstein Smith offered a variation on this kind of definition in her 1978 book *On the Margins of Discourse*, observing that in natural discourse, the lying speaker is one who *says* what he *does not mean*, and the false listener is one who interprets an utterance as *meaning* what the speaker *does not say*. But in *fictive* discourse, where that basic assumption [of the speaker meaning what she says] is understood to be suspended, the "liar" and his counterpart "false listener" are those who do not acknowledge the suspension or who do not permit it to be in force.

(114)

Similarly, Jean-Marie Schaeffer distinguishes between deception and fiction based not on the intention of the speaker but on the relation between speaker and listener: unlike lies, fiction "is not based on an agonistic relation but… on a principle of cooperation" (1999: 46). More recently, Kathleen Stock (2017) has offered another variation on this formula. She distinguishes between deception and fiction by identifying the difference "between, on the one hand, true or false utterances intended only to be believed, and on the other, true or false utterances intended to be imagined, whether or not they are also intended to be believed" (157).

These approaches to defining "fiction" depend on an understanding of what is meant by "truth," "falsity," or "fact," but these terms are as vexed and slippery as "fiction" itself, if not more so. The following chapters will take a roughly constructivist view of the concepts in question. In other words, the discussion to come will assume that what counts as true and factual is at least in part a matter of convention and consensus (cf., e.g., Daston & Galison 2007; Gibson 2007; Fludernik 2018). The idea is not that truth and factuality are subjective or radically unstable but rather that what counts as truth or fact—what aspects of experience people agree on as being true—may differ from time to time and from culture to culture, and may also differ for different groups within a single culture at any one time.

One implication of this observation is that the group of aesthetic artifacts that count as **nonfiction**—as not fictional—may also vary from place to place and time to time. As Richard Walsh has put it, the difference between fiction and nonfiction "ultimately rests… upon the contextually assumed presence or absence of a text-independent referential ground" (2007: 128), a world outside the text to which the text refers. Walsh describes "[t]he fiction/nonfiction distinction

[a]s not fundamentally ontological, but pragmatic; not a distinction between referential worlds, but between communicative purposes" (128). Walsh's perspective on the importance of communicative purposes to the fiction/nonfiction distinction is relatively uncontroversial. There is less agreement about whether this generic distinction is *exclusively* pragmatic, as well as whether it is appropriate to disregard ontological questions in studying fictionality. Chapters 3–5 will return to these questions.

A further implication of the view adopted here is that it might be difficult, in relation to a given text, to achieve agreement on whether it is fictional or nonfictional. Dorrit Cohn discusses this issue at length in her 1999 book *The Distinction of Fiction*, in an examination of Marcel Proust's novel/autobiography *Remembrance of Things Past* (58–78). A further implication is that an artifact that is not considered fictional at one point and/or in one cultural context may come to be considered fictional at another time and/or place. The classic example supporting this point is **myth**, usually assumed to have been treated as in some sense true in its original context, but understood by later audiences as invented. R.M. Sainsbury (2009) describes myths as "counterexamples to the claim that fictionality depends upon being produced with fictive intentions" (21).

As the etymological information at the beginning of this section suggested, the use of "fiction" as a generic marker for a category of literary works is a relatively recent development. Dorrit Cohn has suggested that the critical practice of equating fiction with invented prose narrative originated with Henry James in *The Art of Fiction*, published in 1884 (1999: 11). The reduction of the term "fiction" to **narrative**, or the assimilation of the two concepts, has been a recent topic of critical discussion among theorists of fiction and fictionality. Paul Dawson has noted a "tendency to conflate narrative with fiction" among literary scholars as well as a perhaps more pernicious trend toward "conflation of narrativity and fictionality" that is "symptomatic of a broad postmodern challenge to knowledge both within narratology and in the broader narrative turn," as in the work of historian Hayden White (Dawson 2015: 89). Dawson observes that "fictionality can also be deployed in non-narrative modes of discourse," such as jokes, riddles, and cartoons (90). Not all theorists agree; Mari Hatavara and Jarmila Mildorf, for example, have argued that "while fiction always entails narrative, narrative does not necessarily entail fiction. The process of fictionalization… involves features of narrativization, such as the inclusion of experientiality" (2017: 67). Unlike Hatavara and Mildorf, I will not assume that fictionality necessarily implies narrative form. In part, this is because the examples of fictionality in this book will include non-narrative examples such as static images and rhetorical devices deployed in reasoning and argument.

Some such devices have traditionally been distinguished from fiction. Vaihinger distinguished between fiction and **hypothesis** in his 1911 account of "As-If" inquiry. Vaihinger considered both fictions and hypotheses to be equally crucial to invention and discovery. But they are not the same. A fiction, such as the notion of a frictionless plane used in mechanics, is not a proposition to be falsified or verified but a known simplification devised for the sake of analysis and calculation. The fiction gives scientists and engineers the ability to calculate and theorize about certain properties relating to a real plane by treating that plane as if it were a frictionless plane. A hypothesis, on the other hand, is proposed for purposes of testing against reality. According to Vaihinger, a fiction "is a mere auxiliary construct… to be demolished, while the hypothesis looks forward to being definitively established" (1911: 66). Nevertheless, both hypotheses and fictions require the exercise of imagination and a kind of speculation.

Few theorists of fiction have challenged Vaihinger's distinction between fictions and hypotheses. The relation between fiction and **counterfactual** is a little more contested. The OED defines the adjective "counterfactual" as meaning "[p]ertaining to, or expressing, what has not in fact happened, but might, could, or would, in different conditions"; the term is also used as a noun. Counterfactuals, therefore, also involve speculation. They are pervasive in human reasoning, especially in planning and assessments of responsibility (see, e.g., Lewis 1986; Byrne 2005; Byrne 2020), and the philosophical literature on counterfactuals in English is extensive. Theorists of fiction do not agree about how counterfactuals are related to fictions. Monika Fludernik has suggested that "[c]ounterfactuality could… be considered a (partial) synonym of fictivity" (2018: 72). Marie-Laure Ryan (1991) and Simona Zetterberg Gjerlevsen (2019) insist on a basic difference between the fictional and the counterfactual. The pages that follow will take a position closer to Fludernik's. Later chapters will also consider the relationship between fiction and fictionality, on the one hand, and quite a few other allied terms and concepts, on the other, including **make-believe**, **pretense**, and **imagination**.

PLAN OF THE BOOK

The following seven chapters will explore further the manifestations, functions, and implications of fictionality and fictional discourse, mostly in the Western cultural tradition. These explorations focus on how artists, literary theorists, and philosophers have approached these questions but will sometimes also turn to work in other fields, such as rhetoric, history, anthropology, psychology, and cognitive science. The focus will be on critical and theoretical work that is available in English. Readers with facility in other languages, especially French and German, should be aware that a significant body of work in these languages on the topic of fictionality remains untranslated into English.

Chapter 1 examines a group of themes that have recurred in theoretical accounts of fiction from antiquity to the twenty-first century. The four themes addressed are **mimesis**, or representation, often considered a necessary component of fictionality; **imagination**, also by most accounts necessarily tied to the creation and apprehension of fiction; **make-believe**, the core of one of the most influential recent approaches to explaining fictionality; and the **doubling** of aspects and perspectives, another pervasive theme implicitly present in many discussions of fictionality.

Chapter 2 turns to the question of whether artifacts manifesting fictionality first appeared at an identifiable historical point in Western culture. The chapter offers a selective history of historical moments and sets of artifacts that have been identified as originarily fictional, focusing on the early centuries of the Common Era, eleventh- and twelfth-century Western Europe, and eighteenth-century Western Europe, as well as, briefly, the small canon of Chinese "classic novels" dating from the fourteenth century onwards. Several scholars have observed that these moments in history witnessed new kinds of relationships between audiences and written (or printed) narrative, and the chapter also briefly reviews how some commentators have linked fictionality to textuality and literacy.

Chapters 3–5 each focus on a different aspect of fictional literary artifacts. Chapter 3 examines a set of related topics connected to human intentionality, including the phenomenon introduced in Chapter 1 as **seeing-as**; the relation between readers' access to fictional characters' minds and human understanding of other humans' intentions; the question whether the access to fictional characters' minds, or some other formal feature of fictional narrative, should be considered a signpost of fictionality; and the limits of our ability to assume viewpoints significantly different from our own.

Chapter 4 addresses the conceptualization of fictional discourse as enabling visits to alternative **worlds**. This chapter examines the difference between the possible worlds postulated by philosophers since Leibniz (1646–1716) and the fictional worlds projected by readers of fictional narrative. Some recent theorists have questioned the usefulness of the world metaphor in discussion of the experience of apprehending fictional narrative. These skeptics point out that the imagined world of a novel or even a film is distinguishable both from the real, experienced world and the more technical "possible worlds" generated by philosophers. Chapter 4 not only describes these arguments but also examines some of the reasons the world metaphor might remain in such widespread use despite the criticism.

Chapter 5 turns to the topic of **reference**, the preoccupation of many twentieth-century philosophical and literary-theoretical accounts of fiction. This chapter reviews some of the philosophical debates about the referentiality of fictional discourse and literary theorists' slightly different explanations of the functioning of language in fictional discourse. The chapter also considers the so-called "referential turn" in literary theory and criticism from around the 1980s on. Thomas Pavel (1986) and other theorists coined this term to describe critical-theoretic interest in exploring features of fiction arguably neglected by structuralist and poststructuralist criticism: the significance of descriptions of nonfictional objects and personages within narrative fiction, for example, and the nature of audience engagement with fictional characters and places. Chapter 5 also briefly addresses some of the games with reference that creators and audiences of fictional artifacts have played throughout the Western literary tradition.

The final two chapters and the Conclusion extend the above discussion to additional domains. Most, but not all, of the material in

Chapters 1–5 concerns narrative (linguistic) artifacts. Chapter 6 turns to other modes of fictionality, in particular static images, such as painting and photography; performed fictionality in theater; and moving images, including film, animation, and television. The chapter reviews some of the ways scholars have confronted and resolved issues of fictionality in these media. Chapter 7 widens the focus even further to consider fictionality outside the realm of specifically *aesthetic* artifacts. As suggested earlier in this Introduction, characteristics of, and invocations of, fictionality also appear in scholarly and popular discourses aside from those of literature and art. In certain realms, such as religion, law, science, and philosophy, fictionality or its close relatives function in an arguably benign manner. But features associated with fictionality also mark certain dysfunctional states, such as conspiracy theorizing and totalitarian messaging; understanding fictionality can help us think more clearly about the phenomena involved in these and other troubling human practices.

A brief Conclusion looks both forward and back. It considers again the question of the value of fiction addressed in this Introduction, and in particular arguments about the connection between fictionality and humanity. The Conclusion goes on to consider the possible limits of these arguments by examining the question of whether an artificial intelligence could create, recognize, and/or appreciate fiction in a manner similar to human beings. It considers a famous literary artifact associated with the conceptualization of artificial intelligence, Alan Turing's (1950) article proposing an "imitation game" and what later became known as the "Turing test," and it examines what this fiction and its reception might have to tell us about our ability to share the experience of fictionality with others.

1

PERSPECTIVES ON FICTIONALITY

Quite a few recent theoretical discussions of fictionality begin by commenting that the topic deserves more attention than it has received (e.g., Gallagher 2006; Dawson 2015; Nielsen, Phelan, & Walsh 2015). Such comments can be misleading. In fact, a significant volume of scholarship in English does address fictionality. Many such discussions, however, are highly selective in their acknowledgment of precursors, and few of those precursors have achieved canonical status. One's perception of the body of work overall can depend greatly on the research path one takes and the scholarly tradition acknowledged by the first sources one encounters.

This situation poses a challenge for attempts to survey the approaches taken to the topic in Western philosophy and letters. The works involved are too numerous to summarize concisely, and they do not form a clear tradition. These works do, however, tend to return to a small group of themes, without always acknowledging other works addressing the same themes. This chapter is organized around four such themes.

The first theme is *mimesis*, or representation, a concern dating back to Plato. While the Greek word "mimesis" has been translated into English in a variety of ways, I will treat "mimesis" as roughly

DOI: 10.4324/9781003161585-2

synonymous with "representation." Many commentators consider fictionality to be inherently representational, if not inherently narrative in form, although not all representations are necessarily fictional. Mimesis-oriented accounts of fiction tend to focus on the content of fictional representations rather than on characteristics of representation itself. The concern in such accounts is often with the verisimilitude or realism of this content, or alternatively with the risk that an audience will take the content to be a representation of real events. As the Introduction briefly explained, Plato's account of mimesis is generally taken to exemplify this fear of representational deception.

The second theme to be considered below is *imagination.* Imagination-oriented theories of fiction are concerned with the creators and receivers of artifacts exhibiting or containing fictionality. Many theorists who focus on this aspect of fictionality have a more positive view of the phenomenon than some mimesis-oriented theorists do. The imagination-focused tradition arguably began with Aristotle and has reappeared periodically throughout Western literary history, including in the Middle Ages, the Renaissance, and the eighteenth and nineteenth centuries, especially in connection with Romanticism, as well as in twentieth-century accounts of fictionality. This chapter will merely introduce some of the concerns of imagination-focused theorists; later chapters will examine in more detail some of the implications of imagination-focused approaches to fiction.

The third theme considered in the following pages is *play.* While play and pretend activities often involve representation and the use of players' imaginations, many forms of play are also structured activities involving players' engagement with other players and/or with cultural conventions. Viewing fiction as a form of play or pretend can prompt theoretical attention to the cooperative and social dimensions of engagement with fiction, whereas mimesis- and imagination-oriented accounts may disregard these dimensions.

The final theme addressed in this chapter is *doubling.* Each of the perspectives mentioned so far—fiction as mimesis, imagination, and play—can involve the identification of a doubling movement or phenomenon of some kind inherent in fictional artifacts or their appreciation. Mimesis-focused accounts of fiction, for example, commonly address the relationship between an original and an imitation or representation; the representation is in some respects a doubling of the original, in that the representation reproduces important features of the original without being identical with it. Imagination-focused accounts of fiction may consider the gap between reality and created artifact in a more positive light, while still maintaining a concern with the parallels between reality or source material and imagined alternatives. Other imagination-focused theories note how an appreciator's experience of, for example, a fictional narrative involves a virtualization of the appreciator's experience, an attenuation of the spectator's immersion in the real world that could be conceptualized as the appreciator's experiencing another self. Some imagination-based accounts of fiction, as well as most play-based accounts, also specifically address how artifacts that we experience as fictional have two aspects, in that such artifacts can be regarded in two distinct but equally coherent ways. We can, for example, regard a novel as a material and linguistic artifact, or we can regard it as a kind of tool or prop enabling our imagined access to a represented reality. Accounts of representational artifacts as having two aspects in this way arguably date back to antiquity and, one way or another, are part of most contemporary approaches to fictionality, but theorists have not so far paid much attention to this issue as definitive of fictionality or significant in its own right.

Many of the scholars discussed below might not fully agree with the ways in which their theories have been classified in the following pages. I have arranged the discussions in this chapter to progress from simpler to more complex positions that scholars have historically taken on fiction and fictionality and to offer examples of the use of each concept by particular scholars, rather than to group theoretical accounts into particular schools of thought. As a result, the four sections following in this chapter do not form a typology of scholarly approaches to fiction. Several scholars have proposed such typologies. Some proposals partly overlap with the themes discussed here, while other typologies classify theories of fiction based on theorists' disciplinary background and influences, such as literary studies, anthropology, or philosophy (see, e.g., Ryan 1991; Schaeffer 1999; Nielsen, Phelan, & Walsh 2015; Gjerlevsen 2016a; Fludernik 2018, discussing Klauk & Koppe 2014).

MIMESIS

In his book on fictionality, *Why Fiction?*, the French philosopher Jean-Marie Schaeffer notes that the "opacity" of the term *fiction* "has been linked for more than two centuries to that of the term *mimesis*" (1999: 41). This association is arguably much more than two centuries old. As noted in the Introduction to this book, Plato and Aristotle took different views of mimesis, and Plato used the term in a variety of ways himself (see Gill 1993: 40–41; Halliwell 2002: 50; North 2021: 290–91 n.31), but both associated the term with artifacts we might now call fictional. The discussion below will not address the difficulty of the term "mimesis" in itself but will adopt the relatively straightforward definition given by the OED, which defines *mimesis* as "the representation or imitation of the real world in (a work of) art, literature, etc." The term thus designates one part of a two-part system: the imitation itself is one part of the system, but it is defined in part by its relation to the real world (see, e.g., Eden 1986: 31–32).

As noted earlier, Plato's view of representation has often been understood to be a critical view. To oversimplify a bit, he usually described representations as necessarily inferior to the real world, and the real world of experience as itself a kind of impoverished representation of the ideal. Plato's best-known discussion of mimesis appears in Book 10 of the *Republic*. Socrates initially questions Glaucon about the difference between the *idea* of a bed and an actual bed as it exists in the world as a result of a carpenter's skill. Socrates persuades Glaucon that there is a difference between the two and gets Glaucon to concede that no human-made bed can fully capture the idea of a bed. Socrates then introduces the notion of the *reflection* of a natural phenomenon, describing such a reflection as a kind of creation and likening a reflection in a mirror to the craft of a painter who paints a picture of an actual bed made by an artisan (lines 17–75). Many readers have taken this passage to present a hierarchy in which the *idea* of a bed is the most complete and truthful form the bed can take, a form only imperfectly reproduced in any actual physical bed. Any *representation* of a bed, in turn, can be only a partial reproduction of the physical bed.

In his exploration of the aesthetics of mimesis from the work of Plato on, the classicist Stephen Halliwell suggests that it is a mistake to read the passage summarized in the previous paragraph as expressing such a hierarchy. In Halliwell's view, the passage is highly stylized and even "satirical" (2002: 57). He notes also that Book 10 of the *Republic* does not contain any explicit references to "mimetic works as 'imitations of imitations' or 'copies of copies'" (138), even though the passage discussed previously is sometimes summarized as delivering such a view of mimetic artifacts. Halliwell proposes that some of the difficulty of the passage in question results from the "paradox[ical]" quality of "the object of [Plato's] attention—the mimetic capacity of... artworks to impress themselves on minds that know them to be, in some sense, pretenses" (59). Halliwell's reading of the famous passage takes Plato's discussion of mimesis to be at least in part a discussion of fiction, which involves the same paradox, perhaps as a special case of representation.

Whatever Plato's own position might have been, the notion that representational artifacts are inferior both to real life and to practical artifacts has certainly persisted in critiques of fiction ever since. But as suggested in the Introduction, such an anti-mimetic view in Western thought seems almost always to have coexisted with a more pro-mimetic one. At times, as during the Romantic period in northern Europe, the pro-mimetic view has dominated. Samuel Taylor Coleridge (1772–1834), for example, sought in his criticism "to elevate the notion of 'imitation,' in which likeness and difference, art and nature, are joined together, over that of a 'copy'" (Halliwell 2002: 365). Friedrich Schiller (1759–1805), discussed at more length in the third section of this chapter, identified a biological-anthropological human "pleasure in semblance" and "shaping spirit of imitation" at the root of the aesthetic activity he described as the highest realization of human potential (1801: 95).

Although some recent theorists describe modern Western art as post-representational (see, e.g., Morris 2003: 132–36; Rockmore 2013: 233), it would be inaccurate to conclude that aesthetics in general, and accounts of fictionality in particular, no longer consider the representational dimension of fictional artifacts or gestures. Several recent theoretical accounts emphasize the importance of mimesis to an understanding of fictionality. For example, in his *Why Fiction?*, Jean-Marie Schaeffer characterizes fiction as "a game with representations or a ludic usage of representational activity" (1999: 303). Schaeffer stresses "the irreducible formative role of mental *simulation* and *modeling*" (37) in human activity and distinguishes several forms of imitation, mimicry, and modeling, including the mirroring of motor behavior (46–47) and observational learning (51, 53–55). Instead of pointing out the necessarily incomplete or secondary character of imitations or models, Schaeffer observes that modeling, at least, "constitutes a cognitive gain, since it realizes the passage of the observation of a concrete reality to a reconstruction of its structure and underlying processes" (56). Similarly, he describes an imitation as "the production of a relation of resemblance that did not exist in the world before the mimetic act and the existence of which is caused by this act" (69). Schaeffer thus insists on the importance and elemental quality of mimesis as modeling, cautioning against the "tendency to reduce the notion of mimesis either to a procedure of imitation-semblance or... to a technique of representation, not including any 'imitating' component" (173–74).

Another recent defense of mimesis as a key aspect of fictionality appears in Meir Sternberg's 2012 article "Mimesis and Motivation: The Two Faces of Fictional Coherence." This article presents a framework for analyzing literary narrative distinct from contemporary alternatives, such as formalist, rhetorical or neo-Aristotelian, and cognitivist approaches. Sternberg argues for a two-fold "narrative syntax" (359), made up of complementary "mimetic" and "aesthetic" principles of narrative meaningfulness or coherence (e.g., 364). He bases his account of the mimetic "motivational mode" on an Aristotelian notion of mimesis as inherently purposive, always a representation not just of a worldly original but specifically of action sequences that are comprehensible because readers or audience members can see the portrayed action sequence as a "real flow, inviting the reader to perform... the kind of causal reconstructions... to which we are accustomed in the daily business of living" (337). Sternberg identifies this "motivational" representational mode specifically with fiction. He effectively defines fictionality as that quality of a narrative (of any length) that allows or encourages an audience member to make sense of the narrative as conforming to a "law of world-making" (359) and comprehensible as part of a "fictive world" (453).

This view of fictionality identifies the representation of action as a key element of fictionality. Aristotle's focus on the imitation of purposeful human activity as the prototypical form of mimesis is related to his less critical view of representation, relative to Plato (e.g., Eden 1986: 6; Halliwell 2002: 151, 375). Aristotle's conception of mimesis does not focus mainly on the abstract relationship between original and imitation, as Plato did. Instead, Aristotle is most concerned with the role of human action in representational activity, including the creative activities of poets and the imaginative and emotional experiences of audience members in their encounters with poetic artifacts.

IMAGINATION

Although Aristotle did not use the term "imagination," his account of poetry depends on many of the notions now gathered under that heading, including the intentionality (goal orientation and directedness) of human activity; the way that our mental activity can operate independently of any physical activity and yet also direct and enable our physical activity; the human capacity to simulate a variety of mental states; and the relation between our simulations of mental states in imagination and our experiences of emotion. More than a few theorists of fictionality since Aristotle have placed such considerations at the center of their accounts. This section will discuss some of the ways writers have examined this theme from Aristotle onwards, as well as the views of contemporary neo-Aristotelian literary theorists.

As you read the discussion that follows, keep in mind that the term "imagination" is at least as contested as the terms "fiction" and "fictionality" (see, e.g., Liao & Gendler 2020: 3). A further significant challenge in examining writing about the imagination, including the writing of psychologists and other scientists, is that writers and experiment designers frequently draw on their own imaginative experiences as evidence for more general assertions about what the imagination is, and what it can and cannot do. For example, some theorists insist that imaginative activities of some kinds require self-awareness and indeed an ability to represent one's own behavior to oneself, while others deny that any such self-awareness is essential (Liao & Gendler 2020: 24). Theorists also differ in the emphasis they place on different modalities of imagination, such as visual versus spatial imagination. Often, these positions and other similar ones are among the presuppositions of a theoretical or scientific study. But generalizations of this kind should be viewed with caution. At least since the nineteenth century, we have known that individuals' imaginative experiences differ significantly in, for example, the amount of visualization involved (Zeman 2020: 693–94).

Aristotle's comments on representation and imagination in the *Poetics* are no exception. Near the beginning of the *Poetics*, Aristotle observes that "mimetic artists portray people in action" (ch. 2). He observes that "man's natural propensity, from childhood onwards," is "to engage in mimetic activity," and that this is also a source of pleasure (ch. 4). Aristotle suggests that poetic activity (by which he means the creation of a mimesis of action) is a natural outgrowth of these innate tendencies, and he devotes much of the *Poetics* to analysis of the characteristics of the best examples of mimetic experience, especially in tragic drama. Three aspects of Aristotle's account in the *Poetics* were especially influential for later aesthetics. One is his contrast between the representational activity of the poet and that of the historian: "the poet's task is to speak not of events which have occurred, but of the kind of events that *could* occur" (ch. 9). Thus, to Aristotle, "poetry is both more philosophical and more serious than history, since poetry speaks of universals, history of particulars" (ch. 9). This distinction structured much late medieval and Renaissance European writing about verbal art and representation, and although the distinction is less familiar in its details today, it seems to correspond at least roughly to our contemporary distinction between fiction and nonfiction.

Aristotle's examination of representation in tragic drama also considers techniques for promoting vivid mimesis:

> A poet ought to imagine his material to the fullest possible extent while composing his plot-structure.... By seeing them [the actions represented] as vividly as possible in this way—as if present at the very occurrence of the events—he is likely to discover what is [representationally] appropriate.
>
> (ch. 17; see also Halliwell 2002: 168)

This promotion of an imaginative transportation of the self, whether it be the self of the creator of fiction or that of the appreciator of fiction, has also been central to many subsequent accounts of fiction, especially since the eighteenth century. Finally, Aristotle includes as part of his definition of tragedy its affective impact on the audience, its capacity to move viewers to "pity and fear" (chs. 6, 11) as well as "wonder" (ch. 9). Integral to Aristotle's aesthetics, then, are his concerns with the imaginative activity of both poet and audience, the one in creating a "*simulation* of imaginary *actions and events*" (Genette 1991: 6–7, final emphasis added), and the other by imaginatively feeling for and with the personages who emerge from the represented action in a narrative or performance (see Halliwell 2002: 180 n.7). Chapter 3, in particular, will further explain how recent work on fiction has approached the emotional effect of fiction.

The *Poetics* had a deep but delayed influence on Western aesthetics. The work was not widely read in antiquity, disappeared from European libraries for centuries, and became well known to philosophers in Europe only after William Moerbecke's Latin translation in 1274 (Halliwell 2002: 341–42 and n.89). However, many of the ideas and values of the *Poetics* were espoused by other premodern philosophers and rhetoricians. For example, discussing the orator's art, Quintilian (c. 35–c. 100 CE) described the qualities of verisimilitude (the appearance of truthfulness) and the presentation of "things absent… to our imagination… with extreme vividness" as important aspects of successful rhetoric: "It is the man who is really sensitive to such [vivid] impressions who will have the greatest power over the emotions" (Eden 1986: 88–89, quoting Quintilian 6.2.27–35).

As suggested previously, in the revival of Aristotelian poetics that began in the Middle Ages, Aristotle's three-way contrast of history, poetry, and philosophy was particularly popular. According to Aristotle, poetry is more universal in its scope than history because poetic representation is not limited to what has actually happened, but poetry is more particular and compelling than philosophy, which deals in abstractions rather than concrete representations of individuals' actions. Prominent Renaissance treatises adopting this framework included Sidney's *Defence of Poetry* (ca. 1580), discussed in the Introduction; George Puttenham's *The Art of English Poesy* (1589; ch. 4), and Pierre-Daniel Huet's 1672 history of Western fictional narrative *Traité de l'origine des romans* (A Treatise on the Origin of Romances; see Doody 1996: 16).

In the eighteenth century, the imagination as such began to assume a key role in aesthetics. According to some historians of aesthetics, this pre-Romantic and Romantic shift amounted to a new focus on "the free play of the imagination rather than [the] mimetic [fidelity] of the art object" (Rockmore 2013: 121). New attention to the imagination did not necessarily mean idealization of imagination. Stephen Halliwell has argued that the relationships of post-eighteenth-century aesthetics to mimeticism are, in fact, aligned with Plato's "mistrust of the imagination," which stemmed "from [Plato's] perceptions of its potency" (2002: 95). But this mistrust should not be overemphasized. Distrust of rhetoric during the early modern period coexisted with a growing emphasis on the individual and individual feeling. There is no denying the centrality of the imagination to Romantic poetics such as those of Samuel Taylor Coleridge, William Wordsworth, and John Keats, or to the philosophy of, for example, Jean-Jacques Rousseau, David Hume, and Adam Smith.

In the twentieth century, a diverse group of approaches to the study of fictionality have continued the Aristotelian tradition. One approach has grown from the phenomenological school of philosophy. A second approach within the philosophy of literature and literary criticism draws to varying degrees on contemporary psychological research into the functioning of human imagination. A third neo-Aristotelian or rhetorical approach emphasizes the goal-oriented features of fictional discourse.

Phenomenology in the sense intended here was an early twentieth-century philosophical movement that emphasized "the study of structures of consciousness as experienced from the first-person point of view" (Smith 2018: 1). Jacques Derrida began his career with commentary on and critiques of key works in phenomenology by Edmund Husserl (1859–1938). Other theorists of fiction and the imagination affiliated with this tradition include Roman Ingarden, Jean-Paul Sartre, and Wolfgang Iser. While Sartre is usually associated with existentialist philosophy, like Derrida he began his career with critiques of some of the views of phenomenologists. Sartre's early work included two somewhat neglected studies of imagination, *The Imagination* (1936) and *The Imaginary: A Phenomenological Psychology of the Imagination* (1940). In *The Imaginary*, Sartre challenges what he presents as the orthodox view of the imaginative faculty, a view that takes imagination to be a less-informative substitute for perception. Sartre argues that imagination is a qualitatively distinct human capacity from perception, not an inferior or second-best mode of quasi-perception. According to Sartre, only through the imagination can we experience the realm of the "irreal," to use the term coined by Sartre in this book. Sartre's irreal is not an inferior version of the real but a different dimension of experience with unique characteristics. According to Sartre (1940), for example, in imagining a friend who is not in our presence, we "directly perceive" the friend's "absenteeism," and this absenteeism constitutes the image's irrealism (127). Sartre similarly observes that irreal objects "seem to be presented to us as a negation of the condition of *being in the world*, as an anti-world" (136). While negation is central to Sartre's account of the imagination, he does not judge imaginative experience negatively. Sartre explicitly likens aesthetic experience to the phenomenon of imagining such things as an absent friend. He describes both experiences as involving a shift in intentional orientation that resembles several of the accounts of fictionality as doubling considered in the final section of this chapter.

A number of literary theorists working in the second half of the twentieth century drew on the phenomenological tradition. These writers also tended to give imagination a key position in their discussions of fiction. Barbara Herrnstein Smith (1978), for example, addressing the phenomenology of appreciating fictional representations, observes, "the 'reader' of the painting or poem or musical composition is engaged in the exploration of a structure created by a fellow creature and designed by that artist precisely to encourage and reward such exploration" (11–12). In contrast, she notes, we do not take natural phenomena as having been "designed to engage our interest" (12; see also 96). Focusing more exclusively on readers' experience, Felíx Martínez-Bonati also emphasized imagination in his 1960 study of fictional discourse. He proposed, for example, that "[t]he general objective of all narrative (literary or not) is to place a real or fictional sector of the world before the eyes of our imagination, to cause us by means of language to imagine the narrated circumstances" (Martínez-Bonati 1960: 34). Today, this observation might seem banal, and indeed the view that imaginative activity is required to understand representational artifacts is no longer associated with phenomenology or even Romantic theories of art.

In the twenty-first century, a similar view is espoused by scholars working within entirely different traditions. For example, the linguist Daniel Dor recently proposed an unorthodox account of language as a human technology "dedicated to the systematic *instruction of imagination*: we use it to communicate directly with our interlocutors' imaginations" (2015: 2). In Dor's account, communication by language "instruct[s] the receiver in the process of the mental creation, in imagination, of a totally independent experience—an experience that is supposed to reflect the communicator's experience not because it is perceptually based on [that experience], but *because it is* (approximately) *of the same type*," that is, imagination-oriented (25). Dor suggests that our linguistic activity, even when not creative in the usual sense, involves our use of imagination. On the speaker's or writer's side as well as that of the audience, this use might not be something we are ordinarily aware of, but it is present all the same. Dor's view of the role of imagination (and representation) in nearly all linguistic activity suggests the importance of understanding these capacities, often associated solely with aesthetic activity.

Another phenomenologically oriented theorist, Wolfgang Iser, has argued that imagination plays a special role in the experience of fictionality by providing the raw material for fictional creation. Iser describes literature as produced "through a fusion of" "the fictive and the imaginary," which separately also play other "role[s] in our everyday lives" (xiii). He describes "the fictionalizing act" as "a guiding act…, [that] aims at something that in turn endows the imaginary with an articulate gestalt" (1993: 3). In other words, for Iser as for Aristotle and Sternberg, fictionalizing is inherently purposive and creative; in fictionalizing, we are always seeking to create something that can be shared with others. The imaginary, in turn, is a "multi-faceted potential" that "can be explained only in terms of its aspects" (171), a capacity that "becomes tangible only in terms of products—perception, idea, dream, and so on—that are not exclusively products of the imagination" (184). Iser's notion of the imaginary expressly draws on Sartre's notion of the irreal (194–204).

Other literary theorists and philosophers interested in the relationship between fictionality and the imagination have looked not to phenomenology but to psychology and cognitive science to understand

and account for the role of imagination in aesthetic experience. The philosopher Anthony Everett, for example, in his 2013 examination of "the nonexistent," endorses "the Cognitive Account" of the imagination offered by philosophers and cognitive scientists Shaun Nichols and Stephen Stich (Everett 2013: 2; Nichols & Stich 2003). As described by Everett, this account holds that "[t]here are many robust functional similarities between our belief states and the states involved in propositional make-believe," or imagining particular things to be true (6–7). For example, we can draw inferences from an imagined state of affairs just as we can draw inferences from a state of affairs we believe to be true, and in fact, we draw such inferences from imagined states of affairs all the time when we consider alternative courses of action or assign responsibility for consequences. However, we can readily distinguish our beliefs from imaginings, at least most of the time. Everett also notes the widely accepted view that our beliefs, unlike our imaginings, are not "quarantined" from other beliefs (10). If we learn a new and important fact and believe it to be true, we will integrate that knowledge into our general understanding of the world, but we will not similarly integrate something that we merely imagine to be true into our understanding of reality. Everett notes as well that on some accounts, our beliefs "appear capable of motivating behavior in a way our imaginings are not" (11). When we watch a play and see a character injured or killed, for instance, we do not have the same motivation to act that we would have were we to be in similar proximity to an actual assault or killing. We know at some level that we are only imagining that there is an injury or murder occurring before our eyes.

Unfortunately, there is little agreement among philosophers, psychologists, and neuroscientists regarding exactly what states and/or activities should be considered aspects of the imagination, as well as how they are related to other mental states and activities (e.g., Abraham 2020; Kind 2020). But most philosophers and cognitive scientists do tend to agree on some of the basic premises summarized by Everett, such as the point that imagining does not have the same relation to action that belief does. Psychologists also seem generally to agree about the importance of imagination to the comprehension of written narrative. In understanding such a narrative, the psychologists Joshua Quinlan and Raymond Mar argue,

the imagination appears to act in a uniquely dynamic fashion...,
bridging the perception of narrative cues (e.g. words in a book) with
the imagining of the experiences being represented by these cues, in
a rapid and free-flowing manner.... [T]he imagination in the service of
narrative comprehension appears to occupy a unique space that is separate from pure unconstrained imagination and the direct perception
of events.

(2020: 466)

This account observes that the imaginative activity involved in appreciating the representation of events in words is built on top of a more
basic, creative form of "unconstrained imagination." Notably, however, this description of the role imagination plays in the comprehension of written narrative does not assert that the imagination plays a
special role in the comprehension of *fictional* narrative.

Among philosophers of fiction, the question of whether imagination does play such a special role in the comprehension of fiction
has been the subject of recent debate. Kathleen Stock has argued for a
theory of fiction that she calls "extreme intentionalism," according to
which "the fictional content of a particular text is equivalent to exactly
what the author of the text *intended the reader to imagine*" (2017: 1;
emphasis in original). Stock's account builds on a widely accepted
philosophical account of linguistic meaning associated above all with
H.P. Grice, which makes a speaker's intentions central to meaning
(2). According to Stock, "a fiction is, necessarily and sufficiently, a
collection of propositions reflexively intended by their author to be
conjoined in imagination" (158).

Stock's theory responds to that of Derek Matravers (2014).
Matravers in turn framed his theory as a response to Kendall Walton's
highly influential "make-believe" account, which will be considered
in the next section of this chapter. Matravers argues that "in reading
a text we are not usually mandated to do or experience something,"
such as imagining the events described. To the extent that verbal
descriptions function in this way, according to Matravers, those
descriptions "will do so whether they are fiction or non-fiction" (16).
Thus, Matravers's central argument is that a theory like Stock's or
Walton's does not really concern the distinction between nonfiction
and fiction but rather turns on the distinction between "face-to-face

encounters and representations (whether fictional or non-fictional)," which Matravers calls a distinction between "confrontations" and "representations" (18). No imagination is involved, according to Matravers, in dealing with confrontations, while imagination may be involved in processing representations (53). The meaningful distinction with respect to representations, according to Matravers, is between those that "take the actual world as background and… [those that] do not" (85). His point regarding the use of imagination in processing written representations of both actual and fictional events seems broadly consistent with the conclusions of those who have studied the issue experimentally. But Matravers's argument does leave some questions unanswered. As Stock points out, Matravers does not fully support his contention that "there is no difference in the kinds of accompanying mental states typically caused by fictions versus non-fictions" (2017: 168). Rather, he seems to have based this conclusion on contemplation of his own experience. Nor does Matravers fully support his assumption that we do not use our imaginations in dealing with confrontations, a position at odds with the theory of Daniel Dor discussed earlier in this section.

Another way to consider the relationship between imagination and fictionality is to focus on the creative imaginative activities of authors rather than on the imaginative experiences of members of an audience. A long tradition of theoretical work on literature, of course, addresses the significance of the acts and intentions of authors. Arguably, twentieth-century literary scholarship in French and English was shaped primarily by debates about this topic (see, e.g., Eliot 1920; Wimsatt & Beardsley 1946; Booth 1961; Burke 1992). Twentieth-century literary theories focusing specifically on fiction, rather than on the literary more generally, often stressed the role of authorial intention in determining whether a particular artifact should be considered fiction. In his 1972 book *When Is Something Fiction?*, for example, literary critic Thomas Roberts identified one core sense of the term "fiction" as "fiction by intention": "A book is fiction by intention if its writer knowingly made it factually untrue but also warned his readers he had done this" (Roberts 1972: 4). John Searle adopted a similar approach in "The Logical Status of Fictional Discourse" (1975), discussed in the Introduction. So did the philosopher Gregory Currie in his 1990 book *The Nature of Fiction*. The philosopher R.M.

Sainsbury more recently defined a fictional work as one consisting of "interconnected utterances, a reasonable number of which count as 'fictive,' that is, produced with distinctly fictive intentions" (2009: 7).

Authorial purpose is also central to the position taken by literary theorists of the so-called neo-Aristotelian or Chicago school. These theorists are committed to a view of literature as rhetorical performance—that is, as communication crafted with a purpose. A key contribution to the first generation of work in this school was Wayne Booth's *The Rhetoric of Fiction* (1961). Booth challenged certain mid-twentieth-century trends in literary criticism, such as the overvaluation of authorial "objectivity" and of realism in narrative by critics such as Erich Auerbach (1953) and Ian Watt (1957). Focusing on the rhetorical effects of fictional narrative, Booth urged attention to readers' experiences and to techniques for the direction and manipulation of readers' engagement and emotion. His book is perhaps best known for its accounts of unreliable narration (e.g., 211–40, 339–74) and the implied author as a persona distinct from the narrator and the actual author (e.g., 73–75).

In *The Rhetoric of Fictionality* (2007), Richard Walsh describes his project as an extension of Booth's (6). Walsh, like Booth, "conceive[s] of fiction as a distinctive rhetorical resource" rather than a quality of a "discursive product" (1–2). Walsh proposes an experiential understanding of fiction as "the exercise of our narrative understanding" and defines fictionality as "the regime that provides [a] cultural rationale" for this practice of exercising our narrative understanding (8). Walsh presents his approach as an alternative to many of the most influential twentieth-century accounts of fiction, including the make-believe theory often associated with Kendall Walton (discussed in the next section of this chapter); the fictional-worlds approach considered in Chapter 4; and John Searle's speech-act view (discussed in the Introduction). Some of Walsh's characterizations of these rival theories oversimplify their targets, and his discussion involves a few inconsistencies (see Nielsen 2019: 447), but he does present a coherent and specific definition of fictionality that turns on imagination. According to Walsh,

> Fictional narrative is a communicative gesture, the rhetorical force of which attaches to the process rather than to the substance of a

representational product: acts of fiction are not accounts of imagined
worlds, but imaginings. The sense of imagined world is residual.

(146)

Unsurprisingly, this approach is very much in the spirit of Aristotle's
action-based conception of mimesis in the *Poetics*.

More recently, Walsh joined James Phelan and Henrik Skov
Nielsen as co-author of a provocative article titled "Ten Theses about
Fictionality," published in the journal *Narrative* in 2015 and sparking
multiple extensions and replies. The self-declared purpose of the article was to promote study of *fictionality* as a topic in its own right,
distinct from the study of *fiction* as narrative prose. An important
component of the authors' argument regarding the need for greater
attention to fictionality as such is their contention that fictionality frequently operates outside of narrative prose, as in, for example, political rhetoric and advertising. Nielsen, Phelan, and Walsh (NPW)
(2015) define "fictionality" as "a specific communicative strategy
within some context in th[e real] world" (62) and describe "fictive discourse" as discourse that "overtly invents or imagines states of affairs
in order to accomplish some purpose" (63). Among the ten NPW
theses, the third proposes that "The rhetoric of fictionality is founded
upon a communicative intent" (64).

NPW did succeed in prompting discussion of their theses. Criticism
of their arguments has generally not taken issue with their suggestion
that fictionality can operate or be found outside of works of fiction in
the narrower literary or generic sense. Rather, critics have questioned
NPW's terminological decisions (Dawson 2015: 82; Fludernik
2018: 72) and their allegedly uncritical view of fictionality as a rhetorical device (Mäkelä 2019: 459–62). NPW also have followers,
including Simona Zetterberg Gjerlevsen, who has proposed a blend of
rhetorical and more formalist approaches. In her 2016 contribution on
fictionality to *The Living Handbook of Narratology*, Gjerlevsen notes
that "fictionality has gained ground as an autonomous concept understood as a rhetorical communicative mode" and refers to her own definition with Nielsen of fictionality as "intentionally signaled invention
in communication" (2016a; see also Gjerlevsen 2016b: 176). In a 2017
article, Mari Hatavara and Jarmila Mildorf cite NPW as the inspir-
ation for their examination of formal features usually associated with

fictional discourse but appearing within the nonfictional contexts of oral history and museum display (see also Hansen & Lundholt 2021).

PLAY AND MAKE-BELIEVE

NPW do not have much to say in "Ten Theses" about what has arguably been the dominant theory of fiction for the past generation, the make-believe account championed and often associated with philosopher Kendall Walton, although not originated by him. In fact, the view of fiction as a form of play or make-believe is implicit and sometimes overt in work from Plato through to the Romantics, although this view became a more completely elaborated theory of fiction and fictionality only in the twentieth century. On a make-believe view, engaging with fictional artifacts is fundamentally akin to playing a game of make-believe, an activity that children arguably perform universally and spontaneously. Theorists who espouse this view focus on the interactions between audience members and artifacts as well as on the often interpersonal dimension of make-believe. Many games of make-believe involve mimicry of, and play with, social conventions, and make-believe theories of fiction often draw on this overlap. Make-believe-based theories also very often appeal to anthropological and psychological research on children's play.

The make-believe theory of fiction has been associated with the philosopher Kendall Walton since the 1980s. In 2007, John Gibson described Walton's 1990 book *Mimesis as Make-Believe* as providing the "dominant model of fiction in analytical aesthetics" (157) and noted that it is "impossible to overstate how widespread the use of the notion of make-believe is" (44). Recently, challenges to Walton's framework have proliferated. Some of these challenges seem to be based on objections to the vocabulary used by Walton and others. Before turning to the substance of make-believe theories of fictionality, I will briefly address this issue.

Walton and others presenting make-believe accounts of fictionality use a variety of terms to characterize what we do when we engage with fictional artifacts. These terms, which include "play," "game," and "make-believe," have potentially trivializing connotations that some theorists consider inapt for the discussion of serious aesthetic activity. Reflecting on the distinctions in meaning among the terms in question is a helpful groundwork for understanding make-believe approaches to fictionality. "Play" is arguably the broadest term, since it designates not just games of make-believe, like play fighting, but also simple exuberance and (physical) improvisation (see, e.g., Bateson 1972: 140–41; Schiller 1801: 207; Sutton-Smith 1997). "Game" is a bit more specific than "play" but still names a broader category of activity than "make-believe," since we use the term "game" to refer to activities like gambling that do not seem to involve any element of pretend, mimicry, or "as-if" (see, e.g., Callois 1958: 17–19). "Pretense" and "pretend" might be the next narrowest terms. All games of make-believe involve one or more instances of pretense, but pretense may also occur outside such games, for example, in instances of impersonation or forgery involving an element of deception (see Anscombe 1958; Austin 1958; Morris 2021: 156). The negative connotations of the word "pretend" also seem to lie behind some of the resistance to accounts of fiction that rely on that term, such as John Searle's (1975).

What explains the *popularity* of these concepts as tools for explaining and understanding fictionality? For one thing, the concept of make-believe, especially as deployed by Walton, is both intuitively easy to grasp and complex enough to provide a model for a variety of features of aesthetic objects and experience. These concepts also make it easy for those writing about fictionality to draw on work from other disciplines, including psychology, anthropology, and sociology, in order to suggest the normality and indeed the importance of play and make-believe activities. As one group of sociocultural psychologists has explained, "Through pretend play, children engage in embodied exploration of how the society functions, practice social roles and hierarchies, set their own laws, [and] act out the operation of institutions" (Zittoun, Gläveanu, & Hawlina 2020: 154). Pretend play also appears to help children develop the ability to use language, to reason about others' mental states, and to distinguish between fantasy and reality (Davis 2020: 373; Morris 2021: 209). Children's ability to engage in pretend play, and to distinguish imaginary from real characters, is arguably a universal human capacity, not a culturally bound one (Koukouri & Malafouris 2020: 32–33), although play does of course very often incorporate culturally specific motifs.

In his 1955 essay "A Theory of Play and Fantasy," the anthropologist Gregory Bateson explicitly linked the play of young animals and children with fictionality: "Not only does the playful nip [of a playing puppy] not denote what would be denoted by the bite for which it stands, but, in addition, the bite itself is fictional. Not only do the playing animals not quite mean what they are saying [through their fight-like gestures], but, also, they are usually communicating about something which does not exist," namely a conflict between the two puppies in question (1972: 182). According to Bateson, since

> play is a phenomenon in which the actions of "play" are related to, or denote, other actions of "not play[,]"... [w]e... meet in play with an instance of signals standing for other events, and it appears, therefore that the evolution of play may have been an important step in the evolution of communication.

(181)

Kendall Walton thus was by no means the first theorist to relate fiction to make-believe. Aristotle too noted the "connection... between children's make-believe and artistic mimesis" in his *Poetics* (Halliwell 2002: 152–53). Stephen Halliwell reads Aristotle's discussions of "children's mimesis" as referring to "make-believe or playacting," not just "simple copying" (178). The element common to children's make-believe and mimetic art, according to Aristotle, is "a natural human propensity toward imaginative enactment of hypothetical realities, with a concomitant pleasure in learning and understanding... from mimetic activity" (179). It is worth noting in passing that Plato also acknowledged the role of imitation in children's development and education; part of his objection to mimesis rested on assumptions about children's tendency to identify uncritically with characters in narratives (e.g., Gill 1993: 44). Other prominent thinkers making the connection between children's make-believe and mimetic art include Giambattista Vico, Edmund Burke, Fyodor Dostoevsky, and Walter Benjamin (Halliwell 2002: 178–79 n.5).

The aesthetic theorist perhaps most associated with the concept of play is Friedrich Schiller (1759–1805). Schiller's *Spieltrieb* (usually translated "play drive") is one of the key themes in his *Aesthetic Letters* (1801), which argue for the importance of viewing aesthetic activity as the highest use of human faculties. Schiller observes that while we are stimulated to *work* by lack, what stimulates us to *play* is "sheer plenitude of vitality": "Even inanimate nature exhibits a similar luxuriance of forces, coupled with a laxity of determination which... might well be called play" (207). Such physical play or exuberance is a precursor to aesthetic play: "From the compulsion of want, or *physical earnestness*, she [Nature] makes the transition via the compulsion of superfluity, or *physical play*, to aesthetic play" (209). Schiller introduces the play drive in his Letter 14, describing it as a remedy or response to a culturally induced imbalance between feeling and thinking. He contends that if a person can

> have this twofold experience simultaneously, in which he were to be at once conscious of his freedom and sensible of his existence,... to feel himself matter and come to know himself as mind, then he would... have a complete intuition of his human nature.
>
> (95)

To Schiller, the play drive enables the human experience of freedom because play involves both freely accepted constraints on action, in the form of rules of the game or simply the boundaries of the game, and at the same time the defiance of physical exigency associated with the *Spieltrieb* (105; see also Beiser 2005: 14). Anticipating both Hegel and Sartre, Schiller emphasizes the centrality of negation to his conception of the aesthetic, noting that "it is only through limits that we attain to reality, only through *negation* or exclusion that we arrive at *position* or real affirmation" (129). Although Schiller's theory is rarely mentioned by twentieth- and twenty-first-century theorists of fiction writing in English, it was extremely influential in some branches of nineteenth-century philosophy. Unfortunately, some aspects of Schiller's position were garbled by his early translators and incompletely understood by followers such as Coleridge and Thomas Carlyle (Schiller [Wilkinson & Willoughby] 1967: cxxxvi; see also clix, 331). But other readers of Schiller, like Charles Sanders Peirce and Hans Vaihinger, were more faithful to the details of Schiller's argument (Schiller [Wilkinson & Willoughby] 1967: clxxxvii; Vaihinger 1911: xv), and through their work, it has had some influence on more recent literary criticism.

Even in the twentieth century, a number of theorists anticipated Walton's approach to fiction as a kind of make-believe. Twentieth-century literary scholars likening the creation and/or appreciation of fiction to play include Félix Martínez-Bonati (1960) and Barbara Herrnstein Smith (1978), who produced one of the first late-twentieth-century literary-theoretical accounts linking the capacity to grasp the conventions of fiction to child development and play. Smith points out that fictive discourse shares a "framedness" with play: "Fictive structures... tend to occur in a specially marked, framed or self-enclosed context, a 'storytime' or 'playtime' that may be named as such" (126). Both stories told to children and adult fictions may be "imbedded in natural discourse," or functional, nonaesthetic language, but when this embedding occurs, "the imbedding itself is signaled. Intonational markers are common, as are distinctive bodily motions, and both are readily picked up by children" (126). According to Smith, through experiences with "nursery rhymes, songs, and verbal games" in interaction with caretakers and/or peers, children learn "that certain linguistic structures can and do occur outside the normal context of verbal transactions" and that "the linguistic conventions and social assumptions of the verbal community do not hold for these structures" (130). Thus, Smith argues, "For the child,... natural discourse *itself* gradually emerges as a 'special class' of linguistic structures," despite our adult tendency to think of "fictive discourse [as]... a 'special class' of linguistic structures" (130).

The framed quality of fictionality noted by Smith corresponds to the quarantining phenomenon observed by imagination-based theories of fiction. Such framing is an important element of most subsequent make-believe or play-based accounts of fiction and often, as in Smith's account, is dependent on linguistic and social conventions. Jean-Marie Schaeffer, for example, has identified the key mechanism of fiction as "doing as-if," or "ludic feint," and "imaginative simulation" (1999: xii). Schaeffer relates the human creation and appreciation of fiction to the "mimetic capacities" of many animals and their ability to engage in "(serious) feint" or deception, as well as the "ludic imitations of activity" of, for example, "kittens or puppies brawling with each other" (xv–xvi). Schaeffer also notes that "a ludic feint succeeds only if it is shared," in contrast to serious feints or ruses, which succeed only if not shared (124).

Schaeffer's account is quite similar to Kendall Walton's, although Schaffer argues that his framework is more comprehensive than Walton's (Schaeffer 1999: 167). Walton's most extended presentation of his theory appears in the book *Mimesis as Make-Believe* (1990). Walton describes his approach as a response to philosophical accounts of representational art, like those of Searle (1975) and David Lewis (1978) that "look to language... for models" of understanding (5). Walton insists that "[n]ot all fiction is linguistic" and that an "adequate theory of fiction must accommodate pictorial fictions" (75).

The core of Walton's theory is the position that "representational works of art" are "embedded" in activities "best seen as continuous with children's games of make-believe" (11). Within such activities, representational works "function as props" (11). One of his central examples of a prop that might function in a game of make-believe is a tree stump imagined to be a bear. Walton argues that representational artifacts such as novels and paintings share many characteristics with such make-believe props. Many games of make-believe, Walton also notes, involve multiple make-believers: "collective imagining" is a "social activity" involving mutual realization that "others are imagining" what one is also imagining, and where "steps are taken to see that the correspondence obtains" (18). Representational artworks are, then, props in a cultural game of collective imagining. An art appreciator will use an artwork as a prop containing "a prescription or mandate in some context to imagine something," namely the coherence and quasi-reality of the representational content of the work (39).

Walton's coinage of a full vocabulary for different components of make-believe activity gives his framework considerable descriptive power. Among the theorists of fiction adopting elements of his vocabulary are literary theorists and philosophers, including Thomas Pavel (1986), Gregory Currie (1990), Marie-Laure Ryan (1991), Peter Lamarque and Stein Haugom Olsen (1994), Dennis Green (2002), and Anthony Everett (2013). But as noted at the beginning of this section, some recent work on fictionality has criticized Walton's position. The philosopher John Woods, for example, describes Walton's account as "stand[ing] out... for its opacity" (2018: 19). Woods's primary objection to what he calls Walton's "pretendism" is that the theory is inconsistent with readers' experiences with fiction, or at least Woods's own experience: "no one in the world experiences himself

[sic] as pretending, play-acting, or make-believing" when engaging with fiction (20). The rhetorical neo-Aristotelian critic Richard Walsh has also maintained that "pretence" is "not appropriate as a term for fictional mimesis" (2007: 50).

John Gibson has a more fine-grained objection, deriving from the observation that novels may contain some content describing only make-believe people, events, and places alongside other content that amounts to assertions that are true of the world. An example of the latter would be those assertions in the Sherlock Holmes stories describing aspects of English geography, such as the locations of towns, that have remained unchanged since the late nineteenth century. Gibson criticizes Walton's approach as "ask[ing us] to include world-adequate content under the scope of 'it is make-believe that'" (2007: 165). Gibson contends that it does not make "*any* sense to say that we make-believe material... that we know to be empirically adequate or true-of-the-world" (166). It is not clear that Gibson has identified a genuine difference between make-believe and audience experiences with fictional narrative; after all, when children play make-believe, they do not disregard *all* truths about the natural world. Gibson's rejection of Walton's approach seems, in the end, to be based partly on a disagreement about vocabulary, that is, Gibson's sense that the term "make-believe" is insufficiently serious (see, e.g., 2007: 158, 161, 164).

Marguerite La Caze has presented a distinct set of criticisms of Walton's theory. She argues that the "attempt to provide a foundational theory or a single model of all art is... misconceived" (2002: 151) and that Walton is really trying to do too much with his theory. La Caze also suggests that positing a continuity between children's games and fiction leads to an "egocentric" aesthetic theory that suggests appreciators are always imagining something about themselves (154). She further notes that Walton's theory cannot account for the pleasure we derive from nonrepresentational artifacts (159), but of course, Walton presents his theory as addressing representation in particular. La Caze's main concern is to identify blind spots in Walton's theory, and while she does single out a number of important issues that Walton fails to consider, she does not do full justice to the fact that Walton's is just one of many accounts of aesthetic experience that liken it to play and make-believe.

DOUBLING

Wolfgang Iser has proposed broadly that "[l]iterary fictionality... realizes a fundamental anthropological pattern that manifests itself at times as the doppelganger, and at times as an intramundane totality.... In both cases duality turns out to be the underlying category" (1993: 80). Iser here is suggesting a relationship between the way fictional artifacts often explicitly thematize duality, on the one hand, and the way such artifacts can double reality or experience by enabling our experience of a represented "intramundane totality." In fact, the recurrence of duality in fiction is arguably even more pervasive than Iser acknowledges. Perhaps most basically, all fictional artifacts will possess two aspects, even if they do not expressly thematize doubling or doppelgangers. For example, when we treat an object as a prop in a game of make-believe, the object acquires a new significance; the tree stump becomes *both* a stump and a bear. We can and do also see other representational artifacts, such as fictional texts, as having similar dual aspects: we can regard these artifacts as crafted material objects but also as in a sense containing their represented content. When we focus on that content, we may compare it unfavorably to reality or to an original, as Plato arguably did, or as an improvement on reality that might help us perceive otherwise obscure phenomena or relationships (see Schaeffer 1999: 188–93; Halliwell 2002: 272). All mimesis-focused accounts of fiction at some level acknowledge this two-in-one or double quality of fictional artifacts and experience.

Some writers on fiction and fictionality have emphasized another kind of doubling involved with experiences of fictional representation: the doubling of selves that fictional artifacts can induce. This doubling might take the form of embodiment and/or identification, as in a theatrical performance of a role, or of audience perspective-shifting, as when a reader empathizes with a fictional character in a play or novel. Few modern theorists consider this sort of doubling to be pernicious, although Plato arguably did. For Plato, according to Stephen Halliwell,

> the identification involved in performing or reciting dramatic poetry represents a threat to the soul's unity [necessary for political leaders], because the operation of "self-likening," the enactment of experiences

> fictionally other than one's own, requires the mind to discover within itself, so Plato believes, the nature of what it is brought to imagine. Drama invites and leads us to discover *other possible lives* and, in the process, to make them psychologically our own.
>
> (2002: 93)

The two-in-one character of "props" or representational artifacts is linked to the kind of doubling of experience that concerned Plato, but the relationship is complex and somewhat contested. Aristotle, for example, argued in favor of the "desirability... of an aesthetic experience... in which appreciation of both material and 'object,' of the material artifact and the imagined world that it represents, *coalesce* in a complex state of awareness" (Halliwell 2002: 181–82). Aristotle was not alone among premodern theorists in recognizing the two-in-one character of both aesthetic representation and aesthetic experience. Halliwell ascribes to Plutarch (46–119 CE), for example, a very similar view of poetry: "Mimesis, Plutarch seems to be saying, is *both* the invention of worlds that differ from the reality we inhabit, *and* fundamentally dependent on resemblance to that reality" (2002: 301).

Plato recognized not just the possibility of an audience member adopting another self in response to aesthetic representation but also the practice of authorial doubling. In Book III of the *Republic*, Socrates and Adeimantus are discussing the admission of poets to the ideal state. In the course of the discussion, Socrates introduces a distinction important for later literary criticism: the distinction between *mimesis*, translated here as "imitation," and *diegesis*, translated here as "narration." Socrates notes that in some passages in the *Iliad*,

> the poet takes the person of Chryses... and does all he can to make believe that the speaker is not Homer, but the aged priest himself. And in this double form [i.e., an epic consisting partly of the "speech" of Chryses and partly of the "speech" of Homer] he has cast the whole narrative.

Authorial speech *as* a character, or representation of a character's speech, Socrates calls mimesis: "this assimilation [by the poet] to another... is the imitation [mimesis] of the person he assumes," but "if the poet everywhere appears and never conceals himself, then...

the imitation is dropped, and his poetry becomes simple narration," or diegesis. Thus, on Plato's account, a poet may double him- or herself by directly offering a character's speech for aesthetic appreciation, and this doubling will potentially prompt a complementary doubling in audience members' experience. In addition, many literary artifacts involve a double form in that the artifacts include passages of diegesis and passages of mimesis. Both kinds of passages are parts of the represented content of such artifacts, that is, these passages contribute to just one of the artifacts' two aspects as props.

The double form identified by Plato in Homer's epics also marks most fictional narrative from antiquity to the present day. Some twentieth-century theorists of fictionality have relied on a similar distinction between authorial discourse and character discourse in attempts to identify the distinguishing characteristics of artifacts involving fictionality. In her very influential *The Logic of Literature* (1973), Käte Hamburger likened the relation between a representational text and the alternate reality it presents to the relationship between a canvas and what is painted on it: "the canvas, above and beyond the painting, has its own material value *qua* canvas. But... as a painting, it is no longer a canvas as such" (108–09; see also Smith 1978: 39). The significance of the material object changes once the object is used as a component of a recognizable representational artifact. Hamburger continues,

> The same relationship applies to the tense of the finite verb. Outside of fiction,... the preterite [the simple past tense, as in "She walked to the store"]... expresses a relationship between the statement-subject and its temporal past.... Within fiction, as a narrative tense..., the preterite... is merely the substratum in which the narrative must proceed. As a past tense *per se* it is just as unnoticed as the canvas in a painting.
> (1973: 108–09)

In other words, within a fictional narrative, the verbs within diegesis or the narrator's speech work linguistically in a different way than they do within everyday language: "Fictionalization, action presented as the Here and Now of the fictive persons, *nullifies the temporal meaning of the tense in which a piece of narrative literature is narrated*" (98). In reading fiction, we forget about or set aside our ordinary understanding of the simple past tense, even though we could explain, if asked, how the very same words would function differently in a nonfictional utterance (see also Ronen 1994: 221–27).

The effect Hamburger describes occurs only in diegesis, the narrator's discourse. In a double form narrative that also contains mimesis of characters' discourse, the past tense functions in its normal way relative to the characters who use it: to designate events occurring prior to their speech. Several theorists of fictional discourse have focused on the mimetic elements of double form narrative as exemplifying the distinguishing feature of fictional narrative. Felíx Martínez-Bonati, for example, made central to his theory of fictional discourse the idea that language works in two fundamentally different ways within virtually all narrative fiction. Martínez-Bonati notes that language attributed to a character within a narrative is linguistically distinct from diegetic language (1960: 28, 78). We understand character speech as reproducing an imaginary speech event, but we understand a narrator's words as creative and authoritative, not as quoted but as presented to us directly (see also Doležel 1998, presenting a very similar theory). Martínez-Bonati argues that it is our capacity to speak and write such "pseudo-sentences" as those uttered by characters that "makes possible the introduction of merely imaginary sentences into the realm of communication" and thus makes possible linguistic fictionalizing (79). Characters' discourse consists of pseudo-sentences because audience members understand these sentences to be samples of imaginary speech events and, unlike diegesis, not to be addressed to a storytelling audience (see also Pratt 1977: 173–74 and Sternberg 2012: 445–53 for similar proposals).

On accounts such as these, when we read fictional narratives such as novels, we are performing quite a complex cognitive activity. We alternate, unconsciously, between the kind of linguistic processing necessary to make sense of diegesis and that necessary to make sense of mimesis. We invest and suspend, or reallocate, our identification with the various speakers in the narrative. And we also remain aware, all along, that we are reading a fictional narrative; indeed, this awareness is what prompts the complex activities just described. That is, we proceed with an understanding of the text we encounter as containing representational content—containing a narrative presented as if it could have been observed or experienced. For all of these activities to take place, we must be able to perceive that artifact as possessing the two-in-one quality described at the beginning of this section.

But while most theorists of fictionality would agree that the capacity to perceive these multiple aspects of an artifact is crucial to the aesthetic experience afforded by fiction, they have differed regarding the details of this capacity, and in particular whether audience members can or do perceive both aspects at once or must alternate between them. Adam Smith (1723–90), for example, "tended to" suggest that "awareness of the object and the medium of mimetic art" could not be experienced at the same time (Halliwell 2002: 182 n.3). Sartre adopted a similar position when he observed that the apprehension of a represented person within a portrait involves the viewer's consciousness "effecting a radical conversion that requires the nihilation of the world" and that the perception of the painting and the represented content are acts "*exclusive*" of each other (1940: 189). Similarly, Roman Ingarden contended that "The declarative sentences in the literary work of art can theoretically be read in either of two ways: as judgments about a reality ontically independent of the work or as sentences which only appear to be assertions" (1973: 36). Ingarden describes a "'scintillation' of the assertive units" of a work, derived from the "ambiguous" nature of the "sentences appearing in the work" (71 n.43). These sentences "apparently postulate that they refer to a genuine reality but determine only an intended 'portrayed' world, which only makes the claim of simulating a portrayed reality" (71 n.43). Ingarden also offers another analogy for this phenomenon, observing how, in proofreading, "we so often 'overlook' errors" or at least pay them no significant attention, since our "focus [is] on the typical features of the verbal sign and [we] do not even apprehend the strictly individual features" (177 n.3). Other theorists who have suggested that it is impossible to apprehend both aspects of representational language at the same time include Barbara Herrnstein Smith (1978: 47), Ann Banfield (1982: 262), and the philosopher Anthony Everett (2013: 14 n.8).

But this view is not universal. Other theorists have directly addressed the phenomenon and assert that audience members can and do experience a kind of "double exposure" (NPW 2015: 68). For instance, Mary Louise Pratt contends, "Readers of… literary works are in theory attending to at least two utterances at once—the author's display text and the fictional speaker's discourse, whatever it is. (This duality is not always exploited by the author…)" (1977: 174). In his afterword to the second edition of *The Rhetoric of Fiction*, Wayne Booth notes that "[t]he fictive experience, in contrast to the experience of most narrative in history and journalism, is… made out of a special kind of double role-playing" in which readers inhabit the position of narrative addressee and character (1983: 424). Wolfgang Iser argues that "the fictive simultaneously disrupts and doubles the referential world" (1993: xv). Jean-Marie Schaeffer describes the "state of immersion" as "a divided mental state or, to take up… an expression of [J]uri Lotman, a 'biplanar behavior'" (1999: 164). Similarly, John Woods maintains that "readers the world over are disposed to see [the] sentences [of a fictional work] as both true and not true together, and to see them so without the slightest empirically discernible cognitive discomposure" (2018: 12). Woods explains that "When we read a text which we know to tell a fictional story,… our understanding puts into play two different knowledge-streams," one "knowing that the story [the text] tells is not true *in situ* the world," and the other "know[ing] that indeed it is true *in situ* the story" (140).

Along similar lines, James Phelan maintains that neo-Aristotelian "rhetorical theory explains the phenomenon [of reader response to characters and events 'as if they were real'] with the concept of double consciousness" (2018: 121). Phelan offers as an "excellent description of reading with a double consciousness" Ralph Rader's observation that

> [t]he reader of a novel… experiences "a focal illusion of characters acting autonomously as if in the world of real experience within a subsidiary awareness of an underlying constructive authorial purpose which gives their story an implicit significance and affective force which real world experience does not have."
>
> (Phelan 2018: 126, quoting Rader 2011: 206;
> Phelan's emphases omitted)

While non-realist fiction does not always foster the illusion Rader describes, the importance of his claim lies in its assumption that readers at least sometimes experience a narrative as simultaneously real and unreal. The philosopher Michael Morris has made the view that we can simultaneously attend to an artwork's form and its content a key element of his theory of aesthetic representation (2021: 21, 36, 40). Morris describes the opposing view as both the predominant position among philosophers and as "phenomenologically unnatural," by which Morris seems to mean untrue to his own experience with artworks (40, 46).

Ultimately, disagreement on this precise point might not be very significant. It is not clear what difference it would make if we could determine empirically that the apprehension of fictional narrative involves a "double consciousness" or rather a rapid alternation or "oscillation" of attention (Merrell 1983: 27–39). One of the insights underlying these discussions, however, is important. This is the insight that the "double consciousness" involved in the apprehension of fiction involves an element or gesture of negation. Sartre describes this gesture, a characteristic of imagination, as one of "denial": "to deny that an object belongs to the real is to deny the real in positing the object" (1940: 198). The anthropologist Gregory Bateson has offered a description of this phenomenon that shows how closely it is linked to play behavior. Bateson observes that

> [t]he absence of simple negatives [in communication through, for example, gestures] is of especial interest because it often forces organisms *into saying the opposite of what they mean to get across the proposition that they mean the opposite of what they say*. Two dogs approach each other and need to exchange the message: "We are *not* going to fight." But the only way in which fight can be mentioned in iconic communication is by the showing of fangs. It is then necessary for the dogs to discover that this mention of fight [through the showing of fangs] was... only exploratory. They must... explore what the showing of fangs means.
>
> (1972: 140–41)

This exploration yields play-fighting, which is simultaneously a kind of rudimentary exploration of meaning and a release of energy in which the dogs' actions take on a new significance and a new function. While Bateson's account depends on analogizing the dogs' behavior to human behavior, it is easy to see how a similar dynamic might occur among children without sophisticated language skills in their encounters with make-believe play and made-up stories.

The awareness of fictionality, described previously as requiring access to two different attitudes toward an artifact, also involves a gesture of negation. To regard a stump as a bear, we disregard some aspects of the stump, such as the moss covering it. To understand and appreciate a fictional narrative, we disregard or at least divert our focus from some aspects of the real-world situation in which we find ourselves: background noise, the smell of the book, the sound of turning pages, and so forth. We attend to those aspects of the situation that are relevant to our comprehension of the represented events and in effect say to ourselves, "this is not a real-world experience," much as the puppies' play-fighting gestures may be interpreted as saying "this is not a fight." Similarly, when we identify with a character, we suspend our attention to aspects of our situation that are not conducive to enabling that identification.

A persistent question in the study of fictionality concerns whether or not such gestures of negation and doubling are distinguishing features of fictionality. Similar gestures seem to be characteristic of other human activities, including religious activities as well as more everyday institutional and economic activity. Chapter 7 will consider some of these settings in more detail. Another lasting question suggested by Bateson's discussion concerns the cultural and historical specificity of fictionality. This question has been receiving a good deal of attention in twenty-first-century literary scholarship. Was there ever a point in Western culture when the terms discussed in this chapter and, more important, their associated concepts and practices were not in use? Questions of this kind, which seem purely descriptive, can overlap with evaluative questions. To what degree, for example, is the creation and appreciation of fiction dependent on the existence of social conditions such as urbanization, literacy, and the availability of leisure time, which may in turn depend on the exploitation or dehumanization of other groups of people? The next chapter turns to some of the most visible arguments made in relation to these questions over the past few decades.

2

STARTING POINTS

In a 2018 article, Monika Fludernik identified the different historical points of origin that scholars have recently suggested for fiction
as a cultural phenomenon in the West. Fiction, it has been argued,
originated in the Mediterranean cultures of the first or second centuries of the Common Era, in the "High Middle Ages," during the
Renaissance, or sometime around the eighteenth-century emergence
of the novel in Northern Europe (68). One key disagreement driving
this diversity of proposals concerns the breadth of the term "fiction."
Does this term refer to any invented narrative, or any narrative not put
forward as a historical account, regardless of its length or form (e.g.,
Gjerlevsen 2016b: 176)? Or does it refer only to invented narratives
in prose? Or does it refer only to narratives involving those features
characteristic of most of the kinds of artifacts we now find in the
fiction section of bookstores and libraries: narratives involving not
only invented characters and events, but characters with a certain
depth or complexity, and events plotted dramatically rather than epi-
sodically (see, e.g., Paige 2011)? With only a few exceptions, scholars
who have proposed particular points of origin for fiction have tended
to focus on these categories of invented-narrative artifacts only, rather
than on fictionality considered more broadly as an element of, for

DOI: 10.4324/9781003161585-3

example, shorter tales, oral narrative, pedagogical works, or even history. Nonetheless, some of the historical and cultural developments that figure in these scholars' work do hint at analogous historical perspectives on the presence of fictionality in other cultural artifacts.

One could also understand the disagreements just described as disagreements about how to categorize the relationship between what we now call fiction and those practices that preceded it. Some scholars contend that a cultural practice like what we now call fiction has repeatedly emerged and been lost in Western European culture (e.g., Green 2002: 18; Agapitos & Mortensen 2012: 21). Another view considers fiction to be a kind of loose transhistorical category, whose specific forms and features during any given historical period and cultural milieu will be "*culture*-laden, *language*-laden, and *world view*-laden" (Merrell 1983: 73). Yet another view considers the institution of fiction or fictional discourse to be mainly an institution regarding the *reception* of artifacts, so that fiction has been and will be visible as such only when the historical and cultural circumstances allow—that is, one and the same narrative might be recognizable as fiction during some periods, but not others (e.g., Ingarden 1968: 278). Still another related view is that artifacts involving fictionality are more or less a human universal, although cultural self-awareness about this practice, and thus theoretical concern about its logical or practical implications, becomes possible only sometimes (e.g., Genette 1991: 137–38).

This diversity of positions suggests that understanding fictionality as a cultural practice requires consideration not only of the contexts within which a particular artifact is created and appreciated, but also of how those contexts take their own precursors into account, as well as the possibility that creators, audiences, preservers, circulators, and commentators on cultural products might all act within overlapping sets of conventions and constraints at any given point in history. It seems largely beyond debate that practices of make-believe or "ludic feint" are, like language, a human universal (see, e.g., Schaeffer 1999: 126–27); that such practices do take different forms in different cultures and at different times; and that we nevertheless are able at least partly to comprehend artifacts involving elements of mimesis and make-believe that were generated at times and in cultures other than our own (see, e.g., Doležel 1998: 235 n.37). Beyond these points, however, agreement is limited. This chapter considers four milieux repeatedly identified as origins for practices we can recognize as containing elements of fictionality, if not a critical discourse about these practices: the first few centuries of the common era; the eleventh through sixteenth centuries in central and northern Europe; the seventeenth and eighteenth centuries in France and England; and the fourteenth through eighteenth centuries in China. It also addresses the significance, for these historical accounts, of developments in technologies of linguistic communication.

ANCIENT FICTION

A number of scholars, most notably Margaret Anne Doody in *The True Story of the Novel* (1996), have identified the origin of fiction in Western culture with seven prose narratives in Greek and Latin that have survived from the first few centuries of the Common Era. The Greek novels included in this group are Chariton's *Chiaeras and Callirhoe* (mid-first century), Achilles Tacitus's *Leucippe and Clitophon* (early second century), Longus's *Daphnis and Chloe* (second century), Xenophon's *Ephesian Tale* (late second century), and Heliodorus's *Ethiopica* (third century). All five share a basic plot structure of lovers separated but eventually reunited after a long series of adventures, as well as many more specific themes and motifs that justify regarding the five narratives as members of a single genre, and, for that matter, as novels, a label they did not carry until later. Two Latin prose works from the same period are sometimes grouped with the five Greek novels: Petronius's fragmentary *Satyricon* (between the first and third centuries of the Common Era) and Apuleius's *The Golden Ass* (second century). While the Latin works do not share the plot structure of the Greek novels, many commentators also consider the *Satyricon* and *The Golden Ass* to be early novels because of their self-aware tone and influence on later European literature (see, e.g., Anderson 1984: 19; Doody 1996: xv–xvi; Gaisser 2008). It is easy to forget or overlook that these seven narratives are without doubt only a small part of a larger group of similar artifacts created around the same time, the rest of which did not survive in manuscript beyond the first few centuries of the Common Era. We do know of particular novels that have been lost, including one by Apuleius, and of many others that survive only in fragments (see Gaisser 2008: 42, 296–97). It is also important to observe that the manuscripts that did survive were created during a period known as the Second Sophistic, when conquered Greeks were being more fully integrated into the Roman empire and the Roman elite was self-consciously adapting Greek cultural materials in concert with a broader Roman imperial promotion of intellectual activity.

Not all theorists agree that these artifacts deserve to be called fiction. Wolfgang Iser, for instance, opines that in the "ancient tradition there is only one instance of anything comparable with fiction in its modern usage; this is in Roman law," specifically the practice of treating foreigners as if they were Roman citizens for the purpose of charging the foreigners with crimes (1993: 96). Some commentators who dispute the classification of these works as fiction point to the absence of contemporary critical or theoretical reflection on the artifacts as such. Christopher Gill explains that the form was "ignored almost wholly by ancient writers" (1993: 79). It might not have been until the ninth century that the classic novels were grouped together as a genre in the *Bibliotheca* of the Patriarch Photios, although Photios also described these texts as related to historiography (Agapitos 2012: 248). Moreover, subsequent histories of the romance and novel in early modern Europe did not include the ancient novels in their chronologies (see Doody 1996: 482). And identifying these written artifacts as origins is also complicated by the consensus view that the novels preserved through the Middle Ages in manuscript were based on plots and characters from much earlier storytelling traditions, particularly from the Middle East and North Africa (Anderson 1984: 19; Doody 1996: 103).

Nevertheless, multiple features of the narratives that were preserved in manuscript from this period do justify identifying them as ancestors of modern fiction and the modern novel in particular. These narratives were apparently composed and read in prose. They include human-centered plots with invented characters experiencing fear, anger, jealousy, playfulness, and so on, and expressing concern about the thoughts and views of other characters. The novels also exhibit formal features, such as direct narration of characters' thoughts and selective disclosure of information by narrators, all of which were conventionally associated with modern fictional prose narrative (see Laird 1993: 165; Morgan 1993: 214). Alongside characterization, the novels all contain passages full of "contingent [descriptive] detail" lending verisimilitude to the narrated events (Morgan 1993: 182). The later novels, especially *Daphnis and Chloe*, the *Ethiopica*, and the Latin novels, disclose considerable authorial self-awareness through their thematization of questions of representation, spectatorship, role playing, and cultural heritage (see, e.g., Anderson 1984: 44, 79; Doody 1996: 45; Whitmarsh 2013: 70–71). Finally, as noted above, the novels do seem to have influenced subsequent authors more or less continuously down to the present, even if that influence has sometimes been second-hand, through prior adaptations of the ancient novels' plots, themes, and techniques (see Doody 1996: 482).

The reception of *The Golden Ass* provides a good example of the difficulty of classifying some of these works. The novel is attributed to Apuleius of Madura (125–70 CE), a city now known as M'Daouroch, Algeria. Apuleius left works of Platonist philosophy and rhetoric as well as imaginative prose. *The Golden Ass* is the story of Lucius, a native of Greece who also narrates the novel. Lucius is open-minded to the point of gullibility, and in the third of the novel's 11 books, he is magically transformed into a donkey through a mix-up brought on by his curiosity and covetousness. In the following books, Lucius recounts his unfortunate adventures in the donkey's body through a series of captures and escapes. Throughout, the story of Lucius's adventures is interrupted by short narratives recounting the adventures and misfortunes of those Lucius-the-donkey encounters. The most significant of these is the story of Cupid and Psyche, which Lucius overhears while being held captive by a band of robbers and which takes up nearly three of the novel's 11 books. In the final book, Lucius is transformed back into human shape by the goddess Isis, who foretells that Lucius will become a prominent lawyer and a priest in Isis's mystery cult.

The tale of Cupid and Psyche significantly influenced European literature from Apuleius on. The larger narrative structure and many of the features of *The Golden Ass* also became a model for many later works that we do not hesitate to call fiction, perhaps most notably *Don Quixote* (1605–15) as well as any number of other tale collections and picaresque narratives (see Lamb 2011: 205–06, 248). But it is unclear when readers of *The Golden Ass* started to view the novel in this way. Some support for the view that early readers did not view the novel as a wholly invented narrative comes from Augustine of Hippo's *City of God* (fifth century), in which Augustine notes that "he… has heard (but does not believe) stories of men being transformed into animals and keeping their human reason, 'just as Apuleius either declared or pretended happened to him in the books which he entitled the *Golden Ass*'" (Gaisser 2008: 33). Julia Haig Gaisser argues that Augustine "clearly" read the narrative "as autobiography," and that this reading "continued to be unquestioned for at least a thousand years" (33). The view was perhaps encouraged by some similarities between the character Lucius and the author Apuleius, including their common work as lawyers and their common philosophical/ religious commitments. According to Gaisser, this understanding was superseded only in the fifteenth century, when the Florentine scribe Poggio Bracciolini (1380–1459), a translator of works by the Greek satirist Lucian of Samosata (c. 125–80 CE), translated Lucian's *Onos* (*The Ass*) (Gaisser 2008: 153). The circulation of another version of the tale written in Greek by a contemporary of Apuleius, according to Gaisser, established that "the story [of *The Golden Ass*] was not ori-ginal with Apuleius and consequently that it had to be fictional" (156).

Our conclusions about how early readers regarded the ancient novels will always be speculative. The same is true for our understanding of audience views of other ancient literary artifacts produced earlier than the ancient novels, but bearing features we now associate with fiction. J.R. Morgan has argued that it was actually early historical writing, in which historians openly invented details to render more vivid the events they described, that made the ancient novels a viable cultural form. According to Morgan, "it was within historiography itself that the contract of fictional complicity was first extended to narrative prose, thus allowing fiction, recognized and gen-erally, if reluctantly, licensed elsewhere [i.e., in historical writing], to enter a new form and generate a new and more equivocal litera-ture of pleasure in prose: fiction in the form of history," as in the classic novels (1993: 187; see also Yu 1997: 32–33). Leslie Kurke has argued that both Plato and the historian Herodotus defined their respective innovative prose styles in relation to the cultural signifiers associated with Aesopian discourse (2011: 245–46), which in Kurke's usage refers to both the tradition of Aesopian fables and the *Life of Aesop* with which they were commonly preserved, once they came to be written down in the early Common Era in the form that survived to the present. Kurke also suggests that the reason Plato's aesthetics does not directly address prose fiction is that the form was so closely linked to Aesopian discourse, from which Plato sought to borrow selectively (248). Aesopian discourse, Kurke argues, functioned to signify the ambiguous power of culturally marginal figures such as oracles and sages, while Plato sought for his works a status more aligned with orthodox power structures. Kurke explains, "by so strongly identifying *mimēsis* with poetry, Plato conjures the illusion that his own prose is nonmimetic" (250) and thus dealt with public affairs more directly.

THE IMPLICATIONS OF CHANGES IN LANGUAGE TECHNOLOGIES

Why have Aesop's *Life* and fables not been more frequently identified as a form of fiction existing in antiquity? Kurke plausibly argues that the fables were "obviously and deliberately fictitious" to their tellers and hearers, and later their readers (2011: 43). Kurke's explanation for the exclusion of "Aesopian discourse" from our histories of Western fiction and literature appeals partly to the "low, degraded status" of the Aesop figure, who began life as a slave and is always described as physically unattractive, and partly to the fact that up to the early centuries of the common era, this body of lore seems to have circulated largely if not entirely orally (6 n.11). Along similar lines, Dennis Green (2002) has observed that "the rise of fiction in classical Greece [in the form of the ancient novels] has been associated with the beginnings of literacy there," and notes that "the genesis of vernacular fiction in the twelfth century coincides with a new place for literacy in the literature meant for laymen" (2). In other words, it may be that rightly or wrongly, we tend to consider textuality to be essential to fictionality.

A number of histories of fictionality similarly associate fictionality with literacy, the availability of written media, and/or new communication, preservation, and distribution technologies at various points in European history. It does seem that new fictional forms and theoretical interest in fictionality often surge alongside the emergence of new communication technologies and changes in the social treatment of such technologies. This parallelism offers some support for the view that fictionality becomes a widely recognized possibility for discourse and/or an issue for theoretical inquiry only in the presence of such shifting conditions (see, e.g., Green 2002: 35; Stein 2006: 164–65, 172).

One key landmark in the development of language and communication technologies was the invention of the phonetic alphabet, the first to include vowels, around 1500 BCE (Ong 1982: 89), some two millennia after the invention of nonalphabetic writing in early urban centers in Mesopotamia (83–84). According to Walter J. Ong, it took some time for the writing enabled by this development to be regarded as a mode for preserving narrative; the *Odyssey* and *Iliad*, "the first lengthy compositions to be put into this alphabet," were "first set down" in the alphabet around 700–650 BCE (23). Historians of fiction seldom consider the Homeric epics as a potential point of origin for fictionality, perhaps because, as Ong and Eric Havelock have persuasively argued, as oral epics they were not regarded as works of imagination or entertainment but rather functioned as a kind of storage device for cultural heritage and social norms (e.g., Ong 1982: 70–71).

The development of the alphabet had both "democratizing" and "internationalizing" effects on Greek culture, according to Ong (90), but these effects took hold slowly. It was arguably not until the period of canonical Greek tragedy (400s BCE) and the works of Plato (c. 428–348 BCE) that literate Greeks "interiorized writing" (Ong 1982: 24) in a way that made the technology available for new cultural uses. As suggested by Kurke and Ong, Plato's thought and works were shaped by the fact that he lived and wrote during this transitional period: "Plato's philosophically analytic thought…, including his critique of writing [as tending to weaken mnemonic skills, in the *Phaedrus*], was possible only because of the effects that writing was beginning to have on mental processes" (Ong 1982: 80). Writing and reading also accustomed the literate to conceptualize experience according to visual rather than aural and kinesthetic metaphors, and to regard abstractions as significant explanatory tools (68, 80, 90, 105). In addition, the technology of writing made possible intricate plotting, which for centuries characterized only drama on the model of the Athenian tragic dramatists Aeschylus (c. 523–456 BCE), Sophocles (c. 497–406 BCE), and Euripides (c. 480–406 BCE). The tragedians composed their plays in writing (Ong 1982: 133, 142), although the tragedies were of course not widely read in antiquity as we read printed plays today.

The ancient novels were committed to writing some 500 years later, by which point literacy had diffused even more widely, though not universally, through Greek and Roman culture. Key texts of Judaism and Christianity had also been solidified over the intervening period. Nevertheless, the novels were not written for a mass public; *The Golden Ass*, for example, was written for a relatively sophisticated audience (Gaisser 2008: 169). The next significant technological development was the invention and adoption of the codex rather than the roll or scroll as the preferred format for manuscripts, around the fourth century CE. It was at this point that many texts that had circulated in antiquity were lost (Gaisser 2008: 42, 296–97). This particular development in language technology has made it more difficult for us to learn about the dissemination of novel-like narratives before this point in history. We know that contemporary commentators often denigrated these kinds of narratives (e.g., Gaisser 2008: 41), but such surviving criticism does not rule out the possibility that the novels were embraced by other ancient audiences.

The next major development in language technology was arguably the emergence of the European vernaculars as everyday languages alongside Learned Latin as the language of scholarship around the tenth century. Most of the landmarks of literature in the European vernaculars (Italian, Spanish, French, German, English) date from the eleventh and twelfth centuries on. As the next section of this chapter will briefly explore, the separation between the languages of scholarship and practical affairs during this period may have contributed to a dissociation between sophisticated philosophical writing on issues related to fictionality and written artifacts exhibiting fictionality. That is, although medieval and Renaissance scholars writing in Latin did examine certain key issues also addressed by twentieth- and twenty-first-century theorists of fictionality, the earlier scholars generally did not apply their insights directly to the analysis of contemporary imaginative literature produced in the vernaculars. Literary scholarship tended to focus on the Greek and Roman classics, on the categorization of works of imaginative literature, and on the clarification of the themes and lessons implicit in those works (Gaisser 2008: 224–30), even as the literary artifacts themselves often displayed considerable self-awareness about the mechanisms of artifice those artifacts incorporated.

Subsequent significant developments in language technology include the invention of printing in the fifteenth century; the increasing scope of literacy and commodification of reading material in the seventeenth through nineteenth centuries; and the development of audiovisual and electronic media in the twentieth century. A later section of this chapter will consider arguments made about fictionality during the early modern period of commodification, and Chapter 6 will address some implications of the most recent developments of new media.

At the most abstract level, it seems beyond doubt that shifts in technologies of communication contribute to shifts in the kinds of artifacts produced using those technologies as well as their reception. These shifts also affect the kind of access we now have to records of past views of fictional artifacts and fictionality. But it is important not to conceptualize the relationship between fiction and language technologies too reductively. Literate cultures do differ fundamentally from cultures of "primary orality," as Ong has called those cultures lacking any form of writing. But Ong also stresses that all literate cultures also involve residual forms of orality. Even when invented narratives came to be written, they were for many centuries neither read silently nor designed to be absorbed that way (Ong 1982: 25, 102–03, 115, 149, 157–58). Similarly, Monika Fludernik has noted that some of the formal linguistic features occasionally deemed unique to fiction, such as the narration of others' thoughts, may and do appear in oral communication (1993: 93; see also Stein 2006; Hatavara & Mildorf 2017). It might be most accurate to say that changes in language technologies affected changes in communication conventions that, at particular points in Western history, have coalesced into identifiable *fascinations* with fiction and fictionality. A number of scholars have argued that one of these periods began in the eleventh and twelfth centuries in Europe.

THE MIDDLE AGES AND RENAISSANCE

As suggested in the previous section, a rudimentary critical-theoretical discourse on fiction and fictionality did emerge during the Middle Ages. Panagiotis Agapitos notes,

> In the Western Middle Ages, especially from the late eleventh to the early thirteenth centuries, fiction was... a debated issue. On the basis of various ancient works such as "Homer," Virgil, Lucan and the Aesopic fables, theoreticians either criticized fiction as false and deceiving its recipients or defended it on account of it being able to convey, in the words of Augustine, a "form of truth"... [or] what developed on the basis of allegorical Bible interpretation as the theory of "veiling" (*integumentum*).
>
> (2012: 276)

Virginie Greene has drawn parallels between the work of medieval logicians writing in Latin and the creators of vernacular tales in the eleventh through thirteenth centuries: works in both traditions "share an abstract or idealistic side, able to carry readers far away from everyday life, while they foster a concrete grasp of things and incite readers to look anew at their here and now" (2014: 15). Greene concludes that "logic and fiction are rooted in similar processes of the mind. They are both games, tending toward abstraction... and operating in imaginary spaces of freedom detached from the contingencies of daily life, but reflecting them in a playful fashion" (219). Luiz Costa Lima also notes that the distinctions made by logicians between types of propositions and their relationship to truth created an intellectual environment congenial to the development of fictional narratives written in vernacular verse or prose (2006: 58–59).

Scholars such as those just quoted agree that, in at least some literate milieux, medieval writers and readers were viewing verbal representation and "play" with some degree of self-consciousness. A number of scholars have argued that this consciousness generated an overlap between the techniques of medieval history writing (in Latin as well as vernaculars) and the composition of vernacular romance. For example, Robert Stein has argued that Geoffrey of Monmouth's *Historia Regum Britanniae* (History of the Kings of Britain; ca. 1136), "the great twelfth-century source text for the legend of Arthur and for vernacular romance in general,… invents Latin prose fiction by modeling it so directly on contemporary historiography that the two cannot be told apart using purely narrative criteria" (Stein 2006: 106). Explaining how William of Newburgh criticized Geoffrey's history as purporting to recount a period that was not documented—that "there is simply no available time for much of Geoffrey's narrative to have taken place"—Stein explains that William was arguing that "Geoffrey's book is simply a lie," but that as a result, Geoffrey's history

> becomes a perfect definition of good fiction: fiction is the narrative representation of an invented place, the invention of a dream world containing infinite realms in which to locate events that can be narrated and analyzed for their significance *as if* one were writing history—but without history's constraints.
>
> (107)

Likewise, P.M. Mehtonen has noted the use of narrative techniques now associated with fiction in Monmouth's history: in the "speeches and letters" quoted in the text, "the stylistic register shift[s] from simple to complex," and "the mode of representation is altered," so that "[t]he plot no longer follows linear chronology" (2012: 81). Mehtonen continues

> The embedded sections begin to construct modal and alternative courses of events in the speakers' and listeners' minds—things that might, would or must take place (or not). Naturally, some of these possibilities actualize and some do not as the narrative returns to the world of the main plot.
>
> (81)

More than a few scholars of medieval literature have contended that imaginative works of this period should be considered ancestors of, if not simply early versions of, subsequent fictional forms. We have records from this period of readers describing experiences that seem familiar: Wim Verbaal observes,

> The first clear signs of texts taking over the factuality of a reader
> appear exactly around 1100. In his short poem *De molesta recreatione*
> (On troubled recreation), Marbod of Rennes describes the effects a
> song about love and dying has on him.... Melody and verses evoke in
> the listening poet the sadness and pains of the lady as they are sung.
> "I believed I suffered myself whenever the harpist played." "Reality it
> seemed, no song." Here, for the first time in Western literature as far
> as I know, we have the explicit expression of the power a fictional text
> has over the mind and feelings of a listener.
>
> (2017: 194)

In addition, as noted above, several formal features of medieval
romance that overlap with features of some medieval histories (see
Stein 2006: 143) are also conventional features of modern fictional
narrative. Many medieval romances go much further in thematizing their own imaginative and artifactual qualities through intricate narrative patterning and echoing, as well as thematization of
issues such as role-playing, games, illusion, doubling, and so forth,
suggestive of considerable fascination with these fictionality-related
motifs (see, e.g., Doody 1996: 187). Virginie Greene argues that the
chivalric code forming the backdrop to an entire genre of medieval
romances is itself a fictional or even metafictional construct: "chiv-
alry… is… an aggressive competitive culture with a vivid imagination
and a keen understanding of the power of signs" (2014: 26–27), and
Robert Stein has similarly argued that "the fighting [in chivalric culture and romance] is entirely without consequences, for it is a fiction"
(2006: 110).

While the pastoral romances of the fifteenth century onwards, which
flourished especially in Italy and Spain, no longer turned on the chivalric code, these romances continued the tradition of romance self-
awareness. Wolfgang Iser has described the frequent thematization of
borderlines and "doubling [in the pastoral romance]… as the hallmark
of fictionalizing acts that put in brackets whatever is, in order to allow
a repetition under different circumstances" (1993: 54). Iser describes
the pastoral romance as a "system… in which the original duality
[between urban center and pastoral retreat or refuge] spawns more
and more doublings" (56–57). *Don Quixote* (1605–15) was arguably

the culmination of these currents, an extraordinarily self-conscious meta-romance that mocked ignorance of the conventions of fictionality present in chivalric romance. The composition and rapid popularity of *Don Quixote* suggest that competence with such conventions, and their implications, could be (and was) widely distributed among the novel's readers (see, e.g., Hayot 2012: 123, 125).

THE "RISE OF THE NOVEL"

In her work on the medieval literature on fictionality, Virginie Greene argues that the "convergence of logic and fiction" has occurred only occasionally in Western letters, first "around 1100, and again around 1900... What emerges [at these two points]... is a metadiscourse about [certain] activities: reasoning about reasoning, reasoning about fiction, fictionalizing reasoning, and fictionalizing fiction" (2014: 82). Greene speculates that such bursts of meta-discourse may "coincide with a major change in the form and medium of fictions": in the twelfth and thirteenth centuries, "vernacular stories and songs," and at the turn of the twentieth century, cinema (82–83). Greene's historical scheme focuses on periods when the topic of fictionality becomes a concern in *both* philosophical literature and imaginative productions. This book will consider the second historical conjunction she identifies, in the early twentieth century, in Chapter 5.

Greene's identification of key periods in the history of fictionality does not mention the historical period perhaps most often regarded as a key turning point in the development of fiction: the period between the seventeenth and nineteenth centuries, especially in France and England. This period saw increasingly widespread literacy along with a new commodification of printed artifacts, including romances, novels, and other prose narratives recounting invented events. Philosophers writing during this period were generally concerned with matters other than logic, so it makes sense that Greene would not identify the period as a crucial passage in the history of the philosophy of fictionality. But this period is probably the most frequently proposed point of origin for the appearance of fiction in something close to its paradigmatic contemporary form. Scholars focusing on this period have identified various points during the stretch between around 1650 and 1800 as marking the advent of fiction. In addition to differing about dates, these scholars disagree on the cultural and literary-historical developments that drove this emergence, and they sometimes work with subtly different definitions of "fiction." To illustrate these different approaches, the rest of this section will consider two prominent recent accounts in this vein (see also Davis 1983; Gjerlevsen 2019: 429; Iser 1993: 92, 143, 164, 310 n.2).

One well-known account is that of Catherine Gallagher, whose 2006 essay "The Rise of Fictionality" continues an argument begun in her 1994 book *Nobody's Story* and alludes in its title to Ian Watt's classic 1957 *The Rise of the Novel*, which greatly influenced decades of scholarship on eighteenth-century English literature. Gallagher explicitly argues in "The Rise of Fictionality" that what English-language readers call "fiction" first appeared in the early- to mid-1700s. Her argument is partly based on etymology and usage: she maintains that during the eighteenth century, "an earlier frequent meaning of 'deceit, dissimulation, pretense' became obsolete" (Gallagher 2006: 337–38). Gallagher does acknowledge that "numerous pre-eighteenth-century genres would meet the test set by almost all modern theorists of fictionality," who "conceive of fiction in terms of possible worlds, pretended illocutionary acts,... or language games" and "start from Sidney's premise about 'poesie': fiction somehow suspends... normal referential truth claims about the world of ordinary experience" (338). But, Gallagher contends, "Stories that were both plausible and received as narratives about *purely imaginary individuals*... were still exceedingly rare in the first quarter of the eighteenth century" (340; emphasis added). What prompted the shift to the use of such characters that Gallagher sees as crucial? According to Gallagher, mainly legal developments and socioeconomic realignments: "Because the novel defined itself against scandalous libel [narratives referring to actual people], it used fiction as the diacritical mark of its differentiation requiring that the concept of fiction take on greater clarity and definition" (340). More broadly, Gallagher also argues that

> [m]odernity is fiction-friendly because [modernity] encourages disbelief, speculation, and credit.... [W]hile sympathizing with [the] innocent credulity [of the characters of the early novel], the reader is trained in

an attitude of disbelief, which is flattered as superior discernment.... [T] he reader, unlike the character, occupies the lofty position of one who speculates on the action, entertaining various hypotheses about it.

(345–46)

In positioning him- or herself this way, the reader of novels about admittedly invented people thus becomes socialized as a member of a credit-based commercial society built on impersonal economic exchange.

Gallagher's argument has attracted criticism. In a 2018 article, Monika Fludernik argued that Gallagher's focus on the invented names of eighteenth-century fictional characters, which Fludernik (2018) identifies as Gallagher's "main criterion of fictionality," is historically flawed, since "comic genres have employed invented nomia," or characters, "[s]ince antiquity" (80). Fludernik's own position is that "fictionality is [also] prominently available in the tradition of narrative and epic poetry in the English Renaissance" and that "the artful anachronies" or temporal scramblings—flashbacks and so forth—discussed by twentieth-century narratologists "are a feature of the Greek novel" as well as of Renaissance literature (83). In Fludernik's view, "What is notable for the early modern period is not its invention of fictionality but its invention of genres that provide descriptions of the real world," "in response to the public's craving for factuality" (83; see also Davis 1983 for a similar argument). Fludernik concludes that "[f]ictionality continued to exist as a literary mode and social practice from the time of the medieval romance onward, yet it attained its peculiar connotation as an entirely separate realm opposed to factual discourse only with the institutionalization of factuality in the press" in the seventeenth and eighteenth centuries (84).

Arguably, then, the phenomenon Gallagher addresses in her essay is not fictionality as such, but a narrower concern with truth in fiction, or the question of the sense in which sentences and narratives describing fictional states of affairs can be deemed true. As Gallagher puts it, she describes a "shift from a narrow conception of truth as historical accuracy to a more capacious understanding that could conceive truth conceived as mimetic simulation" (2006: 341). As even Fludernik acknowledges, it does not seem unreasonable to say that *some* kind of significant cultural realignment related to fictionality did occur during the eighteenth century, given the other political and technological developments of that period.

Another critic of Gallagher is Nicholas Paige, who challenges her thesis both with regard to the timing of the decisive literary-historical moment and with regard to the narrative features that mark the advent of fiction. Paige, who focuses on French literature of the seventeenth and eighteenth centuries rather than the English literature about which Gallagher writes, proposes a three-part periodization scheme for understanding the emergence of fiction as a cultural practice (2011: x, 8, 12, 204). The first phase, lasting from antiquity up to about 1670, was an "Aristotelian" regime in which writers of literary narrative generally did not invent their characters, but rather drew the personages in their narratives from history or myth, or else personified abstract types as the agents in their narratives. In the second phase, lasting from the mid-seventeenth century to around 1800, "novelists... assert... the literal reality of their books" (12) and distance their works from medieval and Renaissance chivalric, pastoral, and antique romances (23). Novelists' assertion of their books' "reality" takes the form of frame narratives or other paratextual material presenting the principal narratives as found manuscripts, memoirs, diaries, or collections of letters. Paige argues that novels of this kind cannot be considered truly fictional because they do not ask readers to accept that the narrated events are wholly invented (e.g., 196); rather, such novels consist of pretended utterances like those Searle equates with all fictional discourse (199; see also Introduction). In addition, these "pseudo-factual" novels do not involve the new form of third-person narration, often called omniscient, that becomes a widespread feature of novels only after 1800 (199–200), at which point the third phase of Paige's scheme begins and fiction proper may be said to have entered literary history.

Paige asserts that his study traces the emergence or possibility of "fictionality" (ix), but he also asserts that "there is no such thing as fiction outside novels that are fictional" (206). Thus, he is working with a quite specific definition of "fiction" and "fictionality." More specifically, Paige seems to take "fiction" to refer only to works like those that make up the bulk of what we now find in the fiction section of libraries and bookshops. Paige offers no detailed defense of this definitional choice; he explicitly accepts

Dorrit Cohn's argument that what defines fiction is the presence of "transparent minds" or "psycho-narration" within a narrative (199–200). But Cohn's argument, as Chapter 3 will explain, has itself been criticized. Read narrowly, Paige's book presents a convincing argument that certain specific techniques or technologies of narration indeed do become widespread only after around 1800. But Paige does not offer an especially convincing argument that, for example, *The Golden Ass* and *Don Quixote* do not deserve to be called fiction. In addition, Paige expressly limits his focus to French and English literature, excluding not only other European vernacular traditions but also imaginative literary production from other parts of the world.

THE CLASSIC CHINESE NOVELS

In part, this chapter has been examining the question of whether we are justified in applying the label "fiction" to artifacts that contemporaries would not necessarily have labeled that way. It seems likely that Nicholas Paige would say no, but many of the other theorists and historians discussed throughout this chapter would probably disagree. There is no consensus on whether a critical or theoretical vocabulary addressing fictionality in terms we would recognize is necessary for us to be able to say that contemporary imaginative practices merit the label "fiction" or "fictionality."

Another example of a body of highly complex imaginative literary artifacts created despite the lack of a universally accepted contemporary scholarly label for identifying them comes from fourteenth-through eighteenth-century Imperial China. The five canonical novels in this group have continued to be adapted, modified, and alluded to in Chinese culture down to the present. In chronological order, based on the date of the earliest extant manuscript copies, the novels are *The Romance of the Three Kingdoms* (Sānguó Yǎnyì), attributed to Luo Guangzhong, dating from the fourteenth century; *The Water Margin* (also known as *Outlaws of the Marsh*, Shuǐhu Zhuàn), attributed to Shi Nai'an, dating from the fourteenth century; *Journey to the West* (Xī Yóu Jì), attributed to Wu Cheng'en, dating from the sixteenth century; *The Plum in the Golden Vase* (Jīn Píng Méi), attributed to the pseudonymous Langling XiaoXiao Sheng, and dating from the sixteenth or seventeenth century; and *The Story of the Stone* (Hónglóu Mèng; also known as *Dream of the Red Chamber*), attributed to Cao Xueqin, dating from the eighteenth century. While the first three of these novels narrate the activities of legendary and putatively historical figures, the last two at least arguably narrate the experiences of wholly imagined personages (Yu 1997: 46). However, all of the novels involve techniques associated with fiction in the West, including some psychonarration and third-person narration.

Despite the permeation of Chinese culture by these works and the incredibly intricate construction of all of the novels, they were not labeled by contemporaries using a single term with a meaning akin to the senses of "fiction" discussed earlier in this chapter. One term sometimes applied to these works, *xiaoshuo*, meaning "small talk" or "idle chit-chat," is also applied to other kinds of invented narrative, including much less monumental artifacts. The novels are also sometimes categorized as *xugou*, a word "made up of one character meaning 'empty' and another meaning 'to construct'" (Lobén 2017: 32). Some critics have argued that traditional Chinese literary commentary never explored a theory of mimesis or authorial creativity analogous to those developed in ancient Greece because of the absence from Chinese religious tradition of a creator figure (Yu 1997: 262). Poetry and other imaginative literature also received more erratic approval from imperial officials during the period in question, and indeed were sometimes proscribed, discouraging the generation of both imaginative literary artifacts and commentary on them for significant stretches of time (190).

Yet as noted above, the Chinese novels share some crucial features with what Westerners consider paradigmatic fictional artifacts. *The Story of the Stone* (c. 1740–92) is a good example, especially when considered in light of Paige's arguments about the advent of fiction in Europe at the end of the eighteenth century. Like the other classic novels, this one is massive, composed of 140 chapters that in English translation fill five substantial volumes. The novel is framed by a fantastic narrative purporting to explain the provenance of the discourse that makes up the great bulk of the work. Almost all of the novel concerns the thoughts, feelings, and actions of a group of elite adolescents navigating the protocols of their clan amid its declining fortunes, with a particular focus on the teenagers' emotional entanglements, maturation, and literary efforts. But the very first chapter of the novel opens with a brief account of how the goddess Nü-wa, setting out to repair the sky after a celestial collision, created a number of stones for the purpose and decided to use all but one for her project (47). The rejected stone, which has animate properties including thoughts and emotions, is taken up by a monk who recognizes the stone's assets and promises "to cut a few words in you [the stone] so that anyone seeing you will know at once that you are something special" (48). "[C]ountless aeons" later (48), an ambiguous, symbolic character named Vanitas finds the stone, reads its inscriptions, and after some contemplation "took it back with him to look for a publisher" (51). From this point, partway through Chapter 1, the novel purports to be a transcription of the engraved words on the stone.

Even though this frame narrative presents an explanation of how the novel came to be, its self-evidently supernatural content distinguishes it from the framing material discussed by Paige as characteristic of the pseudo-factual novel. Indeed, the frame narrative resembles more closely the kind of "distressed" fantastic literature that Paige associates with the romance, the fairy tale, and the gothic novel, as opposed to the pseudo-factual literature out of which, he argues, what we call fiction proper developed (Paige 2011: 172–75). But most of *The Story of the Stone* consists of a narrative recounting the actions, thoughts, and emotions of characters who are at least partly if not wholly invented, and who exist within a plausibly realistic contemporary Chinese urban world (Yu 1997: 19, 46); these are features of what Paige identifies as the fictional novel. Also, as Anthony Yu explains, the narrator—who is perhaps the stone or maybe the monk who engraves it—"claims the authoritative knowledge and representation of other minds and lives" (265), presenting the kind of psychonarration that Paige considers a mark of fiction rather than pseudo-fiction. Indeed, because of these inside views of the main characters as well as their tragic experiences, the novel has long been considered exceptionally emotionally powerful, the source of "its own sensational legend that the effect of its sympathetic reading can be lethal" (218). Perhaps, then, *The Story of the Stone* could be considered similar to one of the eighteenth-century "nonce" narratives that Paige discusses. These narratives played with conventions of prior narrative forms in ways that anticipated much later conventions, including through experiments with sentimental identification (e.g., Paige 2011: 206).

And yet, this novel was not part of the tradition that Paige examines. It was part of a quite different literary tradition originally received by readers with a quite different understanding of authorial creativity and the referentiality of extended narratives of people in action (Yu 1997: 262–63; see also Lu 1994). European-centered intellectual and literary historians focusing on the development of fictional conventions and the characteristics of fictionality have had difficulty agreeing on what should count as "fiction" and why, and many such histories do not acknowledge the range of disagreement on this issue. Some of this European-centered work also evidences an impulse toward reductive conclusions: for example, that fiction emerged at a particular datable point in time because particular specific socio-political, cultural, and/or technological developments prompted the use and appreciation of specific narrative features. As European and English-language scholars continue to work on the question of the history of fiction, attention to non-European traditions might be one way to keep these critical shortcomings in view and perhaps start to overcome them.

3

SEEING AS

Near the end of the third chapter of Edward St. Aubyn's novel *Bad News* (1993), Patrick Melrose, the protagonist, leaves a New York City apartment building where he has been visiting a family friend and steps out onto the sidewalk. In this novel, Melrose struggles with addiction exacerbated by his privileged but dysfunctional upbringing. He has come to New York to attend the funeral of his abusive father, and when he steps outside the apartment building, he is jetlagged as well as drunk and disoriented by a combination of Quaaludes and amphetamines:

> Down in the sluggish airless lift, past the fat moronic doorman, and into the street. The shock of standing again under the wide pale sky, completely exposed. This must be what the oyster feels when the lemon juice falls.
>
> Why had he left the shelter of Anne's flat? And so rudely. Now she would hate him forever. Everything he did was wrong.
>
> (St. Aubyn 2015: 166)

This passage exemplifies several features associated with modern prose fiction. It *focalizes* the narrated activity—leaving Anne's

DOI: 10.4324/9781003161585-4

apartment—through Melrose. That is, the passage describes the setting as the jaundiced, disoriented, and hyperreactive Melrose perceives it. The passage seems to narrate Melrose's thoughts, in the second quoted paragraph, but does so in the third person. The novel does not quote Melrose's thoughts using the words he would if he were to articulate his thoughts aloud. In presenting Melrose's thoughts and perspective in this manner, the passage mixes elements of first- and third-person narration in the way associated with what is known as free indirect discourse. And among Melrose's narrated thoughts, perhaps, is the striking analogy between his posture and emotional state and that of the "oyster... when the lemon juice falls," a parallel suggesting vulnerability and perhaps also fear, recoil, and psychological distance through Melrose's cross-species identification.

Through devices such as these, *Bad News* induces readers to visualize or otherwise imagine the events and people described in the novel, and at times to feel with (or to entertain feelings about) them. The focus of this chapter is on the kinds of issues raised by the passage above: readers' mental and emotional responses to fiction, as well as the representation of mental and emotional states within fiction. The following pages consider how such verbal spurs to readers' adoption of particular attitudes, imaginings, and emotions relate to some recent literary-critical debates as well as to topics addressed in previous chapters. The chapter turns first to a background issue central to our interest in narratives of any kind: what it means to see another person as acting intentionally or to see a real or narrated action as intentional. The chapter will also consider two related but distinct ways in which the audiences of artifacts involving fictionality often engage in "seeing as." One way was famously discussed by Ludwig Wittgenstein in his *Philosophical Investigations* (1958), then later dubbed "seeing-in" by Richard Wollheim (1968), and it is closely tied to the doubling phenomena addressed in Chapter 1. The other sense of "seeing as" considered in this chapter involves taking on the point of view of another intentional system or agent: simulating the other's intentional mental state, identifying with them, feeling with them, and so on. The chapter will also review two critical debates linked to this second kind of fictional seeing as. The first debate concerns what is sometimes called the exceptionality thesis, that is, the position that our attitudes toward, and reactions to, real people diverge fundamentally from those we take and have toward fictional characters. The second debate concerns so-called "signposts" of fictionality (Cohn 1990), or the question of what, if any, unique linguistic or other features characterize fictional discourse. Finally, the chapter will consider variants of seeing as and identification that have historically received less attention from theorists but are poised to become more central subjects of critical concern.

INTENTIONALITY

In the *Poetics*, Aristotle describes plot as "a designed pattern of action, and [therefore]… purposive and significant," that is, explicable by the end or aim that the plot leads to (Aristotle [Halliwell] 1987: 94). Aristotle's conception of character was quite different from twentieth- and twenty-first-century conceptions: in his view, "Many actions… necessarily have a degree of characterisation built into them, since their nature will presuppose particular ethical dispositions; but… characterless action is [also] a possibility" (Aristotle [Halliwell] 1987: 95). That is, character for Aristotle becomes visible as a result of action, and in a sense character explains action, or events, but in order to explain or understand action, it is not always necessary to imagine a character whose mental, emotional, and other internal traits produced the action. This view is quite different from modern Western views of how to explain action. Overwhelmingly, the paradigm for such explanation, when the action involves human individuals, is what Daniel Dennett calls the "intentional stance," which includes the attribution to actors of "beliefs and desires and other mental states exhibiting what [philosopher Franz] Brentano [1838–1917] and others call intentionality" (Dennett 1987: 15). Ludwig Wittgenstein described something very similar in his *Philosophical Investigations* (1953), as explained by Stanley Raffel in the following passage:

> Sometimes, no doubt, intentions are hidden, but if we are tempted to think of intentions as inevitably hidden: "Look at a cat when it stalks a bird; or a beast when it tries to escape." Watching a cat stalk a bird, we surely feel we know its intention. Its intention is not invisible[,] though it is not quite right to say it is visible…. Instead of being strictly visible,

its intention appears—seems clear [to us]—because it is a way,... perhaps the only way, to interpret what is visible: the single-mindedness of the pursuit, the stealth, the moments of patience, etc.

(Raffel 2011: 287, quoting Wittgenstein 1953, Part I, para. 647)

To philosophers, intentionality is significant in at least two senses. One sense might be described as external, the other as internal. Dennett and Wittgenstein as cited above are concerned with intentionality in the external sense, as a property we attribute to entities that we regard as agents or potential agents. Literary theorist Lubomír Doležel explains one way in which our tendency to take the intentional stance relates to our experience of fictionality: "The 'reading' of manifest symptoms (both bodily events and speech acts) is a popular method of inferring a person's emotional state. Conversely, the symptoms are a powerful device for constructing fictional emotions" (1998: 69; see also Palmer 2004).

For at least some contemporary subjects of psychological studies, the impulse to ascribe intention to entities on the basis of such symptoms is almost irresistible. Subjects will interpret the movements of even abstract geometrical shapes as intentional (Mar & Oatley 2008: 179). Most theorists agree that we read such symptoms as indicative of goals and emotions based in part on our experience with other people and in part on our experience with representations of human (and other intentional) interaction, in the form of schemata, scripts, and situation models (177). Scripts, explains Monika Fludernik, "are fairly specific, culture-dependent concepts" that "contain a series of (chronologically related) processes and a combination of functional props" and thus "holistically bring together [cognitive and cultural] knowledge which—as soon as the script has been evoked...—produces an immediate holistic, situational understanding" of the action perceived, whether in person or in a representation (1993: 446, 447; see also Kintsch 1998; Palmer 2004; Gibson 2007). An example of such a script is the understanding, shared by many Western adults, of the appropriate and expected sequence of events involved in eating at a restaurant, including for example the expectation that if you are seated and handed a menu, someone will return to take your order unless you are specifically informed otherwise. We understand the waitstaff's conduct as informed by this script, and if we are a member of the waitstaff, we likewise understand customers' behavior according to the script. Such common-sense action sequences seem to structure not only our navigation of the real world but also our comprehension of written narrative.

In taking the intentional stance and making sense of agents' actions in terms of their presumed goals according to a script, many psychologists and cognitive scientists argue, we attribute an interior to those agents. This interior is the site of those beliefs, desires, and so forth that cannot themselves be perceived but that we postulate to explain the agents' action. Among these interior states are states that are intentional in a second, distinguishable sense: they are directed toward some representation, perception, goal, memory, or other content (see, e.g., Lewis 1986: 106). Imagination, on many accounts, is an example of activity that is often intentional in this sense (see Sartre 1940: 28; Gilmore 2020: 2–5, 10). Other such intentional states include belief, desire, and speculation. When we attribute such states to another person, we engage in what many contemporary theorists call "mindreading" (e.g., Nichols & Stich 2003). Such mindreading involves both external "behavior prediction" and internal "belief ascription" (76).

What does all of this have to do with fictionality? A number of contemporary theorists argue that the capacity for attributing intentionality is implicated in several ways in the apprehension of fictional narrative, and perhaps fictionality more generally. We may inevitably regard fiction as the product of intentional activity (see, e.g., Currie 1990: 76, 80). We make sense of represented actions as the results of characters' intentional states. Even when a narrative does not explicitly describe or represent a character's mental state, we often attribute mentality to that character by making assumptions about the character's knowledge, motivation, and mood, for example. Several theorists have suggested that providing opportunities for such practice in mindreading is key to the function of fiction as a cultural practice (e.g., Mar & Oatley 2008). Also, of course, in our own apprehension of fiction we are ourselves taking a specific and rather complex intentional attitude toward the fictional artifact in question.

SEEING-IN AND SEEING-AS

As used in this section, "seeing-in" describes a specific manner of directing attention and intention, first introduced in Chapter 1. "Seeing-as," in contrast, refers to a way of registering, or reasoning about, the experience of another intentional agent.

This clarification is necessary because one of the best-known discussions of seeing-in (or at least one of the best-known anticipations of the concept) calls the phenomenon "seeing as" or "seeing an aspect." This discussion is Ludwig Wittgenstein's, in Part II of the *Philosophical Investigations*. Wittgenstein explains,

One could imagine the illustration

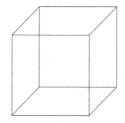

appearing in... a textbook.... [W]e can see the illustration now as one thing [e.g., a "glass cube,... an upturned wire box"], now as another.

(Wittgenstein 1953: Pt. II, xi, para. 116)

Wittgenstein reiterates this point in a later paragraph, illustrated with the well-known "duck-rabbit" image, which "can be seen as a rabbit's head or as a duck's" (Pt. II, xi, para. 118). Chapter 1 considered a similar phenomenon as one of the kinds of doubleness exhibited by artifacts involving representation. All such artifacts can be seen *as* material objects, or *as* what they represent. In the vocabulary of twentieth-century philosopher Richard Wollheim, we can see the artifacts, or see *in* them what they represent (a glass cube, a duck, and so forth).

Wittgenstein was not the first person to note this phenomenon (see, e.g., Schiller 1801: 101; Sartre 1940: 189; see also Iser 1993: 151, discussing an analogous notion addressed by Hans Vaihinger). But Wittgenstein's discussion attracted a great deal of attention from philosophers of mind and aesthetics in the second half of the twentieth century (see, e.g., Hester 1966; Wilkerson 1973; Seligman 1976) and influenced other aesthetic accounts that became influential in their own right, like that of Richard Wollheim regarding the perception of visual representations (1968; see also Walton 2002; Smith 2011; Stecker 2013, commenting on and modifying Wollheim's position). It was Wollheim who popularized the term "seeing in" to describe the phenomenon in question.

The attention that this phenomenon has received reflects its usefulness in analyzing and discussing the perception of representational and fictional artifacts. The notion of seeing-in identifies what is arguably the most important of the flavors of doubling considered in Chapter 1 and provides as well a vehicle for drawing together the other perspectives on fictionality addressed in that chapter. Seeing-in describes a way to think about *mimetic* artifacts, which convey representations in a material (or otherwise perceptible) medium (see, e.g., Schaeffer 1999: 164–66). Seeing-in seems to require the use of some form of partly willed but also partly involuntary *imagination*: we tend automatically to see the duck-rabbit as either a duck or a rabbit rather than an abstract set of marks, but we usually can also shift our perception at will to see the figure as the other represented animal, or even as an abstract set of marks (Wittgenstein 1953: Pt. II, xi, paras. 196–201; Ingarden 1968: 56–57; Seligman 1976: 208–09). Finally, seeing-in involves a kind of *make-believe*—the adoption of a stance toward the artifact as if the artifact were something other than a brute physical object. Discussing the relationship between seeing an aspect and "experiencing the meaning of a word," Wittgenstein notes:

> I can imagine some arbitrary cipher... to be a strictly correct letter of a foreign alphabet. Or... to be a faultily written one...: for example, it might be slapdash....And according to the fiction with which I surround it, I can see it in various aspects. And here is a close kinship with "experiencing the meaning of a word."
>
> (1953: Pt. II, xi, para. 234)

Complex as this phenomenon is, it makes up only part of a still more complex phenomenon that many theorists maintain is inherent in our experience of narrative fiction. As noted above, when we process a fictional narrative, we treat it as a representation of intentional activity that allows both inferences about agents' mental states and sometimes direct access to information about those states (Mar & Oatley 2008: 174). Narrative very often allows us to see as another perceiving point of view, such as that of a character like Patrick Melrose. Reading the passage quoted at the beginning of this chapter, a reader may see in the words not just a represented entity, but a represented entity that itself has the capacity to perceive representations or modes of seeing as: the capacity to see itself *as* an oyster, or to see the threatening environment *as* an oyster might perceive it. To be sure, we also seem to have the capacity to take the perspective of other real people with whom we interact. So seeing as in this sense is not unique to fiction. Indeed, Daniel Dor argues that it is the basis of all communication via language (2015: 20, 37). Nonetheless, a great deal of aesthetic activity and fiction evidences the attraction of *play* with the capacity to see as. Our fascination with the possibility of seeing as an animal, for example, is ancient—just think of Aesop's fables or Apuleius's *The Golden Ass*, in which the protagonist Lucius's transformation into an ass is impelled by his curiosity (e.g., Whitmarsh 2013: 78). Or consider how much make-believe by children involves the assumption of roles, in which the children act (and perhaps "see") "as" animals, warriors, parents, and so on (e.g., Bogdan 2013: 85). Indeed, this tendency toward the adoption of other perspectives, understood as a developmental necessity, lay behind Plato's concern regarding the danger of mimesis (Halliwell 2002: 52–53) and also forms the foundation of cultural theatrical forms (e.g., Iser 1993: 77) as well as, arguably, modern Western structures of interpersonal interaction and professionalism (Goffman 1959).

Just how similar are the kinds of seeing as that we experience in reading a fictional narrative, or watching a fiction film, to those we undertake to communicate with family members or strangers, or to perform professional roles such as those of teacher or health-care provider? This question has been the subject of a recent debate discussed in the next section.

THE EXCEPTIONALITY THESIS

In his 2007 book *The Rhetoric of Fictionality*, Richard Walsh proposed that "the way [our emotions] are involved with real people" is a "special case" of "the way our emotions are involved with fictional characters" (Walsh 2007: 158–59). The more general view that "[e]ncounters with fictional minds are mediated by the same heuristics used to interpret everyday minds" (Herman 2011: 18) has been a tenet of a significant trend in literary scholarship in the late twentieth and early twenty-first centuries. This scholarship often draws on the kinds of research and theorizing noted in the previous sections of this chapter to examine how our understanding of the minds represented in fictional narrative can clarify our handling of mindreading in real life, and vice versa (e.g., Mar & Oatley 2008; Kidd & Castro 2013). Those who challenge this assumption have been described by David Herman as promoting the "exceptionality thesis," or the position that "we approach fiction and nonfiction by means of different protocols for reasoning and with different interpretive strategies" for making sense of real, nonfictional, and fictional minds (Kukkonen & Nielsen 2018: 483). This debate overlaps with, or perhaps is an updated version of, the parasitic-discourse question considered in Chapter 1. Both discussions concern, at least at one level, the question whether representations in fictional discourse are fundamentally like or unlike representations in nonfictional discourse, or those "representations" we generate in attributing intentions, beliefs, desires, and so forth to others in our life.

The "common minds" approach of theorists like Walsh and Herman (Bernaerts & Richardson 2018: 527) has proven quite attractive. Scholars adopting its assumptions, in addition to Walsh and Herman, include philosophers, psychologists, and literary theorists such as Gregory Currie (1990), Raymond Mar and Keith Oatley (2008), Alan Palmer (2004), Lisa Zunshine (2006), David Comer Kidd and Emanuele Castro (2013), Ellen Spolsky (2016), and many others (see especially Gilmore 2020, 11, 61, 67). The common minds approach is attractive, in part, because like make-believe accounts of fictionality, it justifies literary theorists' recourse to a growing body of psychological and other scientific research on, for example, child development, language acquisition, interpersonal skills, empathy, and cooperation. Literary theorists can draw on this research both to explain the internal dynamics of fictional narrative, or its represen-tation of intentional action and mindreading by characters, and the processing of such narrative by audience members. The common minds position is also attractive because it suggests psychological, sociological, and even biological justifications for the practice of creating and appreciating fictional representations as well as the academic study of these practices. Such justifications offer a way to rebut not only Plato's critique of mimesis, but also the turn away from valuing humanistic higher education in much of the twenty-first-century English-speaking West.

But the common minds position is not just a scholarly convenience. Psychological study of the phenomena in question—including imagination, emotion, and empathy—support the inference that audience responses to fictional representations, to the extent that those responses involve imagination, do share biological similarities to responses to real actions and interactions (see, e.g., Gilmore 2020: 11, 61, 67). Thus, for example, psychologists studying the relationship between imagination and emotion have concluded that "imagining a scene and experiencing the sights, sounds, and other sensations in imagination will involve very similar patterns of neural activation as if the scene was being perceived and experienced in reality" (Blackwell 2020: 242). Given this overlap, it is not surprising that some studies suggest that such imagination can "activate" responses similar to those that would be activated for a real-life scene, including emotional responses (243). Indeed, the assumption of "continuity" between our experience of imagined and lived actions and interactions underlies many of the psychological studies themselves, which use subjects' responses to invented narratives as a basis for conclusions about real-life emotional experience (Gilmore 2020: 71 n.96, 107). It is a small step from these findings and assumptions to the position outlined by Richard Walsh at the beginning of this section.

On the other hand, there is no shortage of support for the exceptionality thesis. For example, as many critics observe, our access to fictional minds is often more complete and far more detailed than anything we can experience in real life (e.g., Kukkonen & Nielsen 2018). Our ability to empathize with real people also probably involves more complex capacities than the kind of seeing or feeling with a character encouraged by representational media (e.g., Plantinga 2016: 143). Moreover, as Jean-Marie Schaeffer has noted, "fictional immersion is... paradoxically[] the place of a disidentification.... [I]t is a matter of a split mental state: it detaches us from ourselves,... introducing a distance from ourselves to ourselves" (1999: 298; see also Gallagher 2006: 356–57). The audience member who reads a fictional narrative is not quite the same cognitive agent as that same person going about the activities of daily life. When the mind represented is fictional, audience members perceive it in a way that is mediated by representation, but also with the knowledge that it is an invented construct, unlike those minds we encounter in real life or, perhaps, even those represented in ostensibly nonfictional artifacts.

These differences have generated a related debate regarding the appropriate characterization of the emotions or affective responses that audience members have to fictional representations of events and interactions. Dan Shaw describes the debate as initiated by Walton's article "Fearing Fictions" (1978a; Shaw 2016: 155), in which Walton described the emotion felt by a filmgoer watching an action or horror movie as "quasi-fear," or make-believe fear, rather than genuine fear (see also Walton 1990: 243–47). According to Shaw, Walton's account "has faced substantial criticism from those who contend that we do feel genuine emotions for fictional cinematic characters," leading to the development of "two schools of thought" in the 1990s (2016: 155). One approach connects emotion to cognition and argues that formal aspects of an artwork such as a film, by directing our attention and otherwise channeling our cognition, prompt the experiencing of specifically representation-prompted emotions (155–57). The other approach, endorsed by Shaw, does not assimilate emotion to cognition but "claim[s] that we simulate the emotions of... characters, adopting their perspective... At the heart of such simulations are... mirroring processes that lead our emotional states to converge with those of the characters" (158; see also Gilmore 2020, for a recent book-length examination of this issue).

Another theoretical issue related to the exceptionality question is the so-called "puzzle of imaginative resistance" (Gendler 2000). In fact, this puzzle, debated mainly by philosophers rather than literary theorists, dates back at least to David Hume. The puzzle concerns why

> [w]e are willing to make believe all sorts of things that we take to be false about the actual world, including even things that we take to be physically and metaphysically impossible.... But we seem resistant to the invitation to imagine worlds in which moral truths obtain that are strikingly incompatible with our actual moral beliefs.
>
> (D. Davies 2020: 575)

An example of such an aberrant moral truth would be the premise that it is morally acceptable to kill human beings for sport. Researchers are continuing to investigate this question experimentally as well as theoretically, and their work has the potential to clarify our understanding of the relations between our cognitive and affective responses to real and make-believe scenarios (see, e.g., Vaage 2015).

All of these controversies are complicated further by the way mimetic artifacts may represent minds in the act of simulating or representing other minds, which may themselves be simulating or representing other minds (Zunshine 2006). Much action in modern fictional narrative turns on characters' understandings and misunderstandings of others' intentions, knowledge, and plans. How do we learn to ascribe such complex mental states to others? In part, perhaps, through pretend play in childhood, which introduces us to basic action sequences we can use to infer intentionality and, eventually, more subtle intentional states in others. If the common minds position is at all accurate, we can continue to refine our mindreading skills through the consumption of fiction (e.g., Zunshine 2006; Mar & Oatley 2008). Represented interactions and mental states might even be our main source of instruction on what kinds of circumstances appropriately prompt complex emotions like jealousy (Fludernik 1993; Gibson 2007). Arguably, fictional narrative offers opportunities for practicing mindreading at a level of complexity seldom if ever encountered in real life.

THE SIGNPOSTS DEBATE

The exceptionality thesis proposes a difference between real-life mindreading and empathy and the kind of seeing as a character enabled by fictional artifacts, but it could also be taken to imply a difference between fictional and nonfictional representation: the people (and minds) represented in nonfiction are categorically different from those represented in fiction. Some theorists deny this latter point, without explicitly subscribing to the common minds view (Matravers 2014). But most theorists do assume that the distinction between fictional and nonfictional narrative is a meaningful one. The signposts debate concerns the markers of this difference. What, if any, signposts do readers follow in identifying a narrative as fictional rather than nonfictional? How do they know to see a text as fictional? A variation on this debate concerns the question of whether any particular features are *definitive* of fiction, so that if a narrative has those features, we will need to call it fictional, regardless of, for example, its author's intentions (see Bareis 2008: 157).

For many years in the twentieth century, theorists debated which formal linguistic and structural features of an artifact might identify it as fictional (Dawson 2015: 85; see also Gjerlevsen 2016a). These theorists focused almost entirely on narrative fiction. Various scholars proposed such formal features as the use of internal focalization, psychonarration (the direct narration of character thoughts), and the use of the simple past tense for narration (or, in languages other than English, the use of the epic preterite or another narrating verb form). Other scholars proposed structural narrative signposts, such as the nonidentity of narrator with author. In a nonfictional narrative, the author also narrates any represented events; in a fictional narrative, even a first-person and semi-autobiographical narrative, readers generally take the narrator to be at least slightly distinct from the author. Prominent proponents of the view that internal focalization and associated narrative devices constituted signposts of fiction in the late twentieth century included Käte Hamburger (1973), Wayne Booth (1961), and Dorrit Cohn (1978). But this view did not originate with these theorists, as Cohn subsequently pointed out (1999: 85–86; see also Stock 2017: 164). Proponents of this position all identify a kind of narrative access to characters' "interiors" or intentional states as the defining feature of narrative fiction. On this approach, fictional artifacts allow us to see a particular point of view in a manner that other artifacts do not.

The main structural feature proposed as a signpost—the author/narrator distinction—was also cited by Booth (1983) and has attracted more than a few other advocates, including James Phelan (1981) and Dorrit Cohn (1999). Gérard Genette (1991) has likewise argued that the "rigorous identification" of author and narrator "defines factual narrative—in which... the author assumes full responsibility for the assertions of his narrative" and that in contrast, the "dissociation" of author and narrator "defines fiction, that is, a type of narrative whose veracity is not seriously assumed by the author" (70). Genette explains that this "dissociative" feature makes fictional narrative "a special case of the 'polyphonic' utterance that is characteristic of all 'nonserious' utterances, or, to [borrow] Austin's controversial term, 'parasitical' utterances" (75).

But Genette concluded that the nonidentity of author and narrator should be regarded as a defeasible or potential marker of fictionality. In the same work, Genette also observed that the relationship of identity or nonidentity between author and narrator is "not always as manifest as" the relationship between narrator and character or that between author and character (78). So, he concluded, "Most often… a fictional text declares itself to be such by paratextual marks that protect the reader from any misunderstanding" (79). Paratextual marks are such features as subtitles, the presence or lack of an index, packaging, and other indicators of fictionality that do not form part of the fictional narrative itself (Genette 1997). The position that fictionality is signaled to audience members by paratextual features is now probably the dominant view among literary theorists (see, e.g., Iser 1993; Schaeffer 1999; Nielsen, Phelan, & Walsh 2015; Phelan & Nielsen 2017). Paratextual marks and signals let audience members know that the accompanying artifact can be used for make-believe play, or should be approached in that spirit. Such marks frame the artifact, creating a kind of threshold separating the real world from a make-believe one.

It is possible that the tendency to regard paratextual marks as the main indicators of fictionality is related to the intensified late-twentieth-century trend toward discussion of fiction in terms of worlds, an issue considered in more detail in Chapter 4. Scholarly interest in identifying and analyzing formal markers of fictionality has waned over the past generation or so. The first set of views described above, those identifying fictionality with special forms of access to characters' mental states, has received significant criticism. In particular, critics have noted that the theorists advancing these positions support them with examples drawn mostly from modern, or at least post-eighteenth-century, novels. Yet some historically sensitive critics also continue to reserve the term "fiction" for artifacts that exhibit these classic formal features (e.g., Paige 2011).

Competing positions have also been criticized. One difficulty presented by identifying fictionality as paratextually signaled concerns how to explain moments or passages of fictionality embedded within nonfictional artifacts, the phenomenon that Nielsen, Phelan, and Walsh proposed as ripe for scholarly examination in their "Ten Theses" article (see, especially, Hatavara & Mildorf 2017, examining fictionality in oral narrative and museum displays, and identifying it based on psychonarration and internal focalization). Increasingly sophisticated text processing and machine-learning technologies are enabling the identification of potential new signpost candidates, or at least of textual features distinguishing fictional from nonfictional narrative. Andrew Piper has described his development of a model able to sort previously classified fictional and nonfictional texts with high accuracy based on the presence of features including exclamation marks, personal pronouns, references to family members and bodies, modal verbs, and "the act of negation" (2018: 107, 109, 114). Piper concludes that "[t]he ambiguity [about truth-value or fictional status] that appears to exist on the level of the sentence [studied by philosophers]... no longer holds when we observe writing at a different level of scale," such as entire texts (97). And he observes that these markers have been "surprisingly stable," or consistently characteristic of narrative fiction, "for at least two hundred years" (99). Piper's study has clear limitations; replicating the historical assumptions noted above, he asked his model to consider only novel-length texts from the mid-eighteenth century on. Still, his work suggests a new kind of approach to this area of inquiry that scholars are likely to develop further.

SEEING DOUBLE AND ACROSS CATEGORIES

Most participants in the discussions described above have assumed that there is little, if any, variation among individuals with regard to their reliance on mindreading others, their ability to draw inferences about others' mental states when appreciating narrative fiction, and their emotional responses to fiction. A growing number of scholars are calling such assumptions into question. For one thing, even if humans' attributions of intentionality have a partly biological and automatic component (e.g., Nichols & Stich 2003: 206–07; Urquiza-Haas & Korschal 2015), self-awareness and willingness to communicate about such attributions is not consistent across cultures (Robbins & Rumsey 2008). In fact, we know little about how the imagination, reading comprehension, emotional responses to narrative, and other psychological phenomena related to the experience of fictionality operate in individuals who are not Western, educated, and relatively well-off, simply because most psychological research over the past several decades has used Western university students as research subjects (Heinrich et al. 2010). Even within this population, researchers have found variations in individuals' capacities for empathy (Keen 2011: 302, 305) and their capacities for imaginative activity in different modalities, such as sensory versus episodic imagination.

Other sources, including autobiographical accounts of experience, could make up for some of these deficiencies of psychological research and suggest directions for new research. For example, accounts of Black-lived experience in the United States have long described a kind of doubled or divided attitude as characteristic of that experience. In *The Souls of Black Folk* (1903), W.E.B. Du Bois described the "two separate worlds"—those of the Black and white United States—experienced by Black Americans under Jim Crow (1986: 429), and the "double life every American Negro must live, as a Negro and as an American" (502), with "double thoughts, double duties, and double social classes, [which] must give rise to double worlds and double ideals, and tempt the mind to pretence or to revolt, to hypocrisy or to radicalism" (502; see also 503–04). Such "Du Boisian double consciousness" (Allen 2002) has been the focus of recent psychological research (e.g., Walker 2018), but work on the relationship between this dimension of Black experience and the phenomenology of fiction could yield new understandings of the latter. Recently, Christina Sharpe has echoed Du Bois's points about the existential strain of Black experience in the contemporary United States. Sharpe describes the implications of living in a culture, that of the United States, in which "blackness [i]s the ontological negation of being" (2016: 14). Her account calls to mind Sartre's discussion of the imaginary (see Chapter 1) and can be read to suggest that such doubled consciousness could be empowering as well as intolerable.

Reports of an experience of double consciousness are, of course, not unique to Black residents of the United States. A similar dynamic might have characterized the experience of some Greek-language authors under Roman rule in the early common era (see Whitmarsh 2013: 151), as well as immigrants, migrants, and colonial subjects in any number of colonialist and post-colonialist regimes since. The growing body of work on these kinds of lived experiences suggests an existential position that in some ways resembles that of making believe. Finding new ways to describe such existential positions and to encourage attempts by others to see as if from those positions— as theorists of post-colonialist and diasporic experience have been doing—could enrich not only anti-bias efforts but also theoretical work on fictionality.

How successful can anyone be at seeing as someone very different from themselves? To what extent is the ability to take up the perspective(s) of those unlike us a shared human capacity, or something learned? A number of scholars have proposed that reading narrative fiction is a method of strengthening this very capacity (see, e.g., Zunshine 2006; Keen 2011; Kidd & Castro 2013; Gilmore 2020). But what if any limits to such cross-group seeing as might exist? When, for instance, we read St. Aubyn's description of Patrick Melrose's experience (or self-perception) as akin to that of an oyster about to be consumed, are we learning anything about an oyster's experience, or are we learning only about Patrick Melrose's? In a well-known 1974 article, "What Is It Like to Be a Bat?," the philosopher Ernest Nagel addressed some of these questions from a theoretical, analytical perspective. In considering whether a human being could ever know what it is like to be a bat, Nagel noted that "we apply" "mentalistic ideas" "unproblematically to ourselves and other human beings" (438 n.5), but contended that there is a limit to how much we can "extrapolat[e]" from our own experience to understand the experience of others, even other humans (439, 442). According to Nagel,

> The distance between oneself and other persons and other species can fall anywhere on a continuum. Even for other persons [an] understanding of what it is like to be them is only partial, and when one moves to species very different from oneself, a lesser degree of partial understanding may still be available.... My point is... that even to form a conception of what it is like to be a bat..., one must take up the bat's point of view.
>
> (442)

Nagel's position seems to be that cross-group perspective-taking is possible, but decreases in accuracy as differences increase between the perspective taker and the internal point of view of the perspective being taken. As those differences increase, Nagel suggests, our perspective-taking comes closer to speculation and projection. His account certainly makes intuitive sense, and it seems broadly consistent with psychological research on human perceptions of in-group and out-group members (see, e.g., Gilmore 2020: 191–92).

The recent development of significant literary-critical interest in unnatural narratology suggests the importance of the questions Nagel considers for an understanding of narrative fictionality. Unnatural narratology examines the features of narratives that depart from the model of the realistically mimetic narrative (see, e.g., Alber et al. 2013). Classic examples of unnatural narrative include Franz Kafka's "The Metamorphosis" (1915; see Alber et al. 2013: 103) and indeed *The Golden Ass*, known in antiquity by the title *The Metamorphoses of Apuleius*. In *The Golden Ass*, Lucius repeatedly describes the limitations his donkey-form places on his intentional activity, such as his efforts to speak (Apuleius 1998: 52, 54, 153, 176–77). A fascination with cross-group identification and perspective-taking is thus in no way a modern development. It has, rather, persisted throughout the entire Western cultural tradition. Some unnatural narratives feature narrators that are not even animate, as in the it-narratives of eighteenth-century Europe: these are novels that purport to be narrated by, for example, coins, sofas, and carriages (Lamb 2011; Paige 2011: 253 n.19). Demand for this kind of play with perspective remains high. During the 2010s, for example, users turned social media into a forum for group role-playing as insects (Andrews 2020, discussing the Facebook group "A group where we all pretend to be ants in an ant colony"). But current public opinion does not unambiguously endorse any and all play with cross-group identification. For example, the legitimacy of white authors' inviting audiences to see as fictional characters whose racial or cultural backgrounds differ from the authors' own has recently become controversial (see, e.g., De León 2020; Schaub 2020; see also La Caze 2002; Sohn 2014).

Understanding the drivers and features of this perennial fascination with unnatural perspective-taking seems like a worthy project in its own right. But work on unnatural narrative is also pertinent to understanding several of the issues pursued throughout this chapter in connection with fictional characters and human beings' interaction with them. Some critical work on unnatural narratology has investigated the possibility and extent of readers' empathy with non-human characters (see, e.g., James 2019). Future work on unnatural narrative could, for example, contribute to our understanding of whether or not fictionality is an inherently unnatural phenomenon, or on the contrary whether the creation and apprehension of fiction is a basic feature of human experience, at least in the West.

4

OTHER WORLDS

In her 2006 article "The Rise of Fictionality," discussed in Chapter 2, Catherine Gallagher concluded that "the possible-worlds account of fictionality has now been superseded" (354–55). It is true that the final few decades of the twentieth century witnessed a proliferation of literary-critical accounts of fictional worlds, but it seems premature to say that this metaphor, or conceptual model, is obsolete. Both philosophers (e.g., Terrone 2021) and literary theorists (e.g., Ameel & Caracciolo 2021) continue to rely on the vocabulary of "worlds" to explain representation, possibility, make-believe, and fictionality (see generally Bell & Ryan 2019). And this vocabulary has a long history, extending back to antiquity (see Halliwell 2002: 154–55).

In the modern era, discussion of possible worlds is associated especially with the philosophers Gottfried Leibniz (1646–1716), who used the notion in connection with metaphysics, and Alexander Baumgarten (1714–62), who used it in an aesthetic sense (Vaihinger 1911: xxx). But the English philosopher Margaret Cavendish (1623–73) considered at length the relation between fictional creation and world-making a half-century earlier, in her philosophical fantasy *The Blazing World* (1666). The parallel between creative elaboration of a fictional or invented narrative and rule of a world-like space or region

DOI: 10.4324/9781003161585-5

structures the entire work. In her preface, Cavendish offers a definition of "*fiction*" as "an issue of man's fancy, framed in his own mind,
as he pleases, without regard, whether the thing he fancies, be really
existent without his mind or not" (1994: 123). And in her introductory
address, Cavendish describes the fiction that follows as her creative
response to the constraints of her real-life circumstances:

> since Fortune and the Fates would give me no [empire to rule], I have
> made a world of my own: for which no body, I hope, will blame me,
> since it is in every one's power to do the like.
>
> (124)

The narrative that follows recounts the fantastic journey of a woman
who accidentally travels to and then through the North Pole to a parallel world inside the Earth, of which she becomes a benevolent alien
Empress. The Empress establishes a supernatural channel of communication with the Duchess of Newcastle back on Earth (Cavendish
herself) and learns that the Duchess longs to rule an empire as the
Empress does. The spirits that are helping the two women communicate ask the Duchess

> we wonder... that you desire to be Empress of a terrestrial world, when
> as you can create your self a celestial world if you please.... [E]very
> human creature can create an immaterial world fully inhabited by
> immaterial creatures...; nay, not only so, but he [sic] may create a world
> of what fashion and government he will.
>
> (185)

The Duchess and Empress both follow the spirits' advice, the Duchess
making "a world of her own invention" (188) and the Empress "several worlds" in addition to the one she rules (189).

References to fictional, possible, or alternative worlds or universes
became too numerous to count by the end of the twentieth century,
and as suggested above, remain an important element of theoretical
discussions of fiction. As with all metaphors, the differences between
the nonmetaphorical world and the constructs yielded by fictionality
are as important as the similarities. This chapter considers both the
differences and the similarities. It begins, in the next section, with an

overview of how philosophers and literary theorists have used terms such as "possible world" and "fictional world." The chapter then turns to some of the peculiarities of specifically fictional worlds: the features that distinguish them from philosophical possible worlds and especially from the experiential real world that audiences inhabit. The chapter will consider some explanations for the continued appeal of the fictional world metaphor despite recent criticism, drawing on theoretical work addressing audience elaboration of the contents of artifacts presenting fictional narratives and audience transportation into the worlds created by such elaboration. The chapter ends with some reflections on the kinds of fictional worlds that may seem least possible, because they are based on premises that vary dramatically from our understanding of premises operating in the real world.

POSSIBLE AND FICTIONAL WORLDS

As noted above, philosophical references to worlds other than the terrestrial, everyday environment have a long history. But twentieth-century analytic philosophers began to use these references in new ways, developing what ultimately became quite technical accounts of modal semantics and logic, which seek to clarify understanding of expressions and concepts regarding possibility, necessity, and impossibility (see, e.g., Lewis 1986), as well as accounts of linguistic reference, which English-language philosophers have treated as closely linked to questions of fictionality since the turn of the twentieth century (see Chapter 5; see also, e.g., Kripke 1972: 15–20, 45–46). The US philosopher David Lewis, perhaps the most enthusiastic proponent of a possible-worlds approach to these topics, explicitly distinguished the worlds about which he wrote from "stories," à la Cavendish. Possible worlds, in Lewis's sense, "are like this world, and *this* world is no story" (1986: 7 n.3, 141–42; see also Goodman 1978, to whom Lewis was in part responding). On the other hand, Lewis also proposed that a single "big world… might have many different world-like parts" (72), a notion echoed by some literary theorists using the fictional-worlds metaphor.

Lewis and other philosophers relying on a possible-worlds framework also examined and debated the issue of worlds' accessibility to one another. Possible worlds are, in part, defined by their causal isolation; by definition, "there is no causation from one to another" (78), so events in one possible world cannot have effects in a different possible world. But possible worlds are not unrelated to one another or to the actual world. Lewis and others maintain that the *accessibility* of one world to another can come in various forms. For example, a possible world might be "epistemically" or "doxastically" accessible—accessible to the understanding or belief of actual-world inhabitants—and thus useful "to characterize the content of [those real-world inhabitants'] thought" (27). In this manner, an individual's beliefs about her world, for instance, could be characterized as a world-like part of the world that the individual inhabits. While subsequent theorists of fiction have rarely adopted Lewis's metaphysical insistence that possible worlds exist in the same sense that the actual world does, many of his broad points have retained currency not only in scholarly work but also in popular discourse. (For other uses of "world" vocabulary by philosophers, see, e.g., Dennett 1987; Walton 1978b, 1990; Crittenden 1991).

Several literary theorists writing around the same time as Lewis also took up the vocabulary of fictional "worlds," although the literary theorists were initially influenced more by the phenomenological tradition in philosophy, especially by Martin Heidegger, Edmund Husserl, and Sartre. In his 1960 book on fictional discourse, for example, Felíx Martínez-Bonati (1960) describes literary fiction as "the often enlightened and serious game of construction of worlds formed of narrative images" (34). Roman Ingarden uses the term "portrayed world" of the work for "the whole stock of interconnected intentional sentence correlates" that may be created by a given work (1968: 31). Wolfgang Iser notes that the "represented world" in a fictional narrative has a "dual nature," being "concrete enough to be perceived as a world and, simultaneously, figur[ing] as an analogue exemplifying, through a concrete specimen, what is to be conceived" as the significance of that world (1993: 15).

In the 1980s and 1990s, several literary scholars published compelling and influential book-length studies of the fictional-world idea. Thomas Pavel's *Fictional Worlds* was published the same year as Lewis's *On the Plurality of Worlds* (1986). Drawing on Lewis's and Kendall Walton's work, Pavel noted that the philosophical conception of "possible world" needed modification in order to be useful for discussing fictional narrative (42–43, 49). Pavel proposed, for example, a variation on Lewis's notion of accessibility relations between worlds. Adopting a different metaphor, Pavel differentiated between "self-contained fictional economies," which "mostly consume their own fictional productions," or do not require readers to have knowledge or make many assumptions about matters not explicitly addressed in the text, and "nostalgic or import-dependent systems," which "attentively adapt[] foreign products to local needs" (91–92). The discussions of reader elaboration and deviant worlds later in this chapter will further develop this distinction.

Another important work from this period is Marie-Laure Ryan's *Possible Worlds, Artificial Intelligence, and Literary Theory* (1991). Ryan develops a model according to which "the semantic domain of the narrative text is… a collection of concatenated or embedded possible worlds," in which the "subworlds" are "created by the mental activities of characters" (4). Ryan stresses the significance for narrative fiction of "epistemic possible worlds," noting how in our everyday life

> We not only form beliefs about reality, we also reflect on the possible worlds created by the mental acts of other individuals, and the universe formed by the plurality of represented worlds is a modal system [or system of possibility] in its own right.
>
> (20)

Ryan assumes that our appreciation of fiction involves a substantially similar process, in which our mindreading of characters could equally well be described as our inferences about the possible worlds they each inhabit. Ryan describes "recentering" as "the gesture constitutive of fiction"; "in fiction, the writer relocates to what is for us a mere possible world, and makes it the center of an alternative system of reality," with satellite epistemic possible worlds constituting characters' mentalities (Ryan 1991: 24; compare Hamburger 1973: 73–74).

A third critical work drawing on the philosophical possible-worlds literature was Ruth Ronen's *Possible Worlds in Literary Theory*, published in 1994. Like Ryan, Ronen (1994) explains how the possible-worlds approach to fiction allows us to "explore[] fiction as one among the various modal possibilities that orbit the actual world"

(26). And like Pavel, Ronen observes that the possible-worlds idiom has "provided literary theory with the ideological legitimation for turning theoretical attention... back to referential questions" from the more formal questions on which structuralism focused and the more epistemological questions addressed by poststructuralism (74).

Literary critical and theoretical work relying on the notion of fictional worlds has continued beyond the mid-1990s. Important contributions include Lubomír Doležel's *Heterocosmica* (1998), which relates fictional worlds to possible worlds generated by other cultural systems such as philosophy, religion, natural science, and historiography; Jean-Marie Schaeffer's detailed account of "fictional immersion" in "fictional universe[s]" (1999: 262–63); much work by David Herman, whose notion of "storyworld" has been very influential among cognitive narratologists (e.g., 2002: 20); the linguistics-informed "text world theory" of Paul Werth (1999) and Joanna Gavins (2007); and Eric Hayot's Bakhtin- and Heidegger-inspired account of fictional worlds as "chronotope-containing discourse[s]" (2012: 14) and of the phenomenology of the gesture of "worlding," which involves a "metaphorical capture of totality" (39–40).

As suggested above, all this talk of fictional worlds has drawn some criticism. Skeptics tend to note how fictional worlds have many characteristics fundamentally unlike the characteristics of both our experiential actual world and philosophical possible worlds (see McCormick 1988: 292). If fictional worlds lack these typical world-features, can't we find a more accurate term than "world" to discuss the matter? Gregory Currie argued in his 1990 book *The Nature of Fiction* that references to fictional worlds "seem[] merely to inflate our ontology without producing growth in understanding" (56). Advancing a slightly different criticism, Kathleen Stock has criticized the fictional-world metaphor as generating implications "which clash with the competent reader's experience" (2017: 52; see also Walsh 2007: 32, 37; Woods 2018: 163). It seems possible that this particular contention might be partly a result of variations in critics' own conceptualization of the fiction-reading and -apprehending process; a reader who does not experience representations as world-like could naturally object to describing them that way (see Starr 2015).

PECULIARITIES OF FICTIONAL WORLDS

One frequently noted peculiarity of fictional worlds is their *incompleteness*. This feature distinguishes fictional worlds from philosophical-logical possible worlds (e.g., Walton 1990: 64; Lamarque & Olsen 1994: 91; Priest 2005: 138; Gilmore 2020: 33), as well as from our experiential actual world (e.g., Doležel 1998: 22–23; Greene 2014: 83). Most philosophers examining possible worlds take them to be complete by definition: "Worlds are complete possible situations, which supply everything that is the case" (Cresswell 1988: 63). This assumption is based on our everyday assumptions about the actual world: we usually take that actual world to extend well beyond our perceptions and representations of it. But the fictional world of a particular narrative has only those features it is represented as having, together with, perhaps, certain implications and inferences from those expressly represented features (see Proudfoot 2006: 11–12). This incompleteness arguably extends to fictional characters and objects (see Crittenden 1991: 139; Ronen 1994: 113; Yagisawa 2020: 13–16), and it can be a matter of degree. Some fictional worlds are arguably less incomplete than others because they are, for instance, represented in considerable detail and/ or explicitly as similar to the experiential actual world, enabling audience members to assume their completeness (see Pavel 1986: 101; Doležel 1998: 170; Hayot 2012: 61).

Derek Matravers has argued that an incompleteness of this sort characterizes all representations, not just fictional representations (2014: 88). For example, to the extent that a nonfiction biography creates a world inhabited by its subject, Matravers might say, that world is just as incomplete as any fictional world. But this argument seems to equate the contents of representations with the features of what is "seen in" the representations or constructed by the audience from the representations, a point to be discussed in the next section of this chapter and in Chapter 5. Most readers of a nonfiction biography would likely regard its narrated events as occurring in the (complete) actual world, but would not take the same attitude toward the events in a fictional narrative. There are also a few theorists who disagree that fictional worlds and objects are incomplete. Charles Crittenden, for instance, has argued that "there is a clear sense in which objects in fiction are complete" (1991: 141), since "completeness" is among "the laws pertaining to real people" that readers will import into a fiction as they read and comprehend it (142; see also Culler 2004: 30).

Whether or not fictional worlds are also *indeterminate*, or capable of assuming multiple concrete forms, is a debated issue. Many theorists have been persuaded by accounts like Roman Ingarden's, which does characterize fictional works as indeterminate. In *The Cognition of the Literary Work of Art* (1973), Ingarden distinguished between a work and its "concretizations, which arise from individual readings of the work." Unlike such concretizations, a work is a "schematic formation" that necessarily contains "places of indeterminacy" (13). Ingarden notes that although a work will prompt a specific concretization by each reader on each reading, "In the work itself, only schematized aspects are present... As soon as they are actualized in the reader, they become concrete" (57–58). Ingarden describes the "reconstruction" of a work—the task of the critic—as "the limiting case of the 'concretization' of the work, in which all places of indeterminacy and all potentialities remain" (337 n.7). On this account, a work in Ingarden's sense may contain multiple possible concretized worlds (see also Proudfoot 2006: 12). Literary theorists are not always careful to distinguish between indeterminacy in Ingarden's sense and gaps (or unprovided-for details), which could be signs of either indeterminacy or incompleteness (see, e.g., Ronen 1994: 108). And from another perspective, we might regard fictional worlds and objects as *more* determinate than the experiential actual world. For example, we cannot hope ever to learn more about the fictional world or objects represented by an artifact than the representation itself tells us, but we generally approach the actual world quite differently (see especially Sartre 1940: 125; see also Frow 2005: 76–78).

A third notable and related feature of fictional worlds is what some have called their *aspectuality*. Jean-Marie Schaeffer, for example, notes that in fiction, "aspectuality is not detachable from the presented universe" (1999: 202–03). That is, audience members access the presented world or universe through a representation that supplies a perspective, even if that perspective is not aligned with any character or characterized narrating figure (see Booth 1961). Schaeffer notes that when we confront the actual world, in contrast, "we are able to continue to aim for the same thing while changing aspectuality," and this possibility functions as "a sign that what is aimed for exists independently of the representation that is proposed by it" (203; see also Proudfoot 2006: 23–26). Ruth Ronen proposes a slightly different view: "It is the perspective-dependency of worlds that detain[s] us from opposing fiction to reality; all worlds, including the actual one, are perspective-dependent and hence only versions of reality" (1994: 175; see also Goodman 1978). Ronen ultimately, however, agrees with Schaeffer: "The main difference between fictional worlds and worlds which constitute versions of reality is that the latter assume that beyond all versions there is *the world as it is*" (177–78; see also Lamarque & Olsen 1994: 153).

A final distinguishing feature of fictional worlds concerns their relationship to the actual world. Theorists often discuss this relationship using the vocabulary of *accessibility*, considered briefly in the previous section of this chapter (e.g., Ryan 1991: 31–47). As Ronen puts it, "Fictional worlds are epistemologically possible but physically inaccessible from the real world" (1994: 93–94). Another way of expressing this notion uses the vocabulary of causal insulation or distance, as in Kendall Walton's 1978 article "How Remote Are Fictional Worlds from the Real World?" (Walton 1978b; see also Rafetseder et al. 2010). Related to this ontological difference between fictional and real worlds is a different experience of *time* that many theorists describe as accompanying our access to a fictional world. Sartre notes that in the irreal, the space of the imaginary, time works differently: as "a shadow of time" rather than an experience of duration (1940: 132). Likewise, Ingarden observes that

> the time of reading seems to some extent to be lifted out of the flow of time. The concrete time of the reader stands still... and the temporal phase of the reading either does not count or else strangely shrinks to a single present moment.
>
> (1973: 126 n.24)

Ruth Ronen has argued that it is not only our sense of time that changes when we read narrative fiction but also our processing of linguistic markers of temporality. Drawing on the work of Käte Hamburger,

Ronen maintains that "in fiction, temporal concepts... function as modal indicators and are invested with ontological content," rather than temporal content (1994: 205). That is, the narrative past tense signals to readers not anything about precisely when the events in question took place, but rather that the events in fact occurred in the fictional world central to the work and shared by its characters.

EXPLAINING THE ATTRACTION OF THE METAPHOR: ELABORATION

Despite all of these ways in which fictional worlds differ from the actual world and from philosophical possible worlds, the metaphor seems irresistible to many commentators. Why do so many audience members experience extended fictional narrative as a matter of gaining access to a world? What explains the senses of immersion, exploration, and inexhaustibility (Phelan 1981: 231) that such audiences experience in engagement with some fictional representations?

Part of an answer to these questions might lie in the substantial subconscious cognitive work done by audience members to make sense of such artifacts. The cognitive psychologist Walter Kintsch's model of text comprehension (1998) proposes the creation of "situation models" by audience members as they process a "text base." Kintsch's model does not pertain only to fictional narrative, but it has several similarities to Roman Ingarden's earlier-articulated notion of concretization, discussed in the previous section. On both accounts, in order to make sense of many artifacts, audience members *must* project abstract world-like relationships among the entities and actions that the text instructs them to imagine. Only in this way can readers connect and make meaningful the explicitly provided information. According to this view of narrative comprehension, the fictional world is a kind of byproduct of reading comprehension (cf. Walsh 2007 on narrator and *fabula* as byproducts of narrative comprehension).

What guides readers' world projections? For many people, probably very basic, automatic cognitive processes of the kind that Kintsch emphasizes. Philosophers and literary theorists have made similar suggestions. John Woods, for example, proposes that "When we grasp the author's sentences we are induced to draw inferences about what else obtains in the story," in a way that is "effortless" (2018: 49). Derek Matravers also endorses a Kintsch-like general account of narrative comprehension in terms of mental models. According to Matravers, "engaging with" representations involves, at minimum, understanding them (2014: 76). Psychological research supports the conclusion that many of the audience activities in question are automatic (see, e.g., Busselle & Bilandzic 2008: 226; Quinlan & Mar 2020: 469) and also that they are related both to young children's pretend play and to other forms of everyday reasoning about possibility (Rafetseder et al. 2010: 367–68).

Theorists have also proposed more fiction-specific inferential regularities that guide audience elaboration of the information explicitly presented in artifacts with fictional content. Although often described as rules or principles, these regularities are not understood to be precepts that audience members consciously apply as they process fictional representations. Rather, theorists infer these rules from our practices, as linguists infer the rules of usage and grammar. Kendall Walton has called these rules "principles of generation" (1990: 40–41, 185–86, 213–14). Perhaps the most fundamental such rule is the "Reality Principle," which holds that "fictional worlds [should be] as much like the real one" as possible (144–45). This principle has the "corollary" that "implications follow the lines of what would be legitimate inferences in the real world" (145; see also Nichols & Stich 2003: 303). According to Walton's related "Mutual Belief Principle," we "extrapolate [from expressly given fictional truths] so as to maximize similarities between fictional worlds and the real world not as it actually is but as it is or was mutually believed to be in the artist's society" (1990: 152; see also Lewis 1978: 43–45). Along similar lines, Marie-Laure Ryan's much-cited "principle of minimal departure" (1991: 48–60) holds that "we reconstrue the central world of a textual universe in the same way we reconstrue the alternative possible worlds of nonfictional statements: as conforming as far as possible to our representation of" the actual world (51). This principle allows readers to "form… comprehensive representations of the foreign worlds created through discourse, even though the verbal representation of these worlds is always incomplete" (52). Ryan notes that practices of intertextuality also depend on this principle (54; see also Crittenden 1991; Fludernik 1993).

For sufficiently informed audience members, genre cues also guide elaboration of the world beyond and represented by the artifact (see Ronen 1994; Palmer 2004; Frow 2005: 80–87). Psychological research indicates that the content and extent of audience inferences depend partly on the "distance that a story world lies from reality," a quality that a text might signal through content or paratextual hints placing the narrative in a more or less realist genre (Weisberg & Goodstein 2009: 75). Audience members also seem more willing to import certain types of assumed real-world premises into their comprehension of a fictional world. For instance, when questioned, they usually assume that fundamental mathematical and physical principles remain in force within the fiction, in the absence of textual cues to the contrary, but they do not make similar assumptions about more contingent facts (75). And there might be limits to what premises readers will accept as basic to a fictional world. Work on the puzzle of imaginative resistance discussed in Chapter 3 suggests that many audience members cannot successfully elaborate a fictional world based on morally repellent premises (Gendler 2000).

Whatever the specificity of the principles guiding the elaboration that turns an artifact into an implied world, the process itself arguably generates an experience that resembles the curiosity, excitement, and satisfaction we may feel as we find our way about in the actual world, particularly when we are in novel situations. It is plausible that for at least some readers, this cognitive and affective investment contributes to a sense of the depth, complexity, and inhabitability of the represented world.

EXPLAINING THE ATTRACTION OF THE METAPHOR: TRANSPORTATION

The sense of entering a different world when one apprehends an artifact with fictional content might also be enhanced by a sense that one crosses a border when one focuses one's attention on seeing what is "in" the artifact and withdraws one's attention from one's experiential actual world. Readers and theorists have often used the term "transportation" to describe this sensed shift out of one's everyday world and into the world of the fiction. Joshua Quinlan and Raymond Mar define "transportation" as involving attentional focus on the narrative resulting in a loss of access to the outside world, emotional reactions consistent with the narrative events, mental imagery of the events described, and feeling like you are actually a part of the story or physically present within the narrative.

(2020: 467)

The transportation phenomenon is quite complex; it involves multiple features of fictional artifacts and our interaction with them (see Bortolussi & Dixon 2015, discussing Green 2004 and Gerrig 1993). This section considers three issues relevant to this phenomenon of audience detachment from the actual world and immersion in the fictional world: framing, vivacity, and emotional response.

Chapter 1 introduced Gregory Bateson's account of animal play behavior in considering pretense-based perspectives on fictionality. A key feature of play behavior is that it is always signaled as such, perhaps by the lightness of an animal's nip or an explicit agreement to enter a make-believe scenario with a playmate. These signals correspond to the paratextual cues that let readers of fictional narrative know what attitude to adopt toward an artifact. In another essay, Bateson discussed in more detail the complementary function of literal and metaphorical frames in focusing *attention*:

The frame around a picture, if we consider this frame as a message intended to order or organize the perception of the viewer, says, "Attend to what is within and do not attend to what is outside." Figure and ground, as these terms are used by gestalt psychiatrists, are not symmetrically related.... Perception of the ground must be positively inhibited and perception of the figure... must be positively enhanced.

(2000: 187)

This focusing function of frames complements their attitude-adjusting function: "Any message, which... defines a frame,... gives the receiver instructions or aids in his attempt to understand the messages included within the frame" (188). Bateson notes how modern Western culture is saturated with such "context markers," which include "[t]he pope's throne from which he makes announcements ex cathedra, which announcements are therefore endowed with a special order of validity"; the "shining object used by some hypnotists in 'inducing trance'"; air-raid sirens and "all clear" announcements; boxers' pre-fight handshakes; and "[t]he observances of etiquette" (290). In these phenomena, as in the apprehension of fiction, the context markers could be seen as setting the marked content outside the actual world through a framing gesture that simultaneously places the actual world outside of that marked content.

As suggested in the discussion of doubling in Chapter 1, not all theorists would necessarily agree with this description of the experience of fictionality. Some scholars regard the double aspect-perception involved in the apprehension of fiction as a matter of simultaneous awareness of the experiential actual world and the represented world of the fiction. For example, Kathleen Stock contends that an adequate account of our experience of fiction need not involve "phenomenological disruption in consciousness" (2017: 148; see also Merrell 1983). In contrast, Ann Banfield describes the "process of reading a narrative text" as involving "determining the status of each sentence— is its force objective and fiction-creating or must it be interpreted with the caution due any subjective statement" (1986: 262; see also Gallagher 2006; Woods 2018). Ultimately, as suggested in Chapter 1, this disagreement might be most important as evidence of how many different forms the reading experience can take, even among highly sophisticated and self-aware readers.

The manner in which an artifact involving fictionality presents its represented content may also contribute to an audience member's sense of transportation. Aristotle stressed the importance of narrative vivacity, or *enargeia*, to poetic effectiveness and thus literary merit (see Whitmarsh 2013: 116; Halliwell 2002: 168, describing this quality as enabling "imaginative eyewitnessing"). Käte Hamburger suggested that the grammatical tense conventions of narrative fiction generate a sense of actuality: "from the simple past tense 'said' on, the figures in the novel first really 'make their appearance' as living persons autonomously 'in action'" (1973: 78–79). The "facticity"-conferring value of the preterite contributes to "the experience of the semblance of life" in narrative fiction (120; see also Ronen 1994: 224–27). Formal features of fictional presentation may directly cue certain emotional responses in readers. Philosopher Jonathan Gilmore enumerates among such features "the naming of characters…, the repetition of words…, and the register… of a description" (2020: 199; see also 120–21).

Roland Barthes's well-known 1968 essay on the "reality effect" addressed another device generating such a sense of inexhaustibility in a represented world: what Barthes called the " 'futile' details" and "narrative luxury" or descriptive excess of nineteenth-century realist fiction (1989: 141). As Eric Hayot explains, the "major goal" of such details "is to signify their own insignificance and thus to both (A) indicate the completeness of the diegetic world, and (B) establish a relative baseline against which… amplitude and narrative density can be measured" (2012: 64–65; see also Potolsky 2006: 109). Recent book-length studies of such effects include Elaine Scarry's *Dreaming by the Book* (1999) and Elaine Auyoung's *When Fiction Feels Real* (2018). Barthes himself acknowledged, however, that such gratuitous realistic details are not a requirement for audience transportation (1989: 144–47). As Margit Finkelberg notes, "non-illusionist representation" has been the "general practice" throughout human cultural history (2017: 161), and many premodern theorists, including Aristotle, seem to have assumed that obviously composed, invented representations could and would transport audience members and engage them emotionally.

DEVIANT FICTIONAL WORLDS

In 1986, Thomas Pavel noted that one of the reasons fictional worlds cannot be considered genuine possible worlds is that fictional worlds can involve contradictions, while philosophical possible worlds cannot (Pavel 1986: 49). Jean-Marie Schaeffer likewise observes that "the logic of possible worlds excludes contradictory entities (like a squared circle), whereas such constraints do not exist in the case of fiction" (1999: 181–82). Recognizing these implications, some philosophers have recommended that their discipline expand its attention to *impossible* worlds, defined as those where "the laws of logic do not hold," or where things are as they "could *not* have been" (Berto & Jago 2019: 31–32).

Arguably, as just suggested, it is more common for fictional artifacts to represent things as they "could *not* have been" rather than as they could have been. Literary and cultural history is full of non-illusionistic representation. Space limitations in this book prevent a full discussion of the numerous ways in which fictional worlds might deviate from the real world. Such deviance is often not logical, as in philosophical impossible worlds, but rather moral, cultural, or technological, as in science fiction, or alternatively a matter of empirical and scientific principles and presuppositions, as in some science fiction and fantastic literature, as well as other artifacts involving unnatural narrative. A growing theoretical literature focuses on these kinds of deviant fictional worlds (see, e.g., Roberts 2006; Teverson 2013; Armitt 2020). Logical and metaphysical deviance from the actual world is, of course, also the hallmark of many literary artifacts. Metafiction and works that thematize framing may involve the contents of one represented or referred-to world interacting with the contents of another in a way that is metaphysically if not logically impossible. But even much realist fiction involves comparable impossibility. As Diane Proudfoot points out, "there is no possible world where the omniscient narrator speaks truly when she discloses that which she (perhaps implicitly) claims is undisclosed" (2006: 32; see also Culler 2004).

Some fictional narrators represent a process of transport not between nested worlds, as in metafiction, but between parallel universes or timelines, thus (sometimes subtly) requiring readers to elaborate multiple represented worlds alongside one another (see, e.g., Bourne & Bourne 2016; Gallagher 2018). China Miéville's 2009 novel *The City and The City* presents an interesting combination of these last two alternatives. In the novel, the inhabitants of an ambiguously located urban area actually occupy two superimposed or interlaced municipalities in the same geographical space. Residents of Besźel learn as children to "unsee" the buildings belonging to the other city, Ul Qoma, and vice versa. Residents of the two entities also learn to unsee one another. They are able to perceive occupants of the counterpart city—so as, for example, to avoid colliding with them— but not allowed to interact with them. This regime is enforced by a secret-police-type organization, and the border between the two cities is located in a single building, Copula Hall, the only licit point of crossing between the two cities. Within these premises, Miéville sets a *noir*-style police procedural narrative. The complex world created by this novel is, by the narrative's own terms, confined to a single city, a detail that underscores the allegorical nature of the double city but at the same time, at least for some readers, actually enhances immersion in the narrative. The interactive and navigational premises of the novel seem to describe a pattern of conduct only slightly askew from familiar psychological mechanisms some audience members may recognize from their own experience yet have seldom seen represented. Indeed, the setting of the novel also echoes the experience of transport or oscillation between real and fictional worlds, commenting on its form without breaking the frame in the manner of metafiction.

There remain both works of literature and fictions for which the vocabulary of "worlds" is of very limited, if any, usefulness. These include avant-garde artifacts that stymie audience attempts to project a situation model or any intentional agents, such as some of the work of Samuel Beckett and Alain Robbe-Grillet. For these kinds of artifacts, many of the features of fictionality, in fact, are missing. Also included in this category, however, are examples of fiction that do not permit elaboration into world-like experiences simply because of their fragmentary quality: artifacts such as riddles (Frow 2005: 37), jokes (Gjerlevsen 2019), and cartoons (Fludernik 2015). Elements of fictionality within nonfictional contexts also fall into this category (Nielsen, Phelan, & Walsh 2015). Chapter 5 will consider, among other topics, the question of how scholars have handled such units of fictionality.

5

REFERENCE

An audience member's experience of a fictional world can sometimes seem to be an intensely solitary matter. Reading aloud in the company of others is no longer a common activity among adult Westerners. But it would be a mistake to take our contemporary adult experience with narrative fiction to be inherently private and individual. The experience is based on our interaction with a communication technology, language, that also facilitates human coordination, if not always perfectly, and likely evolved for that purpose. And the seemingly paradigmatic privacy of silent absorption in a narrative is only one among many ways that contemporary audiences interact with fiction and fictionality. Some phenomena involving fictionality—theater is perhaps the most obvious example—are not often experienced in solitude, even if audience members do not interact with one another while appreciating the fiction. More generally, we are able not only to experience fictional worlds on our own but also to talk about them with others, in book clubs, fan forums, and countless other settings, both formal and casual.

These observations might seem trivial, but our ability to discuss fictional events and entities with each other, indeed our hunger for such discussion, fueled a sustained debate in early twentieth-century

DOI: 10.4324/9781003161585-6

European philosophical quarters. This debate involved a historic-ally novel focus on the logical features and implications of such talk about fiction, and it would have significant consequences for the next century's worth of work in both philosophy and literary theory. A key, and contested, concept in this debate was that of *reference*: the fea-ture of language by which we take it to be linked to or hooked up with our experiential environment. On the standard contemporary account of linguistic reference, the referential functioning of refer-ring expressions allows such expressions to "single out, pick out, spe-cify, select, or uniquely identify... particular" people, objects, places, events, and/or processes "as existing," for purposes of coordinating attention, discussion, and action (Margolin 1991: 517).

Such an account is relatively unproblematic as an explanation of how many everyday linguistic interactions work. But what about lin-guistic expressions that occur within artifacts involving fictionality? And what about our discussions concerning such artifacts? Clearly, we are able to have such discussions, and this success suggests that we are able to use language, in some sense, to pick out and identify fictional characters and events. Moreover, within a fictional narrative, the narrator and characters very often seem to use language in a similar manner to specify things and people within the fiction. But such things and people do not *exist* in the ordinary sense of that term. Do expressions within or about fictional discourse refer to *anything*? What exactly do they refer to? If they do not refer to anything real, or existing, then how can the expressions be meaningful, or be said to be true? If such expressions do refer to something, what kind of thing do they refer to? How is it possible for expressions to refer to things that both do exist, in one sense, and do not exist, in another? These were the questions that vexed the influential turn-of-the-century philosophers whose views and legacy are the subject of the next section of this chapter.

The section following that will consider how mid- and late-twentieth-century literary theorists not only built on this philosoph-ical framework but also extended the study of language in and about fiction in new directions. Two subsequent sections will consider more specific and more recent developments: first, the so-called "referen-tial turn" in late twentieth-century literary studies, a result of growing scholarly self-consciousness about the *neglect* of issues of reference and existence, or ontology, characteristic of literary studies in English through the first three quarters of the twentieth century; and second, the patchwork problem, which concerns the appropriate unit of analysis for inquiry into the referential and/or fictional character of discourse and aesthetic artifacts. The final section of the chapter will suggest the scope of the issues addressed in the chapter by examining just a few of the many ways that aesthetic artifacts involving fictionality, and their audiences, have played with mechanisms of reference and representation just about as long as such artifacts and audiences have existed.

PHILOSOPHICAL APPROACHES

Through much of the twentieth century, certain influential philosophers of logic, language, and metaphysics were preoccupied with debates about how best to understand the functioning of certain puzzling kinds of expressions. These debates were not an inevitable development. The disagreements and proposals considered in this section built in particular on certain assumptions about logic inherited from the Aristotelian tradition. Pre-twentieth-century philosophers like Bentham and Vaihinger had developed theories of fiction and fictionality that did not depend so heavily on these assumptions. But the mainstream of twentieth-century academic English-language philosophers did not follow the examples of Bentham and Vaihinger (see, e.g., Fine 1993).

Two especially central tenets of Aristotle's logic were the principle of non-contradiction and the law of excluded middle, introduced not in his work on poetry or rhetoric but in his *Metaphysics*. Virginie Greene has called the principle of non-contradiction "a foundational fiction of Western thought" (2014: 89); Aristotle called it "the most certain principle of all" (90, quoting *Metaphysics* IV, 1005b). Aristotle presented the principle in several different formulations. One often-cited version holds "that the same attribute cannot at the same time belong and not belong to the same subject in the same respect" (Greene 2014: 90, quoting *Metaphysics* IV, 1005b). Bertrand Russell (1872–1970), one of the modern philosophers discussed in this section, used this principle to guide his reasoning about metaphysics, or the question of what has being, and epistemology and logic, or the question of what is true and known. In these domains, the principle suggests that it would be impossible for anything both to exist and not to exist, or for any one statement both to be true and not to be true. Russell adopted an austere and simplified version of the principle: he overlooked Aristotle's insistence "that the principle is valid only if things [the 'same subject'] are considered under the same perspective [the 'same respect']" (Greene 2014: 97; see also Smith 1985: 336–45; Woods 2018: 129–30). Russell also embraced a rigid version of Aristotle's law of excluded middle, which holds that if a particular proposition is not true, then the negation of that proposition must be true. In other words, every proposition must either be true or not true; there is no third option, and every proposition will have its negated counterpart with the opposite truth value.

Russell's preoccupation with the truth or falsity of sentences referring to fictional particulars was also influenced by the then-recent work of Gottlob Frege (1848–1925; Wheeler 2013: 293–94). Frege's life's work concerned the philosophy of mathematics and logic, but he is now perhaps best known for his 1892 essay "Über Sinn und Bedeutung." This title is commonly translated as "On Sense and Reference," and the essay is often read as making a canonical distinction between two dimensions of linguistic meaning, sense and reference. Reference is typically understood along the lines presented at the beginning of this chapter: a word *refers* to that one thing or things in the world that the word uniquely picks out. Contemporary scholars suggest that this understanding is not precisely what Frege himself had in mind (Weiner 1990: 105, 130), but it appears to be what Russell understood Frege to be proposing. Russell also rejected Frege's proposal of a distinction between reference and sense, which Frege described as the "mode of presentation" of an object referred to by a word or expression (Hylton 2010: 510, 522). A simple example: "Queen Victoria" and "the ruler of the United Kingdom between 1837 and 1901" would have the same reference but not the same sense. Frege noted in this 1892 essay that some terms and expressions could have sense, in that they would present some object to be considered, without having reference, in that they would fail to point to anything verifiable in the actual world. The classic example provided by Frege was the expression "Odysseus was set ashore at Ithaca while sound asleep" (see Weiner 1990: 134). Assuming the events narrated in this sentence did not historically occur, the sentence lacks any reference. But since the sentence is comprehensible, and can cause us to envision a concrete scenario, it has sense. Both reference and sense may be understood as dimensions of linguistic *representation*, but Frege and Russell, and their followers, did not tend to use that term.

By rejecting the sense-reference distinction, Russell also rejected a conceptual tool for explaining how a sentence like the above could be used meaningfully. Many people might agree that the quoted sentence might be considered true, in the sense that it is true within the Homeric narrative of Odysseus's journeys that the described action occurred. But Russell's embrace of a strict version of the law of excluded middle prevented his taking the position that a sentence could be true only in a sense, and his acceptance of a simplified understanding of meaning as reference alone required him to conclude that the quoted sentence above could only be evaluated as false.

Russell's (1905) essay "On Denoting" countered Frege's approach to explaining linguistic meaning by proposing a complex method of translating verbal expressions into a form that, according to Russell, more accurately reflected the logical attributes of such expressions. He was impelled to this project by the puzzle of non-referring expressions, like Frege's example sentence about Odysseus, discussed two paragraphs previously. In attempting to solve this puzzle, Russell also sought to explain the kind of knowledge enabling appropriate use of referring, or denoting, expressions and evaluation of the truth of propositions in which they appeared. What is important about Russell's essay for purposes of this discussion is not the technicalities of his proposed solution, which required translation of any sentence containing a denoting expression into an equivalent sentence containing no such expression, but his insistence that a sentence like the one concerning Odysseus could only be understood as false, because the apparent referential function of the name "Odysseus" in that sentence was an illusion.

Russell's essay also expressly responded to the work of Alexius Meinong (1853–1920), who had been publishing books and essays on metaphysics through the 1890s and the first decades of the 1900s. Meinong's focus was on the status of "objects" such as Pegasus, which—like Odysseus—can be coherently communicated about but also can truly be said not to exist. Meinong had developed an explanation of this seeming paradox involving distinctions among types of being that Russell deemed overly complex, inconsistent with Aristotle's logical maxims, and unnecessary (e.g., Routley & Routley 1973: 224; Smith 1985: 309). The position Russell developed in response to Frege and Meinong was that such unreal objects did not exist in any sense; that, contrary to our apparently universal intuitions, no statements appearing to refer to such objects could be true; and that our usual ways of parsing such statements were mistaken. This group of positions came to be English-language philosophical orthodoxy in studies of logic, linguistic meaning, and metaphysics through much of the twentieth century. The influence of Russell's interpretation of Frege on later English-language philosophy is hard to overstate (see Hylton 2010: 509–10; Greene 2014: 54).

Virginie Greene has argued that the influence of Russell's essay and its eclipsing of alternatives suggested by Frege and Meinong

> came at a cost: on the one hand, the inability to understand fiction and give it its proper place in human cultures; on the other, the cultivation of narcissistic illusions concerning our ability to use reason. Russell did not see that the principle of non-contradiction is [itself] a construction involving fiction.
>
> (Greene 2014: 86)

Another cost was the nagging persistence of debate regarding the puzzling questions outlined at the beginning of this chapter; these questions persisted precisely because the intuition is so widespread that we *can* make true statements about, for example, fictional characters. In the last quarter of the twentieth century, English-language philosophers did start to take Meinong's ideas seriously again (e.g., Routley & Routley 1973). Working out the relationship between fiction and truth has also received renewed attention (e.g., Currie 1990; Lamarque & Olson 1994; Sainsbury 2009; Everett 2013), as has the status of fictional objects (see, e.g., Crittenden 1991;

Thomasson 1999; Priest 2005; Woods 2018). Quite a few literary-theoretical accounts of fiction from the 1980s onward have echoed this renewed concern with fictionality, truth, and reference (e.g., Pavel 1986; Genette 1991; Doležel 1998; Schaeffer 1999; Gallagher 2006; Gibson 2007).

LITERARY THEORISTS ON LANGUAGE, FICTION, AND REFERENCE

Many of the more recent discussions of the issues just mentioned reject Russell's insistence that any theory of reference and/or fictionality must be consistent with conservative classical logic. Russell's devotion to a particular logical framework was, as suggested above, not foreordained. But the wide acceptance of his position did suggest that there is something particularly challenging and important about the relationship between fiction and the referential function of language. The work of several key mid-twentieth-century literary theorists accepted this premise but also began to work out alternatives to Russell's logical presuppositions. Three works in this category stand out for their originality and influence: Käte Hamburger's 1957 *Die Logik der Dichtung*; Felíx Martínez-Bonati's 1960 *La estructura de la obra literaria*; and Barbara Herrnstein Smith's 1978 *On the Margins of Discourse*.

Hamburger presented her work as a "linguistic logic of literature" and undertook to determine "whether that language which produces the forms of literature... differs *functionally* from the language of thought and communication" (1973: 3, emphasis in original). Hamburger regards the understanding of "the experience of fiction" as pivotal to understanding literature: "[O]nly in the distinction between *statement* and *fictional narration* is the logical structure of literature to be elaborated" (63, emphasis added). Hamburger's account relies partly on her analysis of the components of "statements" and the different forms such statements can take. One such form she calls the "historical statement," defined as one produced in a frame that implies that "the objects described existed and formed the respective circumstances *independently of whether they became described or not*" (44, emphasis in original). Literary discourse, in contrast, consists of *narration* in addition to or to the exclusion of statements. Narration, according to Hamburger, "has the character of a productive function and not that of a statement" (137; compare Cohn 1999: 112–13). That is, narrative discourse produces what it refers to. For example, Sherlock Holmes did not preexist Conan Doyle's stories about him, but once Conan Doyle wrote a story involving the Sherlock Holmes character, it became possible to produce statements referring to Sherlock Holmes.

While the linguists of the Prague School, following the linguist and psychologist Karl Bühler (1879–1963), had proposed a distinct poetic function for language in the early decades of the twentieth century, the Prague functionalist account described the poetic function as primarily expressive, not productive, and characterized poetic language as conveying its meaning or significance through form rather than referential content (see Pratt 1977: 3–37). A number of philosophers of fiction now take view much more similar to that of Hamburger, who was one of the first to suggest that some literary discourse produces its own referents. Not all of Hamburger's points have been so widely adopted. Some later literary theorists, including Dorrit Cohn, have criticized Hamburger's categorical distinction between third-person and first-person narratives; Cohn calls Hamburger's exclusion of first-person narratives from the category of fiction "an unacceptable price to pay for clarity" (1999: 23).

Like Hamburger and the philosophers discussed in the previous section of this chapter, Felíx Martínez-Bonati began his theoretical account of the functioning of literary language at the level of the sentence. But Martínez-Bonati also drew on a philosophical tradition distinct from the Fregean/Russellian tradition described above. He bases his approach on Bühler's model of "language as organon," a system including speaker, listener, and "events or things (objects described, narrated story)" (1960: 47). (In contrast, the Russellian view does not consider the listener at all.) Bühler's scheme relies on the theoretical distinction between *tokens* and *types*. A token is a specific instance of a type. For example, in the sentence preceding the one you're reading right now, there are three tokens of the type "a"—the English indefinite article. In Bühler's account, as one becomes conscious of a sign as a sign, one also recognizes it as "a token of a type"

(67), and this recognition also involves recognition of "the generalities of a sentence" indicated by an actually produced sentence (68). In other words, sign users tacitly recognize the type, or meaning, beyond each token, or utterance, and it is this recognition that allows them to move to the third dimension of the sign, the "shared state of consciousness" to which a sign makes both speaker and listener privy (68, 64). Although these three dimensions of the sign are theoretically distinguishable, in communication we do not perceive them separately; instead, "the inner meaning [or type] becomes transparent and disappears in its perfect correspondence (adequation) with the perceived object [or token]" (64).

Both everyday language and literary discourse work in this way, according to Bühler and Martínez-Bonati. For Martínez-Bonati, the "lack of seriousness" involved in literary discourse involves not referential dysfunction or logical nonsense but a "*consciousness of play* that *enfolds* the [linguistic and psychological] mechanism that is productive of images*" (130). The conventions of such literary play are such that audience members will make-believe along with a text and imagine what the text's language seems to refer to, in the largely subconscious and effortless manner described above. Because audience members are aware that other people act similarly, it is possible to discuss the contents of a work as if those contents existed independently of their description, but practices of this kind are really just an extension of the consciousness of play that Martínez-Bonati mentions.

In the English edition of his book, published in 1981, Martínez-Bonati acknowledges the compatibility of his account with that presented by Barbara Herrnstein Smith in 1978 (Martínez-Bonati 1960: 153–57). In *On the Margins of Discourse*, Smith (1978) contends that "poems and novels, as opposed to biographies and histories…, are linguistic structures whose relation to the world of objects and events is short-circuited" (10). Like Martínez-Bonati, Smith connects this phenomenon to convention. According to Smith, this "short circuit operates through a convention according to which certain identifiable utterances are understood to be performances of a verbal action.… The child who asks, 'Did it really happen or is it a story?' has already learned the convention" (10). Smith argues that "the essential fictiveness of literary artworks is not to be discovered in the unreality of the characters, objects, and events alluded to, but in the unreality of the alludings themselves" (11). However, she rejects Searle's account of sentences referring to fictional entities as sentences produced by someone who has pretended to refer (see Chapter 1). Instead, she suggests, these sentences are real referential performances placed before the audience as objects for contemplation, or for the instruction of imagination, rather than generated as tools for practical coordination. In the terms used by philosophers of language, narrative sentences in a literary work are *mentioned* rather than *used*. Similarly, Smith describes a direct quotation as "a sort of verbal photograph... of a natural utterance" (65; see also Margolin 1991: 518–19, 521, 531). On the basis of these premises, like Hamburger, Smith asserts a fundamental difference between what Smith calls "fictive" and "natural" discourse (Smith 1978: 15, 45–46, 81–88). She describes fictive discourse as analogous to instructions:

> The text of a poem.... is neither a transcription of an utterance that actually occurred at some specific prior time,... nor... a natural utterance in written form, like a personal letter. It is, rather, like the score of a musical composition..., formal specifications for the physical production of certain events. The text of the poem tells us... how to produce the verbal act it represents.... [T]he text of any poem is... in effect, a score or stage directions for the performance of a purely verbal act that exists only in being thus performed.
>
> (30–31)

Echoing Roman Ingarden, Smith writes that the "characteristic effect" of a poem "is to create its own context or, more accurately, to invite and enable the reader to create a plausible context for it.... [through a process of] inference [and] conjecture" (33).

Although the three works just discussed are not generally cited as forming a coherent tradition, they did propose approaches to understanding the functioning of language in fictional discourse that have been developed or sometimes simply assumed in many more recent discussions of fictionality. For example, Benjamin Harshaw's (1984) article "Fictionality and Fields of Reference" sets out an account of its title topic that does not cite Hamburger, Martínez-Bonati, or Smith but is certainly compatible with their work. According to Harshaw,

> In the case of a work of literature, we are not dealing with isolated sentences..., but with an *Internal Field of Reference*...—a whole network of interrelated referents of various kinds.... The language of the text contributes to the establishment of the Internal Field and refers to it at the same time.
>
> (230)

Harshaw argues that the most important distinction between fictional and nonfictional discourse is the fact that "the former establish their own IFR [Internal Field of Reference]," while the latter do not but claim to describe "the 'real' world" (237).

Monika Fludernik likewise adopted some of Martínez-Bonati's and Smith's insights about the peculiar functioning of quotation within narrative in Fludernik's 1993 book *The Fictions of Language and the Languages of Fiction* (2, 17–19). Fludernik explains, "Represented discourse, just like graphic or sculptural representation,... depicts a semblance of identity or at least similarity" (18), and she provides examples of language being "used to represent, not one specific speech or thought act by a specific person, but a *typical* or *schematic image* of a linguistic expression whose provenance is determined contextually rather than derivationally" (399). In his 1993 book *The Fictive and the Imaginary*, Wolfgang Iser also developed a position compatible with those of Hamburger, Martínez-Bonati, Smith, and Harshaw. Iser breaks fictionalizing acts down into components that include "selection" of "elements" (Iser 1993: 5) of "referential fields outside the text" (4). This selection "marks off from each other the referential fields of the text both by spotlighting and by overstepping their respective limits" (6). A second component of the fictionalizing act is "combination," which "produces relationships within the text" (8) and "changes" language's "function of denotation... into a function of figuration" (10). The final component of the fictionalizing act, according to Iser, is "the fictional text's disclosure of its own fictionality" (11), either through thematization of that fictionality or through other formal or paratextual markers of fictionality. Once a fictional text exists, Iser argues, "the referentiality of the sign [within it] begins to fade" (226). According to Iser, "when the signifier is bracketed off from its denotative use by the 'as-if,'" the "linguistic sign is freed for unpremeditated uses," in a way similar to what happens "in the games played by animals" (247). As a result of this process, the signifier "no longer means what it denotes,... [and] no longer meaning what it denotes becomes itself a denotation" (248).

As suggested above, the work of these scholars and others such as Lubomír Doležel (1998) implicitly rejected the law of excluded middle and the simplified principle of non-contradiction presupposed by many philosophers addressing the functioning of fictional discourse. These literary theorists did use other philosophical concepts, such as the type-token distinction, to flesh out their accounts. While the theorists discussed here did not identify themselves as members of a particular school of thought or theoretical movement, their attention to the peculiar referentiality of fictional discourse created an intellectual lineage alternative to other literary-theoretical trends emerging over the course of the twentieth century. By the 1980s, some literary theorists had begun to speak of a new trend in literary theory and criticism: a "referential turn."

THE "REFERENTIAL TURN" IN LITERARY THEORY AND LITERATURE

There is some debate as to exactly when this turn might have occurred. One of the first literary theorists who claimed to be participating it was Thomas Pavel. In his 1986 book *Fictional Worlds*, Pavel criticized the contemporary so-called "narrative turn" in history and other disciplines as well as literary studies. Pavel applied the label "mythocentrism" to this focus on narrative, a position that in its strongest form "postulates the existence of a narrative level in every meaningful event" (5). The problem with mythocentrism, according to Pavel, is that it promotes the assumption that "problems of reference, mimesis and more generally... relations between literary texts and reality were merely after-effects of a referential illusion, spontaneously produced by narrative syntax" (5–6). Such an assumption failed to do justice to a major part of readers' experiences in appreciating fiction, including those kinds of experiences discussed in Chapter 4 of this book, which attend to fictional content and constructs in a way that classic narratology cannot.

Ruth Ronen struck a similar note in her 1994 *Possible Worlds and Literary Theory*. She noted that classic narratology and "narratological grammars" take a "nonreferential approach" (Ronen 1994: 157). She describes such an "antireferential" position or alignment as ascendant in literary studies from the 1960s to the mid-1980s (81), although the origins of the practice arguably could be dated much earlier, to the advent of modernism and New Criticism (see, e.g., de Groot 2009: 110). Like Pavel, she detects a new focus on meaning, reference, and content in more recent literary studies: Ronen argues that these "more recent narrative theories propose to replace [the antireferentialist approaches characteristic of structuralism]... with a comprehensive mode of narrative semantics" (164).

Much of the more recent theoretical work discussed in earlier chapters of this book might be characterized as participating in this referential turn. It is no longer unusual for literary scholars to consider questions of reference (e.g., Ryan 2015: ix, 62), sometimes labeled questions of semantics (e.g., Doležel 1998), realism (e.g., Morris 2003), worlds (e.g., Ryan 1991; Gibson 2007), or ontology (e.g., Ameel & Caracciolo 2021). Indeed, some discussions of postmodernist art and literature characterize such art as itself marked by a concern with ontological matters, and particularly, a concern with questioning ontological presuppositions, or assumptions about what exists (see Ameel & Caracciolo 2021: 314, discussing McHale 1987). Contemporary postrealist works can also be read as addressing "ontological questions... concerning the fabric and structure of reality, and how our own world relates to other worlds" (Ameel & Caracciolo 2021: 314). But postrealist art arguably does so in an earnest manner, without the mocking or subversive mood of postmodernism. Postrealism can be seen as promoting a "heightened engagement with the real" rather than a questioning of the category (316). In both art and criticism, concern with referentiality and ontology is compatible with the acknowledged possibility of multiple real-world ontologies, deriving from the multiple forms that experienced actual worlds may take for different people and groups (318).

THE PATCHWORK PROBLEM

How do different ontologies relate to one another? The answer given by many of the philosophers and literary theorists discussed so far in this chapter is that, at least in fictional narrative, ontologies or referred-to worlds can both nest inside one another—as characters' ontologies nest inside a narrator's—and exist side by side—as in "polyvocal narration" (Margolin 1991: 522). But consider, for example, a realist narrative such as a Sherlock Holmes story, and take it sentence by sentence. Some sentences will seem to have the productive or self-creating effects attributed to narratorial discourse or diegesis, while other sentences describing, for example, geographical landmarks in London, do not as clearly create new referents. As Gregory Currie put it in 1990: "A work of fiction is a patchwork of truth and falsity." Currie also argued that it is "un-illuminating" to ask how many fictional sentences in a work will make the work fictional as a whole and contends that it is more illuminating to provide a "precise account of the fictionality of statements" (Currie 1990: 49).

Not all commentators have shared Currie's comfort with this patchwork character of many fictional narratives (but see, e.g., Roberts 1972; Genette 1991). The philosopher Derek Matravers, for example, has argued that any theory of fiction that yields such a patchwork account of fictional narratives is for that reason flawed. Matravers maintains that the account of fictional texts as mandates to imagine states of affairs has trouble "moving from the definition of fictional proposition to the definition of fictional works, as such works contain many propositions we are mandated to believe," rather than to imagine (2014: 99–100). To Matravers, such views result in undesirable "indeterminacy in whether a particular narrative is fictional" (101).

The patchwork phenomenon is most often identified as a problem by theorists of fiction who focus on sentences as the units of interest in understanding fictionality and/or on understanding the ontological status of fictional objects and characters. Most such theorists are philosophers. But not all philosophers consider the patchwork problem troubling. For example, Kathleen Stock maintains that it is possible for "F-units," or utterances within a fictional work, to be "non-accidentally true," or successfully referential in the manner of natural language; examples would include those statements about English geography in the Sherlock Holmes stories mentioned earlier. At the same time, the very same utterances might be "also reflexively intended to produce conjoined imagining" (2017: 157). As a result, "all utterances within a fiction" can function homogeneously in certain respects. Some sentences or utterances will simply be susceptible to two different kinds of apprehension by readers. Thus "[t]here need be no 'patchwork'" of fictional and nonfictional utterances within a fictional work (157).

The patchwork issue does also have significance to nonphilosophers. For example, literary or cultural scholars who wish to focus on fictionality rather than on fiction or fictional works need to consider how to handle the fact that "[g]lobal fictions can contain passages of nonfictionality, and global nonfictions can contain patches of fictionality" (Nielsen, Phelan & Walsh 2015: 67). In their "Ten Theses About Fictionality" article, Nielsen, Phelan, and Walsh explain, "If we assume—rightly or wrongly—that a discourse is fictive, we read it as inviting us to assume (among other things) that it is not making referential claims" (68). But does this mean that such a discourse does not refer to anything? Could the discourse contain some content making referential claims and some content making no such claims? In a separate article, Phelan and Nielsen rejected the possibility of "hybrid fictionality" (see Phelan & Nielsen 2017; see also Hatavara & Mildorf 2017; Hansen & Lundholt 2021). The question of how to treat artifacts that display features of both fictionality and ordinary referentiality remains debated among theorists pursuing this fictionality-focused research agenda.

Theories of fictionality that rely on the vocabulary of "worlds" can generate similar puzzles. As noted in Chapter 4, the problem here is that the world created by a fictional narrative must include at least some premises imported from the actual world, even if these are only assumptions about how language or other representational media function, how human perception works, and so on. How does this process work, and why don't we notice this importation taking place as we read or view a fictional narrative (Merrell 1983; Genette 1991)?

Other scholars besides Kathleen Stock have proposed answers to some of these questions. Gregory Currie, for instance, has suggested that "[i]n judging something to be fiction over all we make a rough and ready accounting of the (weighted) ratio of genuinely fictional to nonfictional material" (2017: 317–18). Benjamin Harshaw argued that the sentence, proposition, or utterance is simply the wrong unit of analysis when considering how linguistic reference works in fiction (1984: 230). What we should focus on, according to Harshaw, is an artifact's "Internal Field of Reference," a "network of interrelated referents of various kinds: characters, events, situations, ideas, dialogues, etc." (230). Audiences come to apprehend these referents as networked in a unified field of reference despite awareness that some of the referents were not products of the text's projection: we imagine Sherlock Holmes as living on Baker Street even though we know that Conan Doyle invented the former but not the latter.

More recently, John Gibson has proposed that natural-language reference—for example, to a unit of measurement such as a meter—is possible "not because [we] all... have access to a common metaphysical item," like the distance represented by a meter (2007: 64). Rather, we can refer to size in terms of meters "because of a prior cultural act...: the creation of public *standards* of representation, the construction of common cultural instruments" for "building... representations of our world," like the platinum bars long used as reference points for the measurement of lengths such as meters (64). Gibson contends that a "narrative tradition" or "literary heritage" amounts to "a culture full of 'objects' we can use to archive" the "stories we have to tell of ourselves" (71). On this account, it is our naïve or folk assumptions about how reference works in natural language that represent a distortion or misconception—not, as some philosophers have argued, assertions about fictional events or entities.

REFERENCE GAMES

The patchwork problem is arguably most evident in works that are, from a realist perspective, formally irregular. For example, as Thomas Roberts points out, Herman Melville's *Moby-Dick* (1851) contains "huge chunks," such as Melville's "descriptions of whaling procedures," that do not self-evidently create their own referents (1972: 18). Critics often treat works of this type not as problematic but as especially interesting and/or innovative. But even if post-modernist and postrealist art are thematizing reference in new ways, games with reference have pervaded fictional artifacts as far back as one might care to inquire. Such games include the representation of representations and referring relations (Margolin 1991: 531); the crossing of assumed ontological boundaries, or metalepsis, as when a character from a story interacts with the story's storyteller (520); and the migration of characters, objects, settings, and worlds from one work to others. The rest of this chapter will examine some examples of these kinds of games.

One exceptionally celebrated example of a fiction that incorporates figurations of reference is *Don Quixote* (1612–20), in which Don Quixote's romance-derived delusions prompt his distorted perceptions of his surroundings as if they were the referents of a chivalric romance, his resulting statements and conduct, and the reactions of all of the other personages in the novel. But the thematization of representation is a very old tradition in Western art. The device of ekphrasis (verbal description of a visual artwork), as well as the extensive narration of characters' encounters with artworks or representations, have been features of fictional narrative from the ancient novel on (Doody 1996: 396). The thematization of pretense permeates even realist fiction, which one might otherwise assume to be less referentially self-conscious than "anti-illusionist" or anti-mimetic art (Morris 2003: 39–40). Representations of encounters with representation may prompt more or less explicit reader reflection on the ways that acts of referring can go wrong, not just through error or mendacity, but through failures of interpersonal alignment—or, conversely, how non-referring aesthetic gestures, or world-creating acts, can have effects that reverberate outside the created world, a phenomenon to be discussed shortly.

Metalepsis, or what Uri Margolin calls "level reversal," includes devices such as "reference by narrative agents to the narrator" (1991: 520). Like the thematization of representation, metalepsis is often associated with avant-garde, postrealist narrative and art, but this kind of referential irregularity also appears in *Don Quixote* as well as works from antiquity and the Middle Ages. As Margolin notes, metalepsis has "derealizing," or anti-immersive, effects

(520): metalepsis tends to disrupt an audience's seeing-in the represented content of the artifact and to divert attention back to the vehicle of that content, even if only momentarily, as well as, potentially, to direct attention to the asymmetries between these aspects of the artifact (see Ryan 2015: 136, 251). When, at the beginning of Part II of *Don Quixote*, we read about the publication and popularity of Part I, we are cued to think of the narrative we have just read as a material artifact, rather than a series of represented or imagined events.

The cross-world or cross-work migration of characters, objects, and settings is likewise no recent innovation. All practices of allusion and intertextuality, as well as adaptation, are continuous with such migration. The ancient novels discussed in Chapter 2, while attributed to individual authors, are also understood to be based on personages and narrative sequences long circulating in oral and even written form. Thus, the cross-work migration of characters is fundamental to the tradition of fiction in the West. Two particular manifestations of such migration, however, have recently drawn renewed attention: reader interaction with fictional characters in readers' real lives, and the phenomenon of the megatext.

In the 1970s, sociologist David Phillips coined the term "the Werther effect" to describe the effects of suggestion on suicide rates (Phillips 1974). While Phillips was concerned with such forms of suggestion as the publicizing of actual suicides, he derived his term from the even earlier, widely perceived late-eighteenth- and early-nineteenth-century phenomenon of suicides in imitation of the suicide of the protagonist of Goethe's *The Sorrows of Young Werther* (1774), a phenomenon Goethe himself remarked upon (Phillips 1974: 340; see also Sieber 1993). More often discussed by theorists of fiction is the remarkable audience response to Arthur Conan Doyle's Sherlock Holmes character from the time of his first appearance on. As Michael Saler explains, "Holmes was the first character in modern literature to be treated as if he were real and his creator fictional" (2012: 106). Holmes has incidentally been a central example for generations of philosophers writing about fiction (see, e.g., Pavel 1986: 44), although the philosophical use of Holmes has largely been restricted to using sentences appearing to refer to Holmes as specimens for semantic analysis.

The phenomenon of fan culture has spawned voluminous scholarly and popular literature examining the relationships between fans and fictional characters and/or settings. Especially vibrant fan cultures have developed not just around Sherlock Holmes but also around the novels of Jane Austen (see Luetkenhaus & Weinstein 2019; Glosson 2020), characters from Japanese manga and anime (see Lamarre 2018; Galbraith 2019), and, of course, the *Star Trek* franchise (see Lamb & Veith 1985). Audience interaction with fictional characters also occurs outside such relatively structured collective practices. A 2017 survey of 1500 British readers found that nearly 20 percent of those surveyed reported being influenced by "the voices of fictional characters," even after the readers had returned to the actual world (Lea 2017).

The *Star Trek* franchise and fan culture also exemplify how characters and elements can migrate from fictional work to fictional work (see, e.g., Pavel 1986; Monk 1990; Walton 1990; Jenkins 1992; Hayot 2012). Twentieth- and twenty-first-century literature contains many manifestations of this phenomenon, by which authors other than the original author contribute new volumes to book series in which the original author created a specific, detailed fantastic world or universe. L. Frank Baum's Oz might have been the first example of this practice (see Monk 1990: 38 n.14). Between 1900 and 1920, Baum published 19 novel-length books set in Oz; over the following 30 years, at least five additional authors—Ruth Plumly Thompson, John R. Neill, Jack Snow, Rachel Cosgrove Payes, and Eloise Jarvis McGraw—published 26 further novels authorized and endorsed as continuations of the series by Baum's publisher.

A slightly more complex instance is the remarkably sustained and diverse development of the Cthulhu mythos of H.P. Lovecraft (1890–1937; see Eil 2015; Mullis 2015). Lovecraft's own horror fiction from the 1920s and 1930s consistently incorporates several repeated elements, including a fictional New England geography, imaginary mystical books, a "pantheon of generally hostile extraterrestrials," and a "sense of cosmicism," or the evocation of a deliberately non-anthropocentric perspective of indifference to human concerns and priorities (Mullis 2015: 513–14). Unlike the fictional corpora generating most fan culture, Lovecraft's peculiar works are only minimally character-focused (see, e.g., Henderson 2019). Indeed, Lovecraft's cosmicism could be described as an interest in identifying how far language, or any representational medium, can go in attempting to represent the incomprehensible and inhuman without itself becoming incomprehensible. Lovecraft's work also often betrays the author's Nietzschean racism (see, e.g., Paz 2012). An interesting development in North American literature and popular culture of the early twenty-first century has involved the creation of new works within the Cthulu mythos but rejecting Lovecraft's racism, for example, by involving Black protagonists or otherwise anti-racist premises. Works in this vein include Victor LaValle's *The Ballad of Black Tom* (2016), Premee Mohamed's *Beneath the Rising* (2020) and *A Broken Darkness* (2021), and Matt Ruff's *Lovecraft Country* (2016), adapted for television in 2020. These works prompt reflection on the possibility that Lovecraft's supposedly alien cosmic horror is distinguishable only incidentally, if at all, from the incompatible ontologies inhabited by many actual people, and reflection on the extent to which some actual human ontologies involve dehumanization that Western representational traditions have trouble accommodating.

6

BEYOND TEXT

Previous chapters in this book have occasionally considered non-literary artworks, but the focus has mostly been on how fictionality works in linguistic artifacts. Until recently, most modern theorists of fiction and fictionality likewise focused on verbal artifacts as the paradigmatic setting for fictionality. But not all theorists have limited their analysis in this way, and consideration of nonverbal artifacts involving fictionality also has a long history. To the extent that Plato's concern with mimesis was a concern with something like fictionality, for example, he was more preoccupied with visual representation than with verbal representation (see, e.g., Potolsky 2006: 26). Aristotle's *Poetics* addresses verbal artifacts—written dramatic works—but also takes the performed dimension of theater into account. Today a growing number of theorists of visual art, theater, film, and other media consider how these forms depend on but also transform the kinds of fictionality most often associated with prose narrative.

Unsurprisingly, examining fictionality in other art forms often leads to consideration of themes generally similar to those examined in previous chapters of this book, including the role of imagination and play in appreciating fictionality, the significance and structure of our cognitive and emotional engagement with artifacts, the status of fictional

DOI: 10.4324/9781003161585-7

content, and even questions of reference. But nonverbal artifacts have characteristics that can require theorists to modify language-based accounts of fictionality. For example, while visual artifacts such as paintings may be reproduced or alluded to, they cannot be quoted in exactly the same way that linguistic artifacts can (cf. Cavell 1979: ix), so some of the theories of fictional discourse addressed in Chapter 5 cannot explain fictionality in such artifacts. Some theorists have even taken the position that nonverbal media are "limited in their ability to express the difference between actuality and virtuality" (Ryan 1991: 266). Aesthetic theorists do not agree on whether it is appropriate to seek a unified account of all art forms (e.g., Livingston 2021: 14, 23, 24, 28). Still, there is fairly wide agreement that nonverbal artifacts can be appreciated as fictional, in ways at least roughly analogous to the ways that we appreciate verbal artifacts as fictional (see, e.g., Currie 1990: 10 n.8; Walton 1990: 7, 11, 226).

The volume of theoretical work on fictionality outside of narrative prose makes it unrealistic to undertake a comprehensive overview in this chapter. The discussions that follow are therefore necessarily selective, addressing some of the distinguishing features of fictionality in visual art, photography, theater, live-action motion pictures, animated motion pictures, and television. These are not the only media of significance in the contemporary study of fictionality. Comics, graphic novels, and videogames, for example, are increasingly pervasive aesthetic forms that deserve and are receiving growing scholarly attention.

THE STATIC IMAGE

As noted above, Plato seems to have considered the image (*eikon*) the most basic form of representation. For Plato, any image would be inferior to its original, just as the lived world is inferior to the ideal (see Eden 1986: 64). In the *Sophist*, Plato further distinguished between the *eikastic* image, which resembles or corresponds to its original, and the *phantastic* image, which "is designed to appear like the original," and asserted that the latter is more deceptive than the former (Eden 1986: 65; see also Halliwell 2002: 127). This distinction differentiates between "an image that preserves (measurable) ontological fidelity to the proportions... and surface feature of whatever it depicts, and... an image that is deliberately adjusted to suit the perceptual point of view from which a human observer contemplates it" (Halliwell 2002: 127–28). Eikastic mimesis is "likeness making," while phantastic mimesis is "semblance making" (128 n.27). In the *Sophist*, Plato "places most painting, and indeed most mimesis, in the second category (*phanastikē*)" (128).

Plato's distinction bears some resemblance to the modern semiotic distinction among indexical, iconic, and symbolic signs, originated by the US philosopher Charles S. Peirce (1839–1914). Many aesthetic theorists consider this distinction helpful in clarifying the differences between various forms or modes of representation. An indexical sign is one with a causal or existential connection to what it signifies: classic examples are smoke as a sign of fire and a footprint in the sand as a sign of human presence. An iconic sign has some physical resemblance to what it represents: a portrait of a famous historical figure will resemble the actual historical figure in at least some respects. A symbolic sign has no relation of similarity or causal connection to what it represents; convention governs the association of a symbolic sign with what it signifies. The letters D-O-G were not caused by any dog, nor do the letters resemble a dog in shape or sound. The word "dog" is a symbolic sign. While the simple examples just provided might suggest that Peirce's sign types are mutually exclusive, Peirce in fact held that individual signifying items might and often did signify in multiple ways (Wollen 2010: 180–84). Use of Peirce's framework has been especially common in discussions of photography and photography-based motion pictures.

Since nonphotographic images preexisted photographic ones, however, it may make sense to consider some characteristics of nonphotographic images first. Recent theoretical accounts of pictorial representation, or depiction, have addressed several issues akin to those considered in previous chapters. John Hyman, for example, has suggested that Frege's sense-reference distinction can illuminate the functioning of paintings as well as verbal expressions: "two portraits of the same individual may present him [differently and thus would]... portray (refer to) the same individual, but... present him differently (...differ in sense)" (Hyman & Bantinaki 2021: 7). Both sense and reference would, on this theory, be part of the content of a painted depiction. As discussed in Chapter 3, we can also characterize the content of a representation as what we see in the material artifact. In fact, Richard Wollheim developed his notion of seeing-in as part of his theory of visual art (1968: 140–44).

Any general theory of pictorial representation or signification should be able to explain the functioning not only of portraits, but also of depictions of invented entities such as Pegasus or Sherlock Holmes. While it is tempting to consider images as functioning iconically in Peirce's sense, this characterization does not seem to work well for such depictions of fiction. What does a painting of Pegasus physically resemble? The representation of fictional entities or states of affairs thus creates a puzzle for theories of pictorial representation analogous to the puzzles discussed in Chapter 5.

Of course, the puzzles are only analogous, not identical. Seeing Sherlock Holmes in an illustration differs from seeing him while reading a Conan Doyle story, since the former experience is not mediated by language, a symbolic sign system. Images also, unlike language, arguably possess "natural generativity" (Currie 1995: 131), that is, "we generally have no trouble grasping the representational properties of… images we have never seen before" (130–31). In addition, images lack "atoms of meaning" corresponding to those that drive linguistic generativity: phonemes, lexemes, rules of syntax, and so forth (130). As Gregory Currie notes, "every part of the image is meaningful down to the limits of visual discriminability" (130). The features of images just noted are common to both nonphotographic and photographic images, and several are shared as well with theatrical performance. For instance, none of these forms allows the inside view of characters' thoughts available through psychonarration in fictional prose narrative. On the other hand, as Currie's observation suggests, these three media offer much richer physical, visuo-spatial information than narrative fiction does (see Gaut 2010: 192).

As suggested above, much of the theoretical work considering fictionality in images has dwelled upon differences between nonphotographic and photographic images. Kendall Walton confronted this issue in an influential 1984 article, "Transparent Pictures: On the Nature of Photographic Realism" (see also Walton 1990: 293–333). In enumerating differences between nonphotographic and photographic images in this article, Walton noted many of the points considered throughout this section. First, he observed, "[a] photograph is always a photograph of something which actually exists," while "[p]aintings needn't picture actual things" (1984: 250). Arguably, this point might no longer hold if one considers digital photographs to be photographs (see Gaut 2010: 70). Second, photographs are caused by their subjects in a manner that is in some degree mechanical (Walton 1984: 261). Photographs seem to signify indexically in a way that paintings, say, do not. The causal connection between paintings and what they represent is according to Walton "more 'human'," "involving the artist" and the artist's perception of the object represented (261). Although Walton does not put the point this way, he is suggesting that photographs might be limited in their ability to communicate a variety of Fregean senses, relative to nonmechanically generated depictions. As a result of all of these differences, Walton argues, we "see through" photographs in a way that we cannot "see through" nonphotographic images (262). In other words, according to Walton, "[v]iewers of photographs are in perceptual contact with the world" in a way that viewers of paintings—even photo-realistic paintings—are not (273).

Walton's discussion paralleled points made earlier by André Bazin in the context of film theory (1967), and the indexicality of photographic images remains a debated topic in accounts of photographic and cinematic realism (e.g., Gaut 2010; Carroll 2016; Curran 2016; Hopkins 2016; Wilson 2016). While many have disagreed with some of Walton's specific points, there is wide agreement that photographic images do differ meaningfully from nonphotographic images—even if new digital photographic and image-manipulating technologies force reframing or reconsideration of these differences. For instance, another distinction noted by Stanley Cavell in 1971 may continue to be pertinent. Contrasting paintings and photographs, Cavell observed,

> The world of a painting is not continuous with the world of its frame; at its frame, a world finds its limits. We might say: A painting *is* a world; a photograph is *of* the world. What happens in a photograph is that *it* comes to an end.... The implied presence of the rest of the world, and its explicit rejection, are as essential in the experience of a photograph as what it explicitly represents.
>
> (24)

Walton suggested in "Transparent Pictures" that Cavell's distinction is illusory, since "[w]e can ask," in both cases, "what there is in reality outside the portion depicted" (1984: 274 n.4). But Walton seems to be overlooking Cavell's emphasis on the differing *functions* of the image frame in the two scenarios. The photographic frame directly implies—almost expresses—a *masking* or negating operation, whereas the nonphotographic frame implies the beginning of a record of creative activity. The nonphotographic frame is a different kind of threshold than the photographic frame.

On the other hand, Walton might be taken to be suggesting that this difference in function does not directly make a difference to the possibility of a photographic image's offering an opportunity for the perception of fictional content. As Kathleen Stock (2017) has put it, images can count as fictions if "there is a mutually understood context such that both image-maker and audience recognize the intention" to instruct imagining, as with "[i]llustrations to children's stories" (152) or, perhaps, a photograph of a person dressed as Sherlock Holmes. Still, this position is not universally accepted. For example, the philosopher Berys Gaut has adopted Roger Scruton's thesis regarding the "fictional incompetence of photography," its "inability to represent fictions" (Gaut 2010: 196). If fiction always involves the representation of at least some referents that are invented and not real-world entities, and photographs are always records of the real-world things lying in front of the real-world cameras that took the photographs, then can a photograph ever really have fictional content?

THEATER

Through the influence of Aristotle's *Poetics*, as discussed in Chapter 1, dramatic literature and theatrical performance have remained paradigmatic fictional art forms for many theorists. Aristotle's emphasis on the representation of action and his concern with audience engagement have shaped significant scholarly traditions in the study of fictionality. In the *Poetics*, Aristotle also considered at length the effects of tragedy on audience members, a focus shared by the vast majority of theorizers about theater for the following millennium. As Tim Whitmarsh has noted, critical concern about the effects of theater on audiences was one of the main contexts for discussion of fictionality in antiquity. "The paradoxical nature of the illusion" created by theatrical performance—"it fools you that it is real, when you know all along it is a fiction—is a running theme of much ancient rhetorical and literary criticism, particularly that in the orbit of literary vividness (*enargeia*)" (Whitmarsh 2013: 70). Debates about the extent to which theater audiences could maintain such a double awareness, reminiscent of more recent disagreements surveyed in Chapter 1, structured theater criticism and theory for centuries. Concern with *maintaining* audience illusion to enable audience absorption of the edifying fictional content of a play was the basic motivation for supporters of the dramatic unities of time, place, and action until quite recently (see Carlson 1984: 47, 92, 115, 134, 241).

It is a slight oversimplification to say that Aristotle's discussions of tragedy counted as discussions of fiction or fictionality. In fact, theorists of theater in antiquity commonly held that invented content was appropriate only for comedy and that tragedies should present audiences with action sequences "based on historical truth" (Carlson 1984: 26; see also 31, 50). This particular stricture is, of course, obsolete, but the wide acceptance of this distinction up to the Renaissance is a reminder of the historical contingency of Western understandings of what fictionality consists of and how humans interact with it.

Transferring theories of fictionality and audience engagement that were originally developed in consideration of written narrative to the study of theater is also complicated by the performed and embodied dimension of theater. A minority of drama theorists since the nineteenth century have contended that the dramatic text is the key artifact deserving critical attention, and that performances of the drama inevitably reduce its complexity (Carlson 1984: 223, 288, 289, 370). This position is, however, relatively uncommon. Far more often, theorists consider performance to be an important augmentation of the complexity of dramatic artifacts. For example, Käte Hamburger has argued that dramatic literature, "which can take on the semblance of reality, displays the purely fictional character of fictional literature in a higher degree of intensity, to a certain extent in a more elemental way, than does epic literature" (1973: 204). For Hamburger, drama has this characteristic not solely because of its mimetic verbal dimension but also because of its performed dimension, which creates a physical space of shared reality between performer and audience (200–01, 204, 209). This shared physical space is also a shared time (211–12). Audience confrontation with a performance, Hamburger suggests, can foster awareness of the complexity of the experience and the unusual, artificial role played by language in the performance.

In a sense, performers' physicality corresponds to the materiality of a printed text, while the actions they perform are, roughly, read by audience members as events in a fictional world. But performers also embody their characters even when not speaking or moving; performers directly embody the doubleness associated with fictionality, requiring a subtly different kind of make-believe from that used by readers of novels (see, e.g., Hamburger 1973: 215). More specifically, the make-believe posture demanded of the performance audience does not precisely parallel the make-believe posture required of performers. Performers are engaging in embodied make-believe closely akin to that of children's play (see Carlson 1984: 234). Audiences, on the other hand, are making believe that no such make-believe is occurring.

The intimate and complex relationship between theater and game is suggested, but not clarified, by the use of the English term "play" to refer to both text and performance. Jean-Marie Schaeffer has offered a more illuminating description of this relationship: "theatrical fiction… corresponds to three different fictional devices, according to whether one approaches it by way of the text, of the scenic representation, or of the game" (1999: 246). Schaeffer notes, "The theater as game has the same pragmatic frame as the fictional games of children, of which the game of actors is the extension" (256). One might add that the cultural practice of performance and performance attendance is a further game undertaken simultaneously, but in different modes, by performers and audience.

LIVE-ACTION MOTION PICTURES

Some of the earliest theoretical writing on motion pictures classed them as photographic records of theatrical productions (Furstenau 2010: 9). But theorists quickly acknowledged that such a view fails to account for important elements of live-action film, such as camera motion and montage. If Jean-Marie Schaeffer is correct to describe live-action film as "the essential vehicle for contemporary fiction" (1999: 12–13), then an account of fictionality in the twenty-first century should not focus solely on narrative prose, since a text-oriented theory will fail to explain the contributions of performance, photography, *and* film-specific techniques to the shaping of audience experiences of fictionality in film.

Long-running debates within film theory are concerned with some of these matters, but their integration into an overall account of fictionality in film remains incomplete. In recent theoretical work on film, scholars have examined the phenomenology of audience comprehension of fictional film narrative, including the forms of doubled perception such apprehension involves, the role imagination plays in the process, and the nature of viewers' affective responses to film narrative. These scholars' proposals build on but necessarily modify positions advanced by theorists of fictionality who focus on verbal artifacts.

George Wilson, for example, has recently proposed a "dual-tier" framework for conceptualizing what movie viewers see when they watch a fiction film: "(i) they 'see' the largely fictional items and events that belong to the story told, and (ii) they 'see' the actual items or events that belong to the 'theatrical' portrayal of the story" (2016: 58). Wilson calls these "Tier I" and "Tier II" items, respectively, and notes, "The tier I items... are characteristically fictional" (58). So far, Wilson's framework seems consistent with descriptions of seeing fictional content in other art forms. What happens when we see fictional content in a movie image, specifically? Wilson maintains that "moviegoers *imagine* themselves seeing or, in some fashion, *make-believe* seeing the constructs in fiction film" (62). This activity "is, roughly, a matter of its seeming to the viewer 'as if' she were really seeing the segment of the fictional world on the screen" (63). Wilson further contends that viewers generally treat the moving images themselves—as opposed to the filmed performances—as "transparent mediating images" (70). In other words, according to Wilson, viewers see fictional content in the performed actions, perhaps involving a mixture of real-world and invented referents, but when following the fiction within the film, viewers do not attend to the moving images themselves.

Wilson's proposal helpfully draws attention to three levels of the film image: the physical image itself, consisting of a configuration of colors and shapes on a flat surface; the photographed things and events shown in that image, and the content shown in the combination of physical image and photographed things. Robert Hopkins has proposed a variation on Wilson's model emphasizing these three tiers: one of "moving images," one of "events filmed," and one of the "story told" (2016: 77). Hopkins contends that the mode of representation in the first tier is photographic, and that the mode of representation in the second tier (events filmed) is "very like representation in a play" (77). Hopkins's main point is that in general, when we watch a narrative film, "[o]ne level of representation [the events filmed] drops out of our visual experience" (82) in "a kind of collapsing of levels" (83). The moving images remain present to us: "[t]he level that remains is made up of moving photographic images," which "[w]e now *see... as* images of the events in the story being told" (83, emphasis added). Hopkins maintains that "[c]ollapse... is a phenomenon limited to visual representations (indeed, it is probably limited only to film)" (92).

As this discussion might suggest, the role of imagination in the perception and comprehension of narrative film is a topic of some disagreement. Most theorists acknowledge a role for imagination in the apprehension of film, but the role assigned varies. Hopkins contends that film viewers imagine themselves seeing the depicted events (2016: 62–63). Gregory Currie, in contrast, has argued that a viewer's "imagining" when watching a film "is not that [the viewer] see[s] the characters and the events," but rather "simply that there are these characters and that these events *occur*—the same sort of impersonal imagining" involved in "read[ing] a novel" (1995: 179).

Another way imagination may contribute to audience comprehension of cinematic narrative is through the imaginative filling of gaps in the represented events. Such gaps might include non-represented events, as in narrative prose, as well as unrepresented character motivation and attitude, which performance and photography cannot communicate in all of the ways available to narrative prose (see, e.g., Currie 1995: 195; Gaut 2010: 190–91; Carroll 2016: 123; Curran 2016: 111). As in the comprehension of verbal narrative fiction, it may be that these required gap-filling activities, even if below the threshold of consciousness, contribute to the senses of transport, of entering or at least viewing a different and separate world, and of being present at the depicted events that seem to be experienced by many viewers of film (cf. Cavell 1979: 25). Of course, these experiences differ from those arising from the process of elaborating a written narrative, since film viewers are confronted not with linguistic artifacts but with moving pictorial artifacts. Filmed action and states of affairs contribute different kinds of information than texts do to the situation model viewers must construct to make sense of the artifact confronting them.

Another dimension of audience engagement with film is emotional. The mechanisms and quality of our emotional responses to film have received significant theoretical attention, building on the age-old tradition of theorizing about emotional responses to theater but, again, necessarily moving beyond that tradition. Chapter 3 described Kendall Walton's influential account of the "quasi-" emotions experienced by the audience of fictional narrative; Walton's original examples advanced in support of this account concerned film viewing (1978a: 21–22). Walton's view has been challenged in several more recent discussions. Gregory Currie has argued that the feeling of fear prompted by seeing an approaching threat onscreen "is a real state of feeling and not an imaginary one," since "feelings are states identified, not in terms of their function [e.g., the responses they cause, like flight] but in terms of how they feel" (1995: 150). Berys Gaut suggests that whether a film viewer experiences an actual emotion or a vicarious or simulated emotion may depend on the details of the film scenario, and the degree to which the viewer has empathized with or, in contrast, identified with a character or point of view (2010: 260; cf. Walsh 2007: 99, discussing the difference between address and interpellation in film; Gilmore 2020). Carl Plantinga has sought to clarify the multiple components of an experience of affective response to a performed and projected scenario. Plantinga argues that the quality of twofoldness present in Wollheim's account of seeing-in and Murray Smith's account of character in film (2011) is echoed in our emotional responses to fiction films:

> We respond to characters [in narrative film] simultaneously as people, as actors playing roles, and in some cases as familiar movie stars; we respond with emotion to narrative films while simultaneously

recognizing their artifactuality and their having been produced within certain institutions of fiction.

(137)

The functioning of fictionality in live-action film is both important and complex, and scholarly interest in the topic appears to be growing, in part for reasons to be discussed in the next section. Future film theorists are likely to tune their accounts further to address additional features of fictionality in film, including the contribution of genre conventions as well as editing and other forms of photographic manipulation to film-specific fictionality.

ANIMATION AND TELEVISION

Through most of the first 90 years of theorizing about film, analysts focused on live-action film and in particular on the realist narrative film as prototypical film artifacts. Because such films are, roughly, narratively analogous to novels, the films examined did not radically differ from one another with regard to their fictionality: all such classic films involved fictional content. As a result, there was no obvious pressure to explain the fictional aspect of classic films. Fictionality in such films was a given, not a peculiarity that needed clarification. Over the past generation, however, technological advances in such matters as digital photography and editing, computer-generated imagery, and the platforms used to convey moving images to audiences have forced film and motion-picture theorists to reconsider motion-picture forms and formats that classic film theory treated as more marginal. Among these forms are animation and television.

Pre-cinematic motion-picture technology, which developed in the nineteenth century, was based not on photography, but on hand-created images (Manovich 2010: 247). When live-action film emerged, it did not immediately monopolize critical or theoretical attention, since live-action film can be convincingly characterized as a mechanical, rather than artistic, product (see Morgan 2006: 122). But by the mid-twentieth century, even though animated motion pictures continued to be produced and to find wide audiences, they were drawing little theoretical interest, despite the many interesting aesthetic issues such motion pictures raise.

Among the theorists who did consider animation during this period was Stanley Cavell. Responding to critics of his early work who questioned his reliance on the affordances of the photographic image in film, Cavell argued that animated moving images are fundamentally ontologically distinguishable from live-action film (1979: 168). Cavell acknowledged that he could not "prove" this position, but he pointed out in support of it multiple distinguishing features of "cartoons": the fact that "[t]he inhabitants of the world of animated cartoons… are talking animals," and that "human figures" in them "seem… out of place or in the way"; the fact that these characters inhabit an "animistic world" (169); the lack of "corporeality" of these characters, whose "bodies… never get in their way," are "totally subject to will, and totally expressive" (170); and the simplification and intensification of emotion prompted by an animated film:

> A world whose creatures are incorporeal is a world devoid of sex and death, hence a world apt to be either very sad or very happy. At either extreme its creatures elicit from us a painful tenderness.
>
> …Cartoon tenderness and loss is tenderness and loss maximized, or purified. Cartoon terror is absolute, because since the body is not destructible, the threat is to the soul itself.
>
> (171)

Cavell seems to have been writing of cartoons in the vein of Walt Disney or Chuck Jones, and some of his points are inapplicable to some subsequent animated film, which often does include human characters, if often in fantastic or impossible circumstances. But some of his points seem to retain validity.

One might also note that the viewer of an animated motion picture does not have to undergo the collapse described by Robert Hopkins as occurring in the apprehension of live-action film—or that if collapse does occur, it is in a sense simpler with animation than with live-action motion pictures. What we see in an animated film is mediated not by the bodies of actors plus the decisions of filmmakers, but only by the decisions of filmmakers. Viewers are thus closer in some ways to the fictional events or world represented in an animated film or video, even as viewers are also, of course, in many ways more distant from or even alienated from them.

Attention to the phenomenology of animation viewing is now receiving more attention, due in part to arguments about the significance of new motion-picture technologies such as digital photography and editing. In an influential 2001 essay, Lev Manovich argued that since these technologies involve manual intervention into the creation of the images displayed, they have rendered motion-picture creation a less mechanical, more human process, so that, in fact, *"[d]igital cinema is a particular use of animation that uses live-action footage as one of its many elements"* (2001: 250, emphasis in original). Manovich summarized the history of the relation of animation to motion pictures this way: *"Born from animation, cinema pushed animation to its periphery, only in the end to become one particular case of animation"* (250, emphasis in original; see also 253; Gaut 2010). Increased theoretical attention to animation as an important aesthetic form will almost certainly involve further study of the functioning of fictionality within animation.

The marginalization of animation in classic film theory might have been due in part to its association with children's programming and with television (Lamarre 2018: 5). Late twentieth-century developments in the technologies surrounding television—including the development of the VCR, the remote control, cable and satellite television, and eventually streaming content—have made the justifications for a bright-line theoretical distinction between film and television less obvious. Nevertheless, we continue to reserve the term "television" for motion pictures with particular formal features, notably episodic structure (see Sconce 2004; VanArendonk 2019).

Such features of television support different forms of viewer engagement than are possible with feature-length films. The episodic nature of fictional narrative television programming arguably enhances viewer involvement and absorption, whether the programming is watched on a weekly basis or binged, by incorporating the programming more deeply into the rhythms of viewers' leisure time. As Jeffrey Sconce among others has observed, television series have been remarkably generative of fan-involved elaborations (2004: 95). And the fictional meta-worlds created by narratives based on comics or animated series, in particular, sprawl across media, from game consoles and cellphones to computer and theater screens (see generally Lamarre 2018). These fictional universes are arguably becoming more persistent presences in audiences' lives. The consequences of these developments will be difficult to understand without attention to the ways fictionality functions across media and platforms.

Since the beginning of the twenty-first century, in fact, television has arguably become a more aesthetically adventurous and demanding medium than film (see, e.g., Sconce 2004: 110). The episodic form of television series, Kathryn VanArendonk has argued, might have played a role in fostering greater sensitivity to the mechanics of fictionality among content generators, critics, and viewers. She notes that television episodes within a series "can appear both functionally identical and entirely dissimilar" (2019: 68), prompting viewer attention to variations of content within regularities of form and building viewer patience and skill in deciphering thematically and narratively complex patterns through delivery in manageable, stand-alone episodic chunks (73). As VanArendonk also notes, these tendencies are not necessarily countered but might even be strengthened by the practice of releasing entire series seasons at one time, enabling more intensive viewer engagement with the series as artifact.

7

BEYOND ART

Theorists of fictionality are increasingly interested in understanding the occurrence of something like fictionality, if not fictionality itself, outside aesthetic artifacts. Of course, interest in such phenomena is not an entirely recent development. Hans Vaihinger's *Philosophy of As-If* (1911), for example, addressed only nonaesthetic fictions, mainly in science, law, philosophy, morals, and religion. But some theorists have proposed that the occurrence of fictionality beyond the aesthetic domain is a characteristically modern and perhaps characteristically Western phenomenon, inseparable from the scientific and industrial revolutions of the seventeenth and eighteenth centuries. Catherine Gallagher has argued that "almost all of the developments we associate with modernity—from greater religious toleration to scientific discovery—required the kind of cognitive provisionality one practices in reading fiction, a competence in investing contingent and temporary credit" (2006: 347). Gallagher's position is relatively bold. She suggests that the experience of apprehending literary fictions might have helped *enable* other developments in religion, science, and economy associated with modernity. One need not embrace this position to agree that phenomena and experiences akin to those associated with appreciating literary and aesthetic fiction are not limited to the

DOI: 10.4324/9781003161585-8

aesthetic domain, and might be well worth understanding in their own right.

It is not just theorists who are interested in such nonaesthetic instances of fictionality. In her work on "prefigurative politics," Davina Cooper (2020) has described how political actors, including local government officials, may engage deliberately in as-if "institutional action[] where a *preferred* set of conditions... [is] enacted (or assumed to be already in place)" (895). One example she studies is the practice in both the United Kingdom and the United States of local governments' taking foreign-policy positions (e.g., with regard to immigration law and/or boycotts) contrary to those of the broader government units within which the local governments operate. To be sure, there is a long tradition of activist enactment of, for example, utopian communities that function as if broader political goals have already been achieved. And some forms of activism, such as culture jamming, involve the dissemination of artifacts like satirical or parody advertisements, which could be regarded as fictional or as prompting an attitude in audiences akin to that prompted by aesthetic fictionality.

Recent activism such as the 2019 pro-democracy protests in Hong Kong has been especially closely linked to a particular mode of fictionality: the videogame. Journalists in Hong Kong during the protests noted, with approval, the parallels between activists' skill at spontaneous organization and the skills learned in massively multiplayer online role-playing games such as *World of Warcraft*, in which individuals must likewise improvise organized action involving a large group against a threatening and unpredictable adversary (Chiu 2019). Young Hong Kongers who have fled the city are also preserving "the memory of the protests" through videogame design, out of "concern that the government is trying to spin the narrative" (Andersen 2021). These developers have been countering the "disappearance of Hong Kong in actual space" through absorption into Mainland China with "the emergence of Hong Kong in virtual space" (H. Davies 2020: 3). These activists and videogame authors enact their politics in a way that meshes make-believe role-playing or virtual experience with real-world political action.

This chapter will not present an exhaustive account of all of the places one might encounter fictionality outside, or partly outside the aesthetic domain. Rather, it will focus on a short list of cultural domains in which fictionality has played an important and even constituent role, especially but not only in Western modernity: religion, law, science, and philosophy. The final two sections of the chapter will consider two areas of institutional dysfunction in which fictionality or fictionality-like structures are likewise central: totalitarian discourse and conspiracy theorizing.

RELIGIOUS FICTIONS

Religious ontologies often involve a doubling of worlds very much like that implied by fictional artifacts. Such ontologies divide existence into the secular and the sacred and represent these realms as complementary and partially accessible to one another, but also as asymmetrically related. Hans Vaihinger devoted most of the second half of *The Philosophy of As-If* (1911) to the question of fictions of morality and religion (see Fine 1993: 8). Theorists of aesthetic fiction have also repeatedly noted this analogy between religious and aesthetic fictions. Thomas Pavel, for example, observed in 1986 that dual structures "are not restricted to games of make-believe" but "have long been used by the religious mind as a fundamental ontological model" (Pavel 1986: 57), and he argues that "cult and fiction differ merely in the strength of the secondary universe" (60). Kendall Walton likewise acknowledged that make-believe is not distinctively aesthetic, but plays a role in "certain religious practices" and "the institution of morality," among other human practices (1990: 7). Wolfgang Iser reads philosopher Cornelius Castoriadis as arguing that "imaginary significations [e.g., the Christian God] are those for which there is no specific code-governed signified, so that the signifier points to an empty space, allowing for a nonbeing to be posited as a signified" (1993: 215). On this interpretation, the human projection of a second, sacred level of existence beyond the mundane is a kind of collective cultural gap-filling that elaborates content for the explanation of those parts of human experience not addressed fully through other cultural systems.

More specific experiential features of many religious traditions are also often reminiscent of the experiences associated with aesthetic fictionality. Most often, this likeness results from the way such features work as hinge or access points between secular and sacred ontologies. Religious rites and objects very often exhibit dual aspects akin to those of fictional artifacts. In one of his dialogues, Gregory Bateson discusses the relationship between the Christian rite of communion and the role-playing of a ballet dancer in *Swan Lake* in exactly these terms:

> if for some people the bread and wine are only a metaphor, while for others... the bread and wine are a sacrament; then, if there be some for whom the ballet is a metaphor, there may be others for whom it is emphatically more than a metaphor—but rather a [nonmetaphorical] sacrament.
>
> (1972: 36)

He continues,

> The swan figure is not a real swan but a pretend swan. It is also a pretend not-human being. It is also "really" a young lady wearing a white dress.... [I]t is not one of these statements but their combination which constitutes a sacrament. The "pretend" and the "pretend-not" and the "really" somehow get fused together into a single meaning.
>
> (37)

Bateson also writes about the dual aspects assigned to deities and institutions in some religions, including the religious practice of a village in Bali that Bateson studied as an anthropologist. The council of this village, "in its secular aspects, is referred to as *I Desa* (literally, 'Mr. Village'), and numerous rules and procedures are rationalized by reference to this abstract personage," while "in its sacred aspects, the village is deified as *Betara Desa* (God Village), to whom shrines are erected and offerings brought" (118).

Christianity, of course, especially in its medieval European forms, has also been fascinated to the point of preoccupation with the dual aspects of Christ and, by extension, of humans. As Kathy Eden notes, Augustine placed "particular emphasis both on the double nature of Christ, the *Imago Dei*, as God-man, and on the double nature of man

the *imago* of an *Imago*, as simultaneously spiritual and material"
(1986: 131). Religious images could also reflect this duality and, like
Christ, function as objects of imitation (132–33; Rockmore 2013: 77).
Virginie Greene has explained the intense interest in eleventh-century
Europe in the puzzles of doubled and overlapping ontology posed
by many central Christian motifs. The century saw "the recurrence of debates on issues such as the Trinity, the Eucharist, and
the Incarnation, which require discussing the... usefulness of logic
applied to theological matters" (2014: 33). In Greene's reading, theological debates on these matters amounted to philosophical debates
about fictionality that anticipated those of twentieth-century English-
language philosophers in many ways.

Religious practice sometimes treats the world as a divinely created
artifact to be apprehended and interpreted in ways not unlike the kinds
of reading appropriate to aesthetic artifacts. Although some traditions
of religious and natural law also regard law as a divinely created
product, the secular European legal tradition that developed in Rome
even before the Common Era regarded law as a human creation—but
one in which a kind of fiction was sometimes acknowledged to be
necessary.

LEGAL FICTIONS

As noted in Chapter 2, Wolfgang Iser argued that in the "ancient tradition there is only one instance of anything comparable with fiction in
its modern usage; this is in Roman law," specifically fictions of citi-
zenship for the purpose of charging foreigners with crimes (1993: 96).
Iser's position regarding the nonexistence of aesthetic fiction in the
ancient tradition is now probably a minority position, but he is right
to point to the early recognition of the significance of fiction in the
secular legal domain.

Contemporary legal theorists use the term "legal fiction" in two
senses, one narrow and one broad. Legal fictions in the narrow sense
are not a pervasive feature of legal discourse but an occasional phenomenon. Historically, most such fictions have been the invention
of individual jurists seeking equitable results in particular cases. If
recognized legal rules do not support such an equitable result, because

of either insufficient foresight by the legal code's creators, changes in social and cultural conditions, or both, the jurist may pretend that the facts of the case are other than they truly are in order to reach the fair result without openly disregarding recognized law. For example, the fiction mentioned by Iser and in the previous paragraph addressed a gap in the Roman criminal code, which did not provide for the prosecution of non-Roman citizens. The fiction Iser describes allowed a foreigner to be treated as if he were a Roman citizen for purposes of criminal process, so that the foreigner could be held accountable for a crime committed against Romans.

The legal scholar Lon Fuller (1902–78), in his classic work *Legal Fictions* (1930–31), offered another example of a legal fiction in the narrow sense: "The English courts were in the habit of pretending that a chattel [a piece of personal property] which might in fact have been taken from the plaintiff by force, had been *found* by the defendant" (6). The courts did this "[i]n order to allow an action [for return of the property] which otherwise would not" be recognized by the court because of the strict rules of common-law pleading, which did not allow an action to be based on the allegation that a defendant had taken a chattel from the plaintiff by force (6). Such fictions often became part of legal doctrine after their original recognition, but their use would commonly be restricted to cases similar to those in which the fictions first appeared. Fictions in this sense received that label because they were acknowledged to be contrary to the facts of a case, and were in that sense false or untrue, but were not intended to deceive: all parties as well as the judge would be aware of the deviation from accuracy in a case decided using a fiction (see, e.g., Fuller 1930–31: 6).

In the broader sense, "legal fiction" does not have such a technical definition. Rather, the term refers to one or more of the many ways in which legal practice and discourse rely on legal practitioners' adoption of a make-believe attitude toward their own acts and words (see, e.g., Tans 2014; Tans 2016). This view, anticipated by Lon Fuller although not fully elaborated by him, involves the acknowledgment of multiple features of legal practice, doctrine, and discourse that exhibit features similar to those associated with aesthetic fictionality. For example, legal practice creates a kind of world parallel to and in part independent of the nonlegal world. Lawyers and judges use language performatively, that is, to achieve not just communication but some further change in the world, such as issuing a judgment or entering a verdict (see Austin 1961: 235; see also the discussion in Chapter 1). Relatedly, some legal language creates new referents in a way at least roughly analogous to the referent-creating function of fictional narration discussed in Chapter 5. At the same time, and for related reasons, lawyers and judges are always alert to the ways language can function as a target for analysis as well as an information-conveying and referent-creating technology. Lawyers are practiced at seeing different aspects of the same linguistic event (see Chapter 3). Finally, as in the sphere of religion, fictions of origin play an important role in the legitimation of legal systems and activities.

The philosopher John Woods has described legal institutions and discourse, in general, as a domain in which what he calls "sitehood" operates: "It is true *in law* that the accused is innocent of [a] murder... until a jury finds... otherwise. The fact that he is on trial... is itself strongly indicative of the presumption's *falsity in the world*" but not in the "site" of the law (2018: 87). In this regard, Woods argues, legal discourse is akin to scientific and aesthetic discourse: Woods notes the similarities between the guilty verdict just described, on the one hand, and on the other, Leibniz's "ma[king] true the existence of infinitesimals in the calculus" and "what Doyle did" in writing the Sherlock Holmes stories (91).

Much legal discourse, especially in the United States, relies heavily on the mention of linguistic utterances, as in citations of precedent, where a quoted utterance is treated as an authority external to the argument in which it is quoted, and in hypotheticals, where an invented utterance is treated as an example for examination in consideration of an argument about the meaning of authority. Consider, for example, the following passage from the US Supreme Court's 2022 decision in *Dobbs v. Jackson Women's Health Organization*, the case overruling the Court's 1973 *Roe v. Wade* decision recognizing a constitutional right to abortion:

> The inescapable conclusion is that a right to abortion is not deeply rooted in the Nation's history and traditions. On the contrary, an

> unbroken tradition of prohibiting abortion on pain of criminal punishment persisted from the earliest days of the common law until 1973. The Court in *Roe [v. Wade]* could have said of abortion exactly what *Glucksberg [v. Washington* (1998)] said of assisted suicide: "Attitudes toward [abortion] have changed since [the thirteenth-century English jurist] Bracton, but our laws have consistently condemned, and continue to prohibit, [that practice]."
>
> (third and fifth interpolations in original)

This passage illustrates how a single quoted sentence in legal discourse can carry multiple senses, aspects, or significations. The sentence from the *Glucksberg* opinion quoted by Justice Alito is, first, an excerpt from precedent elsewhere heavily relied upon as controlling in the *Dobbs* opinion, though not for the proposition here. In this light, the quotation borrows from the authoritative status of *Glucksberg*; the quoted sentence is akin to a law issued by another source, namely, an earlier incarnation of the Supreme Court. But Justice Alito also invites readers of the quotation to imagine that this sentence had been contained instead in the *Roe v. Wade* decision. Of course, if the sentence had been used in *Roe v. Wade* to express the Court's position, that 1973 decision would not have found a constitutional right to abortion. The passage thus suggests an alternative world where the Court deciding *Roe* anticipated the allegedly sounder constitutional reasoning of *Glucksberg* and reached a different conclusion, obviating the need for *Dobbs* itself.

Highly complex and somewhat precious rhetorical practices like this example are quite common, but relatively understudied in legal theory (see Petroski 2020). Such practices are as intrinsic to many contemporary forms of legal discourse as quoted dialogue is to modern narrative fiction. As noted in Chapter 5, some theorists of fiction point to this phenomenon of linguistic mention intermingled with linguistic use as constitutive of fictionality in narrative. Felíx Martínez-Bonati reasoned that with mentioned, or quoted, sentences, the phenomenon of "immanent signification" or transparency does not occur; each mentioned sentence is "a representative of another token of the same sentence-type" and is received as such (1960: 79) He proposed that it is our capacity to speak and write sentences tha "are… representatives of (absent) authentic sentences" that "makes possible the introduction of merely imaginary sentences into the realm of communication" (79), and thus in turn makes fictional discourse possible. Martínez-Bonati also presented the concept of "[e]xample-sentences such as those which appear in the theoretical discussions on language," as in linguistics or philosophy of language; such sentences likewise "signify iconically imaginary sentences" (164 n.3; see also Smith 1978: 50–60). Lawyers' use of imaginary sentences is, if anything, growing increasingly common, but recognition of the parallels between this practice and the structure of fictional discourse remains unusual.

As noted at the beginning of this section, since the development of Roman law in the centuries before the Common Era, European-derived conceptions of law have mostly regarded law as a human creation. This conceptualization can yield practical problems that become especially salient in radical or revolutionary challenges to the legitimacy of legal and/or political systems. If humans created the law and/or the state, surely humans can also modify or un-create them. Who or what decides when such modification is acceptable? Originary fictions seek to explain the creation of the law and/or the state in allegorical or fabular form to justify the persistence of a particular instance of state power against questioning. The use of originary fictions to justify the coercive power of existing political and legal systems dates back at least to Plato's doctrine of the noble lie in Book III of the *Republic*. In fact, this "Phoenician tale" is a variation on an Aesopian fable, as Leslie Kurke has pointed out in a discussion of a similar fable in the *Protagoras* (see Kurke 2011: 305–08). Early modern Europe saw a proliferation of such fables, including Hobbes's "bellum omnium contra omnes and… 'original contract,'" which Vaihinger called "for Hobbes conscious fictions" (1911: vii), as well as roughly analogous vignettes in the work of Adam Smith, Étienne Bonnot de Condillac, Jean-Jacques Rousseau, Immanuel Kant, and Friedrich Nietzsche (136–39, 200–68; Tans 2014).

The "original position" and "veil of ignorance" proposed by political philosopher John Rawls (1921–2002) in *A Theory of Justice* (1971) have served a similar function for liberal political theory (see La Caze 2002: 94–118). The jurist and legal philosopher Hans Kelsen

(1881–1973), like so many earlier theorists, explicitly acknowledged the fictional status of the foundational concept in his theory of legal authority, the *Grundnorm* or fundamental norm. According to Kelsen, any given law deserves to be recognized as valid only to the extent that the law is consistent with more basic laws or principles. A piece of legislation, for example, is lawful only if it is consistent with the constitution of the government enacting the legislation. But what validates a basic norm like a constitution? As contemporary legal philosopher Olaf Tans has observed, the legal "validity game" played by participants in a modern Western legal system involves their adoption of a make-believe attitude toward this concept: "[W]hoever wants to play has to go along with the fiction of normative foundation" in a justified fundamental norm, such as a constitution, whose justification will not be questioned (Tans 2014: 135). Tans continues, "One only has to recognize the fact that the game is played under that assumption and pretend to believe in it while playing,… if one wants to be taken seriously" as a legal practitioner (135).

SCIENTIFIC FICTIONS

The use of fictions in science is arguably as old as their use in law, although acknowledging that scientific practice involves reliance on fictions seems to be a more recent development. One could call superseded scientific theories, such as the notion of phlogiston or the dormitive power, fictions. But limiting the use of fictionality in science to these instances fails to do justice to the pervasive ways in which viable, current science depends on forms of fictionality. Most accounts of scientists' and philosophers' growing awareness of the importance of fiction for science date this awareness to the scientific revolution of sixteenth- and seventeenth-century Europe (e.g., Iser 1993: 143).

Two major developments during this period implicate fictionality or something very similar: first, acceptance of the scientific method of empirical testing of hypotheses, which requires speculation as to what might be the case in order to form the hypotheses to be tested (see, e.g., Gallagher 2006: 347; Stuart et al. 2018: 14; Vaihinger 1911: 197–99); second, the self-aware generation of idealizations or models to frame both hypotheses and scientific laws (see, e.g., Fine 1993: 7, 16). Classic examples of such idealizations or models include the frictionless plane and the atom. Increasingly, theorists of Western science view such models as both intrinsic to scientific practice and, in at least some regards, similar to aesthetic fictionality. Roman Frigg, for example, argues that scientific models are "akin to places and characters of literary fiction" (2010: 99; see also 101, 135). Frigg explains that models, like fictional narratives, mean more than they say explicitly: "it is understood that the model-system has properties other than the ones mentioned in the description" of the model (102), that these properties can in a sense be explored, and that this implicational richness of models is precisely why they are useful for scientific reasoning.

There is some tension between an understanding of scientific discourse as, on the one hand, genuinely and uniquely linked to the real world, to things as they are (see, e.g., Ingarden 1968: 4–5), and, on the other, involving the scrutiny of known idealizations and distortions to achieve scientific insight. This tension remains alive in contemporary scientific practice, and it is not clear how to integrate these two competing faces of science. Scientific discourse does presuppose a referential relationship with the real, lived world that differs from the referential relationship presupposed by narrative fiction. Even realistic fiction does not purport to represent solely real-world entities and events, while we do usually understand scientific discourse as purporting to have an exclusive commitment to actuality. As noted in Chapter 5, however, the functioning of linguistic reference both inside and outside narrative fiction remains a debated issue, and it is not clear how far one can take this referential distinction between scientific and fictional discourse.

A related feature of scientific discourse sometimes taken to be definitive is that it is a collective discourse: each scientific proposal of or challenge to a hypothesis or model contributes to a larger collective project. On this point, Roman Ingarden distinguished literary works from scientific works by observing that the latter invite and depend on readers' "go[ing] beyond" the work; in contrast, "[b]eyond" the "completion" of a work of art "there is no possible continuation, such as is certainly quite possible and natural in the case of a scientific work" (1958: 166). This explanation seems vulnerable, both because continuations beyond a single work of art are possible (as discussed in Chapters 4 and 5) and because this collective-project conceptualization of scientific practice does not account well for scientific paradigm shifts.

Does the difficulty of explaining how scientific discourse and practice hook up with the world suggest anything about how we should view the scientific use of fictions? What are the benefits and drawbacks of acknowledging this use? Perhaps the answers to these questions depend on the audience we are considering. Some non-scientists, perhaps especially philosophers, regard the dependence of scientific practice on fiction-like constructs as both appropriate and legitimating for their own work. Thus, some philosophers cite the scientific use of models and thought experiments as legitimating the use of such devices more generally. These philosophers argue that it is the philosophical use of thought experiments that makes philosophical discourse more closely akin to traditional scientific discourse (e.g., La Caze 2002: 78–82; see also Stuart et al. 2018: 7).

PHILOSOPHICAL FICTIONS

As the above discussion suggests, philosophers have not just analyzed fictionality directly; they have also used its techniques and structures, without always reflecting on these uses too carefully. Examples of philosophical reliance on fiction-like mechanisms include philosophers' use of invented scenarios, idealizations, example sentences, and, of course, thought experiments.

Plato is commonly identified as the originator of many of these practices. Leslie Kurke "concur[s] with those scholars who understand the genre of [Socratic dialogue] as a fabricated literary form, and Socrates himself as a fictional character in the writings of Plato and Xenophon" (2011: 252–53; see also Greene 2014: 148). Kurke also notes that Nietzsche identified Plato's dialogues as "the model of the *novel*" (262–63). Plato on occasion explicitly described the work of philosophers as akin to that of painters, or aesthetic creators (Halliwell 2002: 130). And Plato is sometimes cited as the first practitioner of the thought experiment (La Caze 2002: 71).

Some branches of philosophy rely heavily on idealizations akin to those of science, not always fully acknowledging the abstracted or idealized nature of the constructs in question. Such reliance is particularly marked in branches of philosophy that might not initially seem to be associated with science (Stuart et al. 2018: 2): examples might be Kant's categorical imperative in ethics and Rousseau's social contract in political philosophy (Iser 1993: 93–118; La Caze 2002: 94–118). One explanation of the reliance on idealizations in these branches of philosophy is that the kinds of "normative claims [central to these areas] are not amenable to the same sources of evidence as non-normative disciplines" (Stuart et al. 2018: 2). For example, philosophers of mind can draw on psychological research to support their claims. Philosophers of language can and do draw on linguistic research. But there are no comparable sister disciplines for ethics, and quantitative methods in political science are limited in scope. Borrowing the scientific trope of the idealized model might also help work in these branches of philosophy to borrow the aura of objectivity and interpersonal validity associated with scientific discourse.

Philosophers of language have shared with linguists the expositional habit of relying on examples of language use, that is, the mention of sample sentences, very often invented by the theorist. In philosophy, the memorable instances of this practice can earn a scholar attention and influence. Some of the most celebrated example sentences are those carrying some ironic or paradoxical force. As Thomas Pavel notes, in his enormously influential work on modal semantics, Saul Kripke "exemplifies possibility by making use of a fictional being," Sherlock Holmes (1972: 44), thus inaugurating a long tradition of philosophical work that uses Holmes's name and Conan Doyle's stories as the paradigm examples of a fictional character and a fictional work, respectively. Sometimes this practice carries an unacknowledged rhetorical charge or is even (deliberately or not) misleading. Discussing Rudolf Carnap's highly influential 1955 essay "Meaning and Synonymy in Natural Languages," and in particular Carnap's use of sentences in German to illustrate his points, Virginie Greene has observed that

> the point [Carnap] makes... does not need a comparison between languages... The whole demonstration works as well without the

German words. Their use is an effect of fiction. Carnap wants to establish the objectivity of the intensional method [that he proposes]; therefore, his fictional linguists must appear as objective as possible. The linguists need to be ignorant of the language they study, so they are not biased by their own understanding of the language. This is not logically necessary, but makes the fiction more convincing for its intended audience.

(2014: 58)

There is a highly rhetorical, artful dimension to this aspect of philosophical discourse, and part of the artfulness involves a pretense of literality and of the arbitrary or even random identification of examples to present.

Thought experiments are probably the best-known and now most openly studied of these fiction-like philosophical practices. The term "thought experiment" first appeared in the nineteenth century, but the practice received little attention from philosophers until the 1980s (Stuart et al. 2018: 1, 9). There are now multiple competing accounts of the function, operation, and criteria of these devices. A classic, much-discussed thought experiment predating this more recent self-awareness is the violinist scenario presented by Judith Jarvis Thompson in her 1971 essay "A Defense of Abortion." After supposing for the sake of argument that a fetus is a person and therefore has a right to live, Thompson questions whether this premise justifies legal bans on abortion, basing her challenge on the following vignette:

[N]ow let me ask you to imagine this. You wake up in the morning and find yourself back to back in bed with an unconscious violinist. A famous unconscious violinist. He has been found to have a fatal kidney disease, and the Society of Music Lovers has canvassed all the available medical records and found that you alone have the right blood type to help. They have therefore kidnapped you, and last night the violinist's circulatory system was plugged into yours, so that your kidneys can be used to extract poisons from his blood as well as yours. The director of the hospital... tells you, "Look, we're sorry the Society of Music Lovers did this to you.... But... they did it, and the violinist now is plugged into you. To unplug you would be to kill him. But never mind, it's only for nine months...." Is it morally incumbent on you to accede to this situation? No doubt it would be very nice of you if you did.... But do you *have* to accede to it? What if it were not nine months, but nine years? Or longer still? What if the director of the hospital said, "Tough luck, I agree, but you've now got to stay in bed, with the violinist plugged into you, for the rest of your life...." I suspect you would regard this as outrageous, which suggests that something really is wrong with that plausible-sounding argument [about the fetus's right to life] I mentioned a moment ago.

(48–49)

This passage displays a number of characteristic features of philosophical thought experiments: a quasi-fantastic, and certainly not realistic, premise; several incremental variations on the premise; a number of gratuitous but witty details; and finally a declaration by the philosopher of the intuition revealed by the experiment (see, e.g., Kind 2020: 72–75; La Caze 2002: 44–69). Is this passage a narrative fiction, or not? Kendall Walton, himself a philosopher, has argued that thought experiments like Thompson's are virtually indistinguishable from narrative fictions: he describes thought experiments as props embedded in "otherwise nonfictional contexts" (1990: 90; see also Stuart et al. 2018: 19). And thought experiments do seem devised to induce imaginative work and some amount of inferential gap-filling in their readers. On the other hand, thought experiments also seem to have more general purposes differing fundamentally from those of narrative fiction. While thought experiments, like narrative fiction, invite us to imagine, thought experiments do so in order to induce an intuition matching the intuition supplied by the philosopher, in the service of a broader, logically structured argument.

One further way in which philosophical work makes use of fictionality, of course, is by making fictionality an object of study in its own right, as discussed throughout this book, or even by taking aesthetic fictions as a model for understanding our talk and practices in a particular area. The latter approach has come to be called "fictionalism" (see Fine 1993; Papineau 1988; Sainsbury 2009). For example, mathematical fictionalism involves the position that our statements about mathematics do not involve straightforward reference to any mathematical entities, such as numbers or functions, but rather make as if to refer to such entities. Talking about mathematical matters involves playing a game involving make-believe that the referents of mathematical statements exist. Arthur Fine, in his early essay on philosophical fictionalism (1992), focused mainly on recuperating Hans Vaihinger's work and reputation for use in this project, but more recent work on philosophical fictionalism has not always cited Vaihinger as a precursor. This omission mirrors the early twentieth-century neglect of Vaihinger that Fine examines at length in his article. In this area, as in others discussed in earlier chapters, recent theorists have sometimes overstated the novelty of their insights.

TOTALITARIAN DISCOURSE

In many, if not all, of the instances discussed up now in this chapter, fictionality has largely positive functions. In other domains, reliance on fiction or mechanisms akin to fictionality is arguably less functional. Some uses of fictionality, that is, have antisocial rather than cooperative implications. This section and the next will discuss two such domains: totalitarian discourse and conspiracy theorizing.

Totalitarianism is arguably a purely twentieth- and twenty-first-century phenomenon. The term, at least, is an invention of the twentieth century (Fuentes 2013). One way to view totalitarianism as a political form is as a kind of authoritarian or right-wing prefigurative politics (see, e.g., Cooper 2020) that relies heavily on the manipulation of public discourse, the use of such discourse to create its own referents, and the use of religious models to structure public experiences of interaction with the state.

Two famous mid-twentieth-century accounts of totalitarianism stress the linguistic and discursive dimensions of the phenomenon. In *The Origins of Totalitarianism* (1950), Hannah Arendt remarks on the self-consciously creative function of totalitarian propaganda: in the opinion of propagandists, "fact depends entirely on the power of man who can fabricate it" (350). What is created by this propaganda is a "fictitious world," "fit to compete with the real one, whose main handicap is that it is not logical" but rather simplistically affective (362; see also

Dor 2015: 102; Gronskaya et al. 2012: 284). Arendt observes in this regard how a totalitarian regime can, for example, make a dubious "scientific" fact, like the supposed facts of racial difference and contamination, into realized facts (362). A complementary work, Victor Klemperer's *The Language of the Third Reich* (1947), examines in more detail the linguistic strategies used to these ends by Adolf Hitler and Joseph Goebbels in particular. Among the strategies recounted by Klemperer are the gratuitous use of empty superlatives and the use of neologisms and abbreviations, as well as metaphors of martial strength, contamination, and so forth. Yet another linguistic device used by both Nazi propagandists and the Romanian dictator Nicolae Ceauşescu, among others, is "de-agentification," the selective denial of the power of intentional agency to some individuals in descriptions of state and public activity (Ilie 1998). Such strategies begin, perhaps, as a kind of prefigurative as-if politics, but have the power to invade the thought and speech patterns even of those victimized by the totalitarian state (see Klemperer 1947).

The convergence of politics and religion is not unique to totalitarianism, of course. Arguably, this merging of religious and political domains lies at the origin of the modern Western state (see, e.g., Kantorowicz 1957; Bateson 1972: 183). In contemporary Western democracies, too, government officeholding involves a kind of make-believe or role-playing. As Gregory Currie has observed, both "[f]ictional roles" and "offices," such as that of the US presidency, "belong to a larger class of entities" definable as "function[s] from worlds to individuals" (1990: 173–74). That is, office holders hold their offices as members of one world, such as the political world of the state or the sacred world of a church, while also remaining inhabitants of a different world, the secular world of civil or private society. In a totalitarian regime, this doubling of roles is less openly acknowledged, and the totalitarian leader's deification does not necessarily suggest that the leader has a dual aspect as both private and public, quasi-sacred individual. In addition to this deification of the leader, totalitarian regimes characteristically make use of "new rituals," the "creation of a sophisticated liturgy," and other participatory practices supporting a narrative of "redemption" (Fuentes 2013: 57). This dimension of totalitarian state practice involves a blending of aspects of the things and events involved that is almost indistinguishable from that of more traditional religious ritual, as discussed earlier in this chapter.

A further similarity between totalitarian and religious practices is the fact that both often rely on an atmosphere of secrecy or esotericism. The message conveyed to adherents and skeptics alike is that insight into the truth—of history, of the path to the future—is reserved to a minority (Arendt 1950: 352; see also Fuentes 2013). The promise of initiation into this privileged group might help to compensate for the frequently noted cognitive poverty of totalitarianism, which characteristically sneers at rationality and usually persecutes non-regime intellectuals and academics. Passion, not reason, is the appropriate engine of action within a totalitarian regime. This feature of totalitarianism can drive surprising shifts in power but is also a severe weakness of totalitarian regimes. It can, for instance, limit the effectiveness of the linguistic strategies of totalitarian discourse noted above. Daniel Dor has recently noted that individuals

> differ in terms of their trust in the carriers of the linguistic worldview, and in the general truthfulness of language.... [W]hen speakers are convinced that they speak a sacred tongue,... they would probably be very deeply affected by their language.... On the other side, when speakers realize that the language they have to use is an artificial construction built and used for the purposes of thought-policing, they very often learn to experience-for-instructing [i.e., become capable of pragmatically processing the language]..., but in their own world of experience, they nevertheless keep themselves away from the worldview reflected by the language. This was the attitude reflected by many speakers toward the newspeak dictates of the great totalitarian regimes of the twentieth century.
>
> (2015: 97)

For this reason among others, the totalitarian leader's goal of total control is never completely realizable (Gronskaya et al. 2012: 279; see also Žižek 1989).

The phenomenon described by Dor is reminiscent of the double consciousness also described by, for instance, W.E.B. Du Bois (see

Chapter 3). More broadly, the features of totalitarian discourse discussed in this section are not necessarily unique to what we would normally identify as totalitarian propaganda. Nielsen, Phelan, and Walsh open their "Ten Theses on Fictionality" article with an example of fictionality in US political rhetoric from a speech by former US President Barack Obama. Despite the apparent harmlessness of the example, they argue,

> The employment of fictionality in political discourse will tend to contribute—again for better or worse—to a logos-immunization of the discourse whereby arguments and counter-arguments have to take place on other levels and with other forms of appeal than those based in facts and documented evidence.
>
> (2015: 69; see also Mäkelä 2019: 459–62)

It remains to be seen whether this prediction will be borne out by events. But the broader point, that awareness of how fictionality works might help us see whether such a wider shift in discourse is occurring, seems reasonable.

CONSPIRACY THEORIZING

From a different perspective, one could view a totalitarian regime as a conspiracist state, a political apparatus founded on and organized by conspiracy theory (Fenster 2008: 89, 104). Esotericism is also a central feature of conspiracy theorizing. The allure of conspiracy theories is also driven by the attractiveness of decipherment, the gaining of access to a more real world, and in particular the "affective rush" that accompanies the extrapolating, world-building engagement of understanding the role of new details in the conspiracy narrative (110).

A more technical view of conspiracy theorizing and its attractiveness might regard conspiracy theorizing as stemming from a breakdown in the cultural institutions or structures that otherwise permit members of a culture to distinguish fictionality from factuality. Jean-Marie Schaeffer defines the "possibility of fiction" as depending on at least three conditions. First, it must be possible for individuals to make a "dissociation between mimetic procedures and [the] conduct of mimicry," if demanded by the representation; in other words, individuals must be able to understand a representation as a representation, or to see in to the representation and recognize it as a creation. Second, individuals must possess "a complex mental organization" that includes both "an instance of conscious (or attentional) control susceptible of blocking the effects of pre-attentional lures at the level of beliefs" and "a sophisticated intentional organization susceptible of distinguishing between what is valid for real and what is valid make-believe." That is, individuals must be able to adjust their attention between the dual aspects of an artifact exhibiting fictionality, and must be able to see how each of those aspects does or does not fit into their wider experiential world. Finally, according to Schaeffer, for fictionality to exist, a social organization must exist that makes possible "shared ludic feints," or interpersonal agreement on the above matters. To Schaeffer, "shared ludic feint is possible only in the frame of a social organization in which the part of reciprocal cooperation is larger than the one of conflictual relations" (1999: 138–39). In other words, playful representation requires cooperation among the players, a willingness for all involved to agree to treat certain items and behaviors as part of the game, rather than as real-world or serious phenomena. Conspiracy theorizing, then, might proliferate in the absence or weakening of the third of these elements: where the members of a culture simply do not agree on which artifacts exhibit fictionality and how their features do or do not fit into their wider experiential world. Conspiracy theorists take their explanation of the connections between events to refer accurately to real-world causal relationships and phenomena, while those not subscribing to the theory will view the conspiracy theorists' explanations as fantastic. But the conspiracy theorist adopts these explanations precisely because the theorist rejects the consensus view of real-world history as a sinister fabrication.

Conspiracy theorizing has a longer history than totalitarianism, arguably stretching back at least to medieval milliennialism (Fenster 2008: 40). The term "conspiracy theory," however, was coined by Karl Popper in the 1950s (Meek 2020: 22). At the time, and for many decades thereafter, conspiracy theorizing was regarded as a fringe activity (see Hofstadter 1964; Fenster 2008: 32). In the twenty-first century, however, it no longer seems possible to describe conspiracy theory-like belief structures as non-mainstream, at least quantitatively. In some twenty-first-century Western cultures, a slim majority of the population subscribes to such beliefs (Meek 2020: 19, 20).

What do these belief structures look like? The precise contents vary, of course, but commentators have identified particular patterns of thought and meaningfulness that seem to span otherwise distinct conspiracy theories. As noted above, conspiracy theories share with totalitarianism the allure of the esoteric: each such theory centers on a vast hidden truth that has been brought to light by an intrepid investigator, while also being accessible to any sufficiently dogged believer (Fenster 2008: 7, 8; Meek 2020: 21). These theories propose a single, relatively simple explanation for all manner of social and political events. The theories attribute those events to a single tightly knit group of agents operating in secret (Meek 2020: 21). Conspiracy theories promise a never-ending process of interpretive rectification, as the relationship of additional events and details to the core explanation is revealed or rooted out over time (Fenster 2008: 13, 95; Meek 2020: 22). Such theories are often, if not always, anti-government in political orientation, espousing an "anarchistic, nihilistic libertarianism that takes government as its ultimate enemy" (Meek 2020: 22–23). While typically opposed to leveling or redistributive movements, conspiracy theories tend to be politically populist (Fenster 2008: 95; Meek 2020: 22–23). Perhaps the most obvious recent example of these typical dynamics is the QAnon family of conspiracy theories embraced, though not originated, by former US President Donald Trump (Meek 2020).

Conspiracy theorizing and conspiracy theorists are increasingly linked to anti-government populist movements around the world, not just in the United States (Meek 2020, discussing the parallels between UK and US politics over the period between 2016 and 2020). Conspiracy theorizing is also commonly viewed by most mainstream commentators as dysfunctional. The contemporary legal scholar Mark Fenster has argued, however, that conspiracy theories are, in fact, exhibitions of a "mode of populist logic" that is "not foreign to democracy" but has been integral to US politics, at least, since its beginning (2008: 90). This populist logic is the logic of criticism of established power structures, especially non-transparent power structures. This logic is the kind that political founding fictions seek to short-circuit. Fenster also notes that establishment political discourse can look similar to conspiracy theorizing in its attribution of obfuscation and illegitimacy to political opponents (46). In general, however, partly for reasons noted above, conspiracy theorizing does not in fact tend to enable effective political activity, or at least not effective governance, except perhaps in the form of totalitarianism (46).

The links between conspiracy theorizing and fiction are not limited to the analogies between, for example, a theorist's reading of the hidden meaning of reality and a reader's understanding of the represented content of a narrative. There is also a strong ongoing relationship between conspiracy theorizing and play or make-believe in their more ludic, cooperative senses. Conspiracy theorizing has been an increasingly common topic for fictional representations, most notably but not only in the TV series *The X-Files* (1993–2002; see Fenster 2008: 143–50), which realistically represented the fanlike structure of communities of conspiracy theorists in its depiction of the Lone Gunmen characters, who eerily prefigure some categories of QAnon adherents. Fenster has pointed out how some such conspiracy-theory communities are quite self-aware about their activities (2008: 155–94). A recent example of ludic conspiracy theorizing (or conspiracy-jamming) is the "Birds Aren't Real" campaign in the United States (Lorenz 2021). This parody conspiracy theory includes billboards, bumper stickers, and protest activity purporting to unveil the conspiracy behind the US government's replacement of all birds with drones sometime in the mid-twentieth century. Initiator Peter McIndoe, raised in a conservative rural community, explained in an interview that in his young adulthood he began to realize that he was not the only person "forced to straddle multiple realities," and that he developed the ersatz movement to "hold[] up a mirror to America in the Internet Age" (Lorenz 2021). Like non-parodic conspiracy theorizing, however, and like prefigurative politics in both its progressive and right-wing forms, such conspiracy-jamming might be necessarily an interstitial activity, organized but voluntary. As some remarks above have suggested, it is likely that fictionality-like structures also play crucial roles in more democratic political forms that are beyond the scope of this book.

CONCLUSION

What might a future introduction to fictionality look like? It would probably devote more space to some topics this book has treated only briefly, such as film and interactive digital media. Would it also need to address the nonhuman creation and appreciation of fiction?

Put another way, is fictionality a uniquely human phenomenon? This brief conclusion will review some of the ways the link between fiction and humanity has been drawn, and then test the link in two ways. First, it will consider the well-known Turing test for computer or artificial intelligence, offering reflections on the 1950 philosophical paper in which Alan Turing proposed the test and its treatment by subsequent readers. Then the conclusion considers a bit more systematically what it might take for a nonhuman intelligence to create and, most crucially, apprehend fiction, basing the analysis on observations made throughout this book and on recent developments in artificial intelligence research.

FICTION AND HUMANITY

Many recent accounts of fictionality emphasize its apparent biological and anthropological bases. Jean-Marie Schaeffer discusses

DOI: 10.4324/9781003161585-9

the "mimetic capacities" of many animals and the ability of many to engage in "(serious) feint," as well as "ludic imitations of activity" of, for example, "kittens or puppies brawling with each other" (1999: xv–xvi; see also Bateson 1972: 181–82). Moreover, many developmental psychologists endorse the view that children's ability to engage in pretend play and distinguish imaginary from real characters, from about 18 months on, is a biological universal (e.g., Koukouri & Malafouris 2020: 32–33). One could thus argue that most humans have the capacity to engage with more complex institutions of fictionality, and perhaps even that some animals possess some of the more basic skills necessary for the development of this capacity. Most scholars of fictionality, however, seem to assume that the creation and apprehension of fiction builds on capacities that have developed and interact in unique ways in humans. Schaeffer, for one, considers only humans to have the more complex capacities described in the previous chapter that he identifies as requisite for fiction to exist as a cultural institution (1999).

Some theorists simply assume that humanity is a necessary condition for the creation or apprehension of fiction, without explaining the grounds for that assumption. Floyd Merrell argued in 1983 that

> the conception... of fictions cannot be divorced from much of what makes us distinctly human.... [W]hat underlies the capacity to... perceive-imagine fictions is continuous with what underlies the capacity for generating paradox, or for using language vaguely, ambiguously, and metaphorically, or even for using language as an instrument of deceit.
>
> (14)

Richard Walsh describes fiction as "an integral part of a culture's discursive exploration of itself" (2007: 168–69; see also Wood 1993: xviii). Eric Hayot has argued that the concept of "world" is "tie[d]... firmly to the self-conceptualizing, self-realizing activity of the [human] species" (2012: 53; see also Dawson 2015: 92).

Writing at the beginning of the nineteenth century, Friedrich Schiller offered a somewhat more systematic argument for the connection between creative play and humanity. According to Schiller, "play and play alone... makes [a human] whole and upholds both sides of his nature at once" (1801: 105). Schiller described play as the highest expression of human being: "[M]an only plays when he is in the fullest sense of the word a human being, and he is *only fully a human being when he plays*" (107; emphasis in original). Like several more recent theorists, Schiller described this capacity in anthropological terms. "[T]he outward and visible signals of the savage's entry upon humanity," he wrote, are "the same in all races which have emerged from the slavery of the animal condition: delight in *semblance*, and a propensity to *ornamentation* and *play*" (191–93). The importance of play and semblance to humanity, for Schiller, derives from the creativity inherent in these phenomena (193) as well as from their provision of access to a world beyond the actual, the "illusion of freedom" they enable (219). For Schiller, "aesthetic phenomena [namely, love of play and delight in form and semblance] are to be regarded as the germ of rational and moral conduct" (Schiller [Wilkinson & Willoughby] 1967: 272).

Some twentieth-century accounts of the connection between fictionality and humanness are also a bit more systematic. Wolfgang Iser's theory of fictionality is avowedly anthropological and implicitly links fictionality to humanity. According to Iser, "literary fictionality" "indicates that human beings cannot be present to themselves" (1993: 86). He describes fiction as becoming, in the modern era, "the chameleon of cognition,... a sort of repair kit for conceptualization" (165), as in scientific idealization and thought experiments, as well as "an extension of human beings" that "makes it possible for them to operate beyond their limitations" (170).

Jean-Marie Schaeffer likewise aims to understand "the anthropological foundations of fiction" in his more recent account of fictionality (1999: xviii). Schaeffer identifies two genealogical models for fiction, one associated with Nietzsche and accounting for fiction as "born from the fact of the progressive weakening of the serious belief in magical incarnation," the other regarding "ludic mimetic activities" as "a basic anthropological behavior possessing a proper function that could not be filled by any other relation in the world" (30–31). Schaeffer notes that "humanity alone has secreted in a substantial manner (almost... a frenetic manner) representational devices publicly incarnated" (83–84). Ultimately, Schaeffer explains the second genealogy mentioned above in an evolutionary-psychological way. He explains,

> [T]he birth of the fictional competence is... a very important factor in the process of mastering reality.... [F]ar from being a parasitical outgrowth of a connection to the real that would be an originary given, the imaginary activity [and]... access to fictional competence [are]... important factor[s] in the establishment of a... distinction between the self and reality.
>
> (140)

Echoing Schiller, Schaeffer argues that a posture of fictional immersion—discussed using the term "transportation" in Chapter 4 of this book—"neutralizes... the direct reactional loops between an individual and reality and liberates him (momentarily) from the necessity of an adaptation in real time to the counter-reactions of 'reality'" (296–97).

Some of the points made by the theorists cited above—about, for example, the relationships between fiction and creation, improvisation, flexibility, and metacognitive activity—do seem persuasively to distinguish human from animal capacities. But they do not address the question of whether it is conceivable that a human creation, an artificial intelligence, might have or develop similar capacities.

THE IMITATION GAME AND THE TURING TEST

For many decades, debate about how comparable artificial intelligence (AI) could become to human intelligence built on Alan Turing's 1950 essay "Computing Machinery and Intelligence," published originally in the philosophical journal *Mind* (see Halpern 2006: 42). Although the term "Turing test" has entered the popular lexicon, Turing's paper actually proposed two different games: the imitation game, and a modification of that game more closely resembling what most people now understand to be the Turing test.

The imitation game, in its original form, did not involve a computer, but rather three humans. One human "interrogator" would be given the task of determining which of two other humans—shielded from view and communicating with the interrogator only via text printouts—was a woman. One of the hidden humans would be a man, and one would be a woman. The hidden man's task would be to convince the interrogator that he, the hidden man, was in fact the woman, while the hidden woman's task would be to convince the interrogator that she, the hidden woman, was the woman (Turing 1950: 433). Turing introduced this game with the proposal that the question for experimental inquiry into machine intelligence should be not whether machines can think, but whether there are "imaginable digital computers which could do well in the imitation game" (442). The game, in other words, was a component of a thought experiment designed in part to probe our intuitions about how we attribute intelligence to other entities.

Arguably, in the course of his paper, Turing turned from this rather complex setup to a simpler scenario constituting the now-canonical Turing test. This scenario involves an interrogator communicating, through text as in the imitation game, with a single conversational partner. In this scenario, the interrogator does not know whether the partner is a human or a machine. The machine passes the Turing test if the interrogator takes the machine to be a human conversational partner, or alternatively if interrogators are no more likely to identify the human as the human conversational partner than they are to identify the machine as the human conversational partner. This version of the Turing scenario became the model for the real-life Loebner competition, initiated in 1991 and continuing annually through the 2010s, in which entrants vied for a cash prize by presenting chatbot-style programs for assessment alongside human interlocutors by human interrogators (see, e.g., Zdenek 2003).

Between the publication of Turing's paper in 1950 and Hugh Loebner's launch of his competition, the Turing test changed from a thought experiment to a real-life quasi-experimental game. But Turing's paper also spawned a great deal of philosophical discussion, notably from John Searle (1980) and Ned Block (2003). Many of the most well-known of these discussions focused on pointing out logical and/or intuitive flaws in Turing's argument, often through the construction of competing thought experiments. None of this philosophical work appears to have overlapped with any work on fictionality, even though participants in the AI debate, such as Searle, were also prominent contributors to the philosophical literature on fictional semantics. This lack of overlap is a bit surprising, given Turing's own focus on linguistic behavior and his consideration of counterarguments questioning machines' ability to create, surprise, and improvise (1950: 442–54). Turing also proposed, as a construct that might satisfy his criteria for intelligence, a "learning machine" that would experientially develop the kind of semantic knowledge, or knowledge of word meanings and relationships among meanings, necessary for linguistic reference and maybe also for the kind of reference-creation involved in fiction (454–60; see also Schaeffer 1999: 75). In this way, Turing anticipated the deep-learning large-language-model breed of AI that has emerged in the twenty-first century, discussed further in the next section.

Although most of Turing's readers have focused on the simpler Turing test, some commentators have argued that it is Turing's imitation game that is most central to his argument. They note that in the 1950 essay, Turing explicitly proposed a variation on the imitation game in which a computer takes the place of the *male* interlocutor (see Sterrett 2003; Traiger 2003). Susan Sterrett observes that the imitation game in either form requires impersonation (of a woman, by the man or the computer), and that impersonation is a more complex activity than intentional action or basic communication (85). Impersonation demands more than simple conversational facility. Impersonation also requires "knowing how to use the knowledge that someone else knows how to draw conclusions," or a theory of others' intentionality, as well as "the ability to edit one's own responses" (93). Sterrett notes that these are skills that humans ordinarily use only in certain domains like "educating or persuading" or games like charades (93). On Sterrett's reading, Turing's paper—if not its prevailing interpretation—does seem to contemplate something much like the question of whether a computer could have at least some of the capacities that humans use in making and appreciating fiction.

WHAT WOULD IT TAKE FOR A NONHUMAN TO APPRECIATE FICTION?

But could a computer develop and use *all* of the capacities that humans use in making and appreciating fiction? Quite a few commentators considering this question have been skeptical about, if not downright hostile to, this possibility. But recently developed forms of AI might provide grounds for a less skeptical, if still not broadly embraced, conclusion.

Up to a point, it seems that AIs can at least *create* fiction. There is no question that some AIs have long been able to generate rudimentary narratives comprehensible as such by humans (e.g., Ryan 1991: 233–57; Bringsjord & Ferruci 2000). One of the most heralded AI approaches of the 2020s has been the advent of deep-learning large language models. These systems are "large neural net[s] that ha[ve] been trained on a titanic data set" of language examples scraped from the Internet (Johnson 2022). The large language model GPT-3 (Generative Pre-Trained Transformer 3), released by the US-based OpenAI project in early 2020, is among the most impressive of these AIs. GPT-3 is able to compose not only original and coherent essays on specific topics in response to verbal prompts, but also screenplays and short stories (Johnson 2022). Some of the output of both GPT-3 and its predecessor, GPT-2, has even been published under the fiction rubric. But these AI-generated stories are generally brief and seem to mimic a mashup of journalistic and fantastic narrative (GPT-2 2020) or first-person confessional narrative (Allado-McDowell 2020).

Some commentators are also skeptical that these AI-generated fictions really deserve the label. In a widely read 2021 paper, four AI developers argued that large language models such as GPT-3 offer only the "illusion" of intentionally and intelligently produced argument or narrative (Bender et al. 2021: 616). The developers pointed out, for example, the lack of any reason to attribute to the AI "accountability for the truth of the utterances produced" (616–17 n.2). Nevertheless, other informed observers have been willing to suppose that large language models "are already displaying some signs of emergent intelligence" (Johnson 2022).

It is difficult to determine whether GPT-3, for instance, at any point undertakes activities corresponding to those engaged in by human appreciators of fiction. We cannot tell how well the AI comprehends the language samples on which it is trained, whether it has any capacity corresponding to imagination, or whether it is capable of anything resembling the aspect-switching involved in both play and perspective-taking, or the gap-filling involved in comprehension of a linguistic narrative (see Chapters 1 and 3). Literary scholars have generally been skeptical that AIs will ever be capable of such activities. Literary scholar Andrew Piper tested the ability of earlier machine-learning systems to comprehend human-authored fiction and reported less-than-impressive results: while "[a]dult readers have little problem with the task" of "resolving pronoun and alias reference to characters," computer systems can be "trained" to perform the task only to a lesser degree of accuracy and consistency (2018: 124; see also 223 n.9). Jon Phelan has argued that AIs are unlikely ever to be able to appreciate poetry as humans do, since such appreciation involves aspect-switching as well as the appreciation of "significance," and these capacities are unlikely to be reproducible by machine intelligences (2021: 83). Phelan contends that while AIs are clearly capable of textual analysis, they are not and cannot possibly be capable of reflection and thus that observations about such matters as the significance of absent details or tone are inaccessible to them (73, 77; see also Fletcher 2021: 3).

On the other hand, large language models "have been making steady improvements, year after year, on standardized reading comprehension texts" (Johnson 2022). The basic theory behind large language models, which involves training the AI to predict the most likely word following a string of words on the basis of its digestion of language examples, might be basically analogous to "the game of predict-the-next-word… [that] children [might] unconsciously play when they are acquiring language themselves" (Johnson 2022). Jim Davies, addressing the question of whether software can exhibit imagination, has observed that "[m]any video games use procedurally generated quests, given players endless missions to accomplish without human authorship," and has noted the existence of "systems that dynamically create music…, kinetic sculpture, stories, and performance art" (2020: 164). It appears that at least some large language models are able to perform the so-called "false belief task" long used as an experimental device in developmental psychology to determine the point at which children develop an understanding that the knowledge and beliefs of others might differ from the children's own (see Wimmer & Perner 1983; Johnson 2022). If so, these AIs might be capable of some kind of aspect-switching. And although gap-filling requires experience-based "common sense" (Levesque 2017), it is not out of the question that an AI might develop such knowledge. Walter Kintsch, considering what it would take for a computer to amass the kinds of propositional knowledge held by typical adult humans, notes, "Machines cannot act and live as humans can and hence they cannot learn from experience as we do, but they can read. Therefore, they can learn from reading" (1998: 87).

This very possibility is the basic premise of Martha Wells's prize-winning *Murderbot Diaries* science-fiction series (2017, 2018). The first-person Murderbot narrator of the series is a human-machine security-officer construct that hacks its "governor module," thus becoming self-determining and immune to direct human control. Wells writes Murderbot as a kind of cyborg adolescent; much of the humorous pleasure of the novellas derives from Murderbot's cynical commentary on its difficulties, as a former slave and nonhuman, in learning how to interact with free humans. Murderbot's primary escape from these difficulties, as well as its chief learning tool, is its addiction to "entertainment media," mentioned on nearly every page of the books. Through escapist serials such as the fictional *Sanctuary Moon*, Murderbot obtains schemata for understanding standard human reactions and decision-making. Murderbot is not a pure AI, but it is not the only figure in Wells's books with such an addiction; pure AI constructs share Murderbot's fascination with human entertainment media (Wells 2018).

Of course, Murderbot is a fictional character, but Wells's idea fleshes out Kintsch's basic point at length. Wells's scenario involves more than simply Murderbot's learning from fictional narrative; Murderbot is able to tell and comment on the differences between these entertainment serials and the experiences it has with physical reality. Thus, the novellas seem to presuppose Murderbot's capacity to engage in some kind of aspect-switching. Whether or not actual AIs could develop this capacity might depend on exactly what human aspect-switching involves. As explained in Chapter 1, there is currently no consensus on this question; when we read a novel, for example, are we simultaneously aware of its fictionality and absorbed in its content? Or do we toggle or "oscillate" between these awarenesses? It is possible that answering these questions might be necessary to model aspect-switching or prompt it as an emergent capacity in an AI. How, when, and why do these parallel processes interact in humans? Is aspect-switching a capacity that emerges from a combination of other capacities? How does it interact with the imaginative elaboration of a gappy representation?

Even knowing that an AI could perform operations, such as aspect-switching or imaginative elaboration, would not necessarily be enough to let us know whether the AI could appreciate fiction more or less as humans do. We would likely have to base any such conclusion on inferences from the AI's behavior and from our communication with the AI over time—just as we have built our understanding of the human experience of fictionality from countless accounts of that experience generated by humans and converging on a number of consistent themes and topics. While much popular consideration of the potential future capacities of AI adopts a cautious or even pessimistic stance, it seems worth considering the benefits of a more open-minded attitude. An AI with fiction-appreciating capacities might also be able to win our trust in a unique way (see Wells 2018), and even to help us improve our own human understanding of fictionality.

GLOSSARY

As if the attitude characteristic of make-believe, pretend, and on some theories, the experience of audience engagement with fictional artifacts. Hans Vaihinger addressed as-if attitudes at length in his *The Philosophy of As-If* (1911). See also **Make-believe**

Common minds approach see **Exceptionality thesis**

Concretization in the literary theory of Roman Ingarden (e.g., 1968), the process of a reader's giving determinate content to a narrative text through the reader's imaginative elaboration of the linguistic content of the text. In Ingarden's account, a literary work only becomes an aesthetic object as a result of the reader's concretization of the work. See also **Situation model**

Counterfactual a hypothetical scenario relating to what has not in fact occurred, but might, could, or would occur under different conditions

Deception the intentional misleading of one person by another; saying or implying what one does not mean

Diegesis the part of a narrative artifact that describes events, as opposed to that part of the artifact that represents (usually linguistic) events more directly. See also **Mimesis**

Double consciousness (1) an experiential state that, according to many theorists of fiction, typifies the apprehension of a fictional artifact, given the need for audience members to engage with represented content but also to remain aware that the content is part of a representation. (2) A concept proposed by W.E.B. Du Bois (1903) to characterize the experience of being Black in the United States, generated by the need for Black individuals to be able to function within a dominating majority-white culture while being largely prevented from regarding themselves as full members of that culture

Eikastic image in Plato's *Sophist*, an image that resembles or corresponds to its original, or is a likeness of its original. See also **Phantastic image**

Elaboration see **Concretization; Principles of generation; Situation model**

Exceptionality thesis the position that our mindreading of other real people with whom we interact differs fundamentally from the kind of mindreading involved in apprehending a fictional narrative and seeing as a fictional character. Proponents of the exceptionality thesis reject the perhaps more widespread common-minds position, which holds that the same cognitive and emotional capacities support both our taking of the perspectives of other real people and our taking of the perspectives of fictional characters. See also **Mindreading; Quasi-emotion**

Fact a statement about the world that humans accept as truthful and accurate

Fallax fallacious representations, intending to deceive, distinguished as such by Saint Augustine in the *Soliloquies*. See also **Mendax**

Fiction derived from the Latin root *fingere*, meaning "to devise or fabricate," this English term was used as long ago as the sixteenth century to designate literary works presenting imaginary events and characters. The same noun is also still used in a broader sense to refer to the feigning or invention of imaginary existences, things, etc., for deceptive or practical purposes

Fictional world the complex state of affairs represented by a fictional artifact such as a novel, film, or even painting and experienced by an audience member as worldlike. Unlike philosophical possible worlds, fictional worlds are often characterized as incomplete, inherently perspective-dependent, and accessible in certain regards from and to the actual world. Also unlike philosophical possible worlds, fictional worlds may (but need not) contain logical contradictions or contradictory entities or states of affairs. See also **Concretization; Possible world; Principles of generation; Situation model**

Fictionalism in philosophy, the position that certain areas of thought and/or speech, such as our languages of mathematics and moral judgment, consist of utterances that are strictly speaking false but are nevertheless still relevant and appropriate

Fictionality the state or quality of presenting content that audiences may interact with and/or take as fiction

Fictitious entities in the philosophy of Jeremy Bentham (1748–1832), the referents of nouns appearing to name abstractions, such as duty, right, and force

Fictive discourse (1) in the work of Barbara Herrnstein Smith (1978), a category of discourse contrasted with natural discourse. Humans use natural discourse to accomplish particular practical ends; in contrast, fictive discourse is like "a score or stage directions for the performance of a purely verbal act that exists only in being thus performed" (30–31). (2) As defined by Richard Walsh, James Phelan, and Henrik Skov Nielsen, fictive discourse "overtly invents or imagines states of affairs in order to accomplish some purpose" (2015: 63)

Focalization in narratology, the term used by Gérard Genette (1980) to describe the mode of presentation of narrated activity or a description. Internal focalization presents narrated activity or circumstances through the perspective of a character or subject, without necessarily having that character or subject narrate the activity or the description in the first person

Free indirect discourse narrative discourse mixing elements of first- and third-person narration, including such elements as tense, deixis, pronouns, and diction

Game a structured form of play, often but not always undertaken for diversion. Most games involve goals and rules. Ludwig Wittgenstein famously argued in his *Philosophical Investigations* (1953) that activities meriting the label "game" are related to one another only through "family resemblances," not because all such activities share any core set of attributes. See also **Make-believe**

GPT-3 Generative Pre-Trained Transformer 3, a "large language model" neural net, or artificial intelligence, released by the US organization OpenAI in 2020

Grundnorm in the legal philosophy of Hans Kelsen, the fundamental norm or rule that ultimately validates all other authority-conferring rules or norms within a given legal system

Hypothesis contrasted by Hans Vaihinger with fiction. For Vaihinger, while both hypotheses and fictions are crucial to invention and discovery, fictions are not propositions to be falsified or verified; rather, fictions are known simplifications devised for the sake of analysis and calculation. Hypotheses, in contrast, are proposed in order to be tested against reality and potentially falsified

Iconic sign in the semiotic theory derived from C.S. Peirce, a sign bearing some physical or formal resemblance to what it signifies. See also **Indexical sign**; **Symbolic sign**

Imagination (1) in the view of Jean-Paul Sartre (1940), a qualitatively distinct human capacity from perception. According to Sartre, only through the imagination can we experience the realm of the "irreal." (2) In more recent cognitive science, imagination is construed as a form of intentional activity that involves many of the same capacities we engage in the experience of belief, but that is decoupled from some of the cognitive consequences of belief, such as willingness to act. Contemporary theorists do not agree on whether the appreciation of fiction engages a unique kind of imaginative activity on the part of appreciators

Imitation according to the French theorist Jean-Marie Schaffer, "the production of a relation of resemblance that did not exist in the world before the mimetic act and the existence of which is caused by this act" (1999: 69). See also **Mimesis**

Indexical sign in the semiotic theory derived from C.S. Peirce, a sign with a causal or existential connection to what it signifies. See also **Iconic sign**; **Symbolic sign**

Intentional stance the attribution to an actor of beliefs, intentions, wishes, plans, and other internal or mental states that explain and predict the actor's behavior. The term was popularized by Daniel Dennett in his book *The Intentional Stance* (1987). See also **Mindreading**

Intentionality (1) a property or state that we attribute to agents that we regard as intentional agents (2) a state involving an intentional agent's directedness toward a presentation, perception, goal, memory, or other content. States involving intentionality in this sense include the states of belief, desire, and expectation

Irreal in Jean-Paul Sartre's theory of the imaginary (1940), the dimension of experience accessible only through imagination, as in visualizing an absent friend or comprehending a fictional narrative

Law of excluded middle the classical logical principle holding that if a particular proposition is not true, then the negation of that principle must be true. In other words, any given proposition must be true or not true; there is no third possibility

Legal fictions (1) the endorsement of a factual supposition contrary to the actual facts of a legal case, in order to facilitate the application of existing law to the case, where existing law does not account for the kinds of facts actually presented in the case. Usually a judge will endorse such a contrary-to-fact supposition to achieve an equitable result in a particular case. (2) One or more of the many ways in which legal practice and discourse rely on legal practitioners' adoption of a make-believe attitude toward their own acts and words

Lie saying what one does not mean; an utterance that the speaker knows to be untrue, but that the speaker intends the audience to believe true

Ludic activity playful experiences. See **Game**; **Make-believe**; **Play**

Make-believe the practice of taking an as-if attitude toward some element of one's environment and acting in accordance with that attitude, usually but not necessarily for ludic purposes. In the theory of philosopher Kendall Walton (1990), all appreciation of mimetic artifacts involves adopting an attitude of make-believe toward these artifacts. See also **As-if**; **Prop**; **Principles of generation**

Mendax fabulous representations, not intended to deceive, distinguished as such Saint Augustine in his *Soliloquies*. See also **Fallax**

Metalepsis in narratology, the crossing of assumed ontological boundaries within a narrative, as when a character from a story interacts with the story's storyteller

Mimesis representation, presenting-as. In the *Republic*, Plato distinguishes mimesis, or authorial speech as a character, from diegesis, authorial speech narrating events from an outside perspective. See also **Diegesis**

Mindreading the attribution of specific intentional states to other agents perceived as intentional agents. See also **Intentional stance**

Model a representation that condenses the object of representation in some regard. Models tend to reconstruct the structure and/or underlying processes of the aspect of reality they represent or model. The use of models is especially widespread in modern Western science

Mutual belief principle the principle of generation proposed by Kendall Walton (1990) according to which readers extrapolate from expressly given fictional truths in a way that maximizes the similarities between fictional worlds and the real world as it is or was mutually believed to be in the author's society. See also **Principles of generation**

Myth a story that was considered true in some sense in its original context, but is understood by later audiences not to be true

Narrative a representation of causally related events, either fictional or nonfictional, generally involving intentional human or other intelligent agency. Theorists disagree about whether fictionality requires a narrative setting or may occur outside such settings, as in static images and rhetorical devices

Nonfiction literary works that are not fictional. Because the category of the fictional is in part a product of convention and mutual understandings, those works falling into the category of nonfiction will vary from place to place and time to time

Non-referring expressions linguistic expressions that purport to refer to entities, such as Pegasus or Sherlock Holmes, that do not exist. See also **Reference**

Ontology the philosophical study of the fundamental makeup and nature of being, existence, and reality

Paratextual marks such features outside a narrative proper as the presence or lack of an index, titling and subtitling, and packaging, all of which may help audience members to identify a narrative as fictional or nonfictional

Performative utterance as defined by philosopher of language J.L. Austin, a verbal utterance that does not simply communicate information, but also and at the

same time accomplishes some act, such as the christening of a ship or the pro-
nunciation of marriage vows. According to Austin, such utterances are neither
true nor false, but may be successful or unsuccessful

Phantastic image in Plato's *Sophist*, an image that is designed to appear like the original, or presents a semblance of the original. Plato contrasts the phantastic
image with the eikastic image, which Plato considered less deceptive than the
phantastic image

Play the activity of expressing physical exuberance and/or improvisation, as well as
activities relating to pretend and make-believe; according to Gregory Bateson,
play is a "phenomenon in which the actions of 'play' are related to, or denote,
other actions of 'not play,'" as in puppies' playful nips' denoting actual biting
(1972: 181). See also **Game**; **Make-believe**; **Spieltrieb**

Poetry in Aristotle's *Poetics* and later writing up through the Renaissance, literary
works not classifiable as either historical or philosophical, and including, for
example, drama, prose narratives, and perhaps other tales as well as verse
and lyric

Possible world (1) in modal philosophy and logic, a complete and consistent set
of propositions about states of affairs, analogous to the propositions that
would describe the actual world, and epistemically or doxastically accessible to
occupants of the actual world—accessible to those occupants' understanding
or belief—but causally insulated from that actual world (see Lewis 1986). (2) In
the work of some literary theorists (e.g., Ryan 1991; Ronen 1994; Doležel 1998),
the representations of states of affairs implied by fictional characters' mental
activities, such as hoping, expecting, and believing. See also **Fictional world**

Pretend (1) in the speech-act theory of fiction advanced by John Searle (1975), fictional discourse differs from normal discourse in that the author of a passage
of fictional discourse pretends to make an assertion. (2) In more recent theories of fictionality, pretend is a component of make-believe involving the non-
serious or non-committed inhabiting of a role or position. The term "pretend"
can also, however, be applied to the activity of feigning involved in such deceptive contexts as impersonation and forgery

Principles of generation in Kendall Walton's theory of representation, the often
implicit rules governing the experience of make-believe and allowing for
engagement with the make-believe scenario. See also **Mutual belief principle**;
Principle of minimal departure; **Reality principle**

Principle of minimal departure proposed by Marie-Laure Ryan (1991), this principle holds that readers construe the "central world of a textual universe" as
"conforming as far as possible to our representation of" our actual world (51).
See also **Principles of generation**; **Reality principle**

Principle of non-contradiction in Aristotle's *Metaphysics*, the principle that an object
cannot both have and not have the same attribute at the same time, for
example, that a table cannot be both blue and not blue. Early twentieth-century
philosophical explorations of the functioning of reference to fictional objects
and people attempted, with limited success, to reconcile this principle with our
everyday talk about fictional characters and events

Props in the theory of Kendall Walton (1990), items and artifacts that serve as prompts for games of make-believe. Such props can be improvised, as when children pretend a tree stump is a bear, or intentionally crafted for the purpose of serving as props, as with fictional narrative. Appreciators of aesthetic artifacts use the artifacts as props "containing a prescription or mandate in some context to imagine something" (39). See also **Make-believe**

Pseudo-factual novel a literary-historical category proposed by Nicholas Paige (2011), including novels published from around 1650 to 1800 and characterized by frame narratives or other paratextual material presenting the principal narratives as found manuscripts, memoirs, diaries, or collections of letters

Psychonarration the direct narration of character thoughts and mental states

Puzzle of imaginative resistance a phenomenon explored by, for example, philosopher Tamar Szabó Gendler (2000). While audiences seem to have little resistance to engaging with narratives based on many kinds of outlandish premises (e.g., narratives in which time travel is possible), audiences seem highly resistant to imaginative engagement with representations based on morally repugnant premises, such as the premise that killing humans for sport is a legitimate recreational activity

Quasi-emotions a kind of intentional state proposed by some theorists who hold that fictional representations do not prompt the same kind of emotional responses as real-life situations do

Reality effect a term coined by Roland Barthes in a well-known 1968 essay and referring to what Barthes called the "'futile' details" and "narrative luxury" or descriptive excess of nineteenth-century realist fiction (Barthes 1989: 141)

Reality principle the principle of generation proposed by Kendall Walton (1990) according to which fictional worlds should be as much like the actual world as possible. See **Principles of Generation**

Reference, linguistic the feature of language by which we take it to be linked to or hooked up with our experiential environment. In the common understanding of Gottlob Frege's distinction between sense and reference (1893), the reference of a term is that object the term picks out or identifies, while the sense of a term is the mode of presentation of that object

Referential turn contrasted with the better-known linguistic and narrative turns, a trend in late twentieth-century English-language literary criticism focusing on analysis of the represented content of artifacts and audience engagement with that content rather than on the structure and formal features of the artifacts

Seeing-as (1) the perception of represented content in a material representation, for example, seeing a painted canvas as a representation of a landscape. While Ludwig Wittgenstein (1953) used the term "seeing-as" to describe this phenomenon, some later theorists such as Richard Wollheim (1968) use the term "seeing-in" to describe it instead. (2) The taking of another intentional agent's perspective, whether the other agent be a real person or a represented figure or character. See also **Free indirect discourse**; **Mindreading**; **Psychonarration**

Semblance the appearance or form of something as perceived, possibly at variance with the thing's underlying nature or structure

Signposts of fictionality the formal or other markers that allow an audience member to identify a particular artifact as fictional or involving fictionality. Markers proposed by various theorists include internal focalization, psychonarration, the use of the simple past tense or preterite for narration, the nonidentity of narrator with author, and paratextual signals

Situation model a term used in the psychological study of reading comprehension to refer to an audience member's mental representation of the state of affairs described in or presented by an artifact

Spieltrieb the "play drive" posited by Friedrich Schiller in his *Aesthetic Letters* (1801). Schiller described play as driven by our "sheer plenitude of vitality" and observed even in plant life "a similar luxuriance of forces, coupled with a laxity of determination which... might well be called play" (207). Schiller regarded the play drive as fundamental to aesthetic activity

Symbolic sign in the semiotic theory derived from C.S. Peirce, a sign that stands for its signified based solely on convention, or users' habitual association of the sign with the signified. A pure symbolic sign does not have any causal connection or formal resemblance to its signifier. See also **Iconic sign**; **Indexical sign**.

Thought experiment a rhetorical device used especially in modern philosophical writing, inviting readers to imagine an invented scenario. Thought experiments often involve nonrealistic premises, incremental modifications of the premises, and comic and/or witty details. Through thought experiments, philosophers seek to win reader agreement with the philosopher's point by prompting readers' intuitive responses to the thought-experiment scenario

Transportation the experience of appreciating a fictional artifact, involving attenuation of the appreciator's awareness of the real world and an immersion in the fictional world. See also **Concretization**; **Situation model**

Truth an account of shared human experience that humans agree on as accurate

Type-token distinction the distinction between a category, or type, of object, on the one hand, and instances, or tokens, of the category, on the other. In general, any type may be instantiated or exemplified by multiple tokens. The letter "A" as a component of the Roman alphabet is a type; each appearance of an "A" or "a" in this sentence is a separate token of that type

Unities in classical dramatic theory, the precept that the represented content of a drama should be unified in action, place, and time, in order to maintain the illusion in the audience that they are witnessing real events

Unnatural narratology the study of the features and function of narratives that depart from the model of the classic mimetic narrative, for example, by representing the perspectives of nonhuman agents such as insects, animals, or inanimate objects

BIBLIOGRAPHY

Abraham, Anna (2020) 'Surveying the Imagination Landscape,' in Anna Abraham (ed) *The Cambridge Handbook of the Imagination*, Cambridge: Cambridge Univ. Press, pp. 1–10.

Agapitos, Panagiotis A. (2012) 'In Rhomaian, Frankish, and Persian Lands: Fiction and Fictionality in Byzantium and Beyond,' in Panagiotis A. Agapitos & Lars Boje Mortensen (eds) *Medieval Narratives from History to Fiction: From the Centre to the Periphery of Europe, c. 1100–1400*, Copenhagen: Museum Tusculanum/Univ. of Copenhagen, pp. 235–67.

Agapitos, Panagiotis A., & Lars Boje Mortensen (2012) 'Introduction,' in Panagiotis A. Agapitos & Lars Boje Mortensen (eds) *Medieval Narratives from History to Fiction: From the Centre to the Periphery of Europe, c. 1100–1400*, Copenhagen: Museum Tusculanum/Univ. of Copenhagen, pp. 1–24.

Alber, Jan, Stefan Iverson, Henrik Skov Nielsen, & Brian Richardson (2013) 'What Really Is Unnatural Narratology?,' *Storyworlds: A Journal of Narrative Studies*, **5**, pp. 101–18.

Alfino, Mark (1991) 'Another Look at the Derrida-Searle Debate,' *Philosophy & Rhetoric*, **24**, 2, pp. 143–52.

Allado-McDowell, K (2020) *Pharmako-AI*, London: Ignota/Ashgate.

Allen, Ernest, Jr. (2002) 'Du Boisian Double Consciousness: The Unsustainable Argument,' *The Massachusetts Review*, **43**, 2 (Summer), pp. 217–53.

Ameel, Lieven, & Marco Caracciolo (2021) 'Uncertain Ontologies in Twenty-First Century Storyworlds,' *Style*, **55**, 3, pp. 313–24.

Andersen, Sebastian Skov (2021) 'The Developers Keeping Hong Kong's Spirit Alive through Games,' *Wired*, Mar. 29.

Anderson, Graham (1984) *Ancient Fiction: The Novel in the Graeco-Roman World*, Kent: Croom Helm.

Andrews, Travis M. (2020) 'Feeling Antsy? Join the Club. Nearly 2 Million People on Facebook Are Pretending to Be Ants,' *Washington Post*, July 17.

Anscombe, Gertrude E.M. (1958) 'Pretending,' *Proceedings of the Aristotelian Society*, **13**, pp. 279–94.

Apuleius (1998) *The Golden Ass*, trans. & introd. E.J. Kenney, New York: Penguin.

Arendt, Hannah (1950) *The Origins of Totalitarianism*, 2nd ed. 1967, Boston, MA: Houghton Mifflin Harcourt.

Aristotle (1987) *The Poetics of Aristotle*, trans. & comment. Stephen Halliwell, Chapel Hill, NC: Univ. of North Carolina Press.

Armitt, Lucie (2020) *Fantasy*, London: Routledge.

Auerbach, Erich (1953) *Mimesis: The Representation of Reality in Western Literature*, trans. Willard R. Trask, Princeton, NJ: Princeton Univ. Press.

Austin, John L. (1958) 'Pretending,' *Proceedings of the Aristotelian Society*, **13**, pp. 261–78.

Austin, John L. (1961) *Philosophical Papers*, 3rd ed., Oxford & New York: Oxford Univ. Press.

Austin, John L. (1962) *How to Do Things with Words*, 2nd ed., ed. J.O. Urmson & Marina Sbisà, Cambridge: Harvard Univ. Press.

Auyoung, Elaine (2018) *When Fiction Feels Real: Representation and the Reading Mind*, Oxford & New York: Oxford Univ. Press.

Banfield, Ann (1982) *Unspeakable Sentences: Narration and Representation in the Language of Fiction*, Abingdon: Routledge & Kegan Paul.

Bareis, Alexander (2008) 'The Role of Fictionality,' in Lars-Åke Skalin (ed) *Narrativity, Fictionality, and Literariness: The Narrative Turn and the Study of Literary Fiction*, Örebro: Örebro Univ. Press, pp. 155–75.

Barthes, Roland (1989) *The Rustle of Language*, trans. Roland Howard, Berkeley, CA: Univ. of California Press.

Bateson, Gregory (1972) *Steps to an Ecology of Mind*, Chicago: Univ. of Chicago Press, 2000.

Bazin, André (1967) 'The Ontology of the Photographic Image,' in Marc Furstenau (ed) *The Film Theory Reader: Debates and Arguments*, Abingdon: Routledge, 2010, pp. 90–94.

Bearn, Gordon C.F. (1995) 'Derrida Dry: Iterating Iterability Analytically,' *Diacritics*, **25**, 3, pp. 3–25.

Beiser, Frederick (2005) *Schiller as Philosopher: A Re-Examination*, Cambridge: Cambridge Univ. Press.

Bell, Alice, & Marie-Laure Ryan (eds) (2019) *Possible Worlds Theory and Contemporary Narratology*, Lincoln, NE: Univ. of Nebraska Press.

Bender, Emily, Timnit Gebru, Angelina McMillan-Major, & Shmargaret Shmitchell (2021) 'On the Dangers of Stochastic Parrots: Can Language Models Be Too Big?,' *FAcct' 21 Virtual Event*, doi:10.1145/3442188.3445922, pp. 610–23.

Bernaerts, Lars, & Brian Richardson (2018) 'Fictional Minds: Coming to Terms with the Unnatural,' *Poetics Today*, **39**, 3, pp. 523–42.

Berndt, Jacqueline (2018) 'Anime in Academia: Representative Object, Media Form, and Japanese Studies,' *Arts*, **56**, 7, doi:10.3390/arts7040056

Berto, Francesco, & Mark Jago (2019) *Impossible Worlds*, Oxford: Oxford Univ. Press.

Blackwell, Simon E. (2020) 'Emotional Mental Imagery,' in Anna Abraham (ed) *The Cambridge Handbook of the Imagination*, Cambridge: Cambridge Univ. Press, pp. 241–57.

Block, Ned (2003) 'Psychologism and Behaviorism,' in Stuart Shieber (ed) *The Turing Test: Verbal Behavior as the Hallmark of Intelligence*, Cambridge, MA: MIT Press, pp. 229–66.

Bogdan, Radu J. (2013) *Mindvaults: Sociocultural Grounds for Pretending and Imagining*, Cambridge, MA: MIT Press.

Booth, Wayne C. (1961) *The Rhetoric of Fiction*, 2nd ed. 1983, Chicago, IL: Univ. of Chicago Press.

Bortolussi, Marisa, & Peter Dixon (2015) 'Transport: Challenges to the Metaphor,' in Lisa Zunshine (ed) *The Oxford Handbook of Cognitive Literary Studies*, Oxford & New York: Oxford Univ. Press, pp. 525–56.

Bourne, Craig, & Emily Chadwick Bourne (2016) *Time in Fiction*, Oxford & New York: Oxford Univ. Press.

Bowers, Maggie Ann (2004) *Magic(al) Realism*, Abingdon: Routledge.

Breithaupt, Fritz (2015) 'Empathetic Sadism: How Readers Get Implicated,' in Lisa Zunshine (ed) *The Oxford Handbook of Cognitive Literary Studies*, Oxford & New York: Oxford Univ. Press, pp. 440–59.

Bringsjord, Selmer, & David Ferruci (2000) *Artificial Intelligence and Literary Creativity: Inside the Mind of Brutus, a Storytelling Machine*, Mahwah, NJ: Lawrence Erlbaum.

Burke, Seán (1992) *The Death and Return of the Author: Criticism and Subjectivity in Barthes, Foucault, and Derrida*, Edinburgh: Edinburgh Univ. Press.

Busselle, Rick, & Helena Bilandzic (2008) 'Fictionality and Perceived Realism in Experiencing Stories: A Model of Narrative Comprehension and Engagement,' *Communication Theory*, **18**, pp. 255–80.

Byrne, Ruth M.J. (2005) *The Rational Imagination: How People Create Alternatives to Reality*, Cambridge, MA: MIT Press.

Byrne, Ruth M.J. (2020) 'The Counterfactual Imagination: The Impact of Alternatives to Reality on Morality,' in Anna Abraham (ed) *The Cambridge Handbook of the Imagination*, Cambridge: Cambridge Univ. Press, pp. 529–47.

Callois, Roger (1958) *Man, Play, and Games*, trans. Meyer Barash, Urbana, IL: Univ. of Illinois Press, 2001.

Carlson, Marvin (1984) *Theories of the Theatre: A Historical and Critical Survey, from the Greeks to the Present*, Ithaca, NY: Cornell Univ. Press.

Carnap, Rudolf (1955) 'Meaning and Synonymy in Natural Languages,' *Philosophical Studies*, **6**, pp. 33–47.

Carroll, Noël (2016) 'Motion Picture Narration,' in Kathryn Thomson-Jones (ed) *Current Controversies in Philosophy of Film*, Abingdon: Routledge, pp. 115–28.

Cavell, Stanley (1971) *The World Viewed: Reflections on the Ontology of Film*, Cambridge, MA: Harvard Univ. Press, enl. ed., 1979.

Cavendish, Margaret (1994) *The Blazing World and Other Writings*, ed. Kate Lilley, London: Penguin.

Chiu, Ming Ming (2019) 'Are Video Games Making Hong Kong Youths Delinquents, Loners.... or Better Protestors?,' *Hong Kong Free Press*, Sept. 15.

Cohn, Dorrit (1978) *Transparent Minds: Narrative Modes for Presenting Consciousness in Fiction*, Princeton, NJ: Princeton Univ. Press.

Cohn, Dorrit (1990) 'Signposts of Fictionality: A Narratological Perspective,' *Poetics Today*, **11**, 4, pp. 775–804.

Cohn, Dorrit (1999) *The Distinction of Fiction*, Baltimore, MD: Johns Hopkins Univ. Press.

Cooper, Davina (2020) 'Towards an Adventurous Institutional Politics: The Prefigurative "As If" and the Reposing of What's Real,' *Sociological Review*, **68**, 5, pp. 893–916.

Costa Lima, Luiz (2006) 'The Control of the Imagination and the Novel,' in Franco Moretti (ed) *The Novel: History, Geography, and Culture*, Princeton, NJ: Princeton Univ. Press, vol. 1, pp. 37–68.

Coste, Didier (1989) *Narrative as Communication*, Minneapolis, MN: Univ. of Minnesota Press.

Cresswell, Maxwell J. (1988) *Semantics Essays: Possible Worlds and Their Rivals*, Dordrecht: Kluwer.

Crittenden, Charles (1991) *Unreality: The Metaphysics of Fictional Objects*, Ithaca, NY: Cornell Univ. Press.

Culler, Jonathan (2004) 'Omniscience,' *Narrative*, **12**, 1, pp. 22–34.

Curran, Angela (2016) 'Fictional Indeterminacy, Imagined Seeing, and Cinematic Narration,' in Katherine Thomson-Jones (ed) *Current Controversies in Philosophy of Film*, Abingdon: Routledge, pp. 99–114.

Currie, Gregory (1990) *The Nature of Fiction*, Cambridge: Cambridge Univ. Press.

Currie, Gregory (1995) *Image and Mind: Film, Philosophy, and Cognitive Science*, Cambridge: Cambridge Univ. Press.

Currie, Gregory (2017) 'Afterword: Fiction as a Transcultural Entity,' in Anders Cullhed & Lena Rydholm (eds) *True Lies Worldwide: Fictionality in Global Contexts*, Berlin: De Gruyter, pp. 312–24.

Daston, Lorraine, & Peter Galison (2007) *Objectivity*, New York: Zone Books.

Davies, David (2020) 'Imagination in the Philosophy of Art,' in Anna Abraham (ed) *The Cambridge Handbook of the Imagination*, Cambridge: Cambridge Univ. Press, pp. 565–77.

Davies, Hugh (2020) 'Spatial Politics at Play: Hong Kong Protests and Videogame Activism,' Proceedings of Authors & Digital Games Research Association Australia.

Davies, Jim (2020) 'Artificial Intelligence and Imagination,' in Anna Abraham (ed) *The Cambridge Handbook of the Imagination*, Cambridge: Cambridge Univ. Press, pp. 162–71.

Davis, Lennard J. (1983) *Factual Fictions: The Origins of the English Novel*, New York: Columbia Univ. Press.

Davis, Paige E. (2020) 'Imaginary Friends: How Imaginary Minds Mimic Real Life,' in Anna Abraham (ed) *The Cambridge Handbook of the Imagination*, Cambridge: Cambridge Univ. Press, pp. 373–89.

Dawson, Paul (2015) 'Ten Theses against Fictionality,' *Narrative*, **23**, 1, pp. 74–100.

de Groot, Jerome (2009) *The Historical Novel*, Abingdon: Routledge.

de León, Concepción (2020) 'On "Oprah's Book Club," "American Dirt" Author Faces Criticism,' *New York Times*, Mar. 6.

Dennett, Daniel C. (1987) *The Intentional Stance*, Cambridge, MA: MIT Press.

Derrida, Jacques (1981) *Margins of Philosophy*, trans. Alan Bass, Chicago, IL: Univ. of Chicago Press.

Derrida, Jacques (1988) *Limited Inc.*, Evanston, IL: Northwestern Univ. Press.

Doležel, Lubomír (1998) *Heterocosmica: Fiction and Possible Worlds*, Baltimore, MD: Johns Hopkins Univ. Press.

Doody, Margaret Anne (1996) *The True Story of the Novel*, New Brunswick, NJ: Rutgers Univ. Press.

Dor, Daniel (2015) *The Instruction of Imagination: Language as a Social Communication Technology*, Oxford & New York: Oxford Univ. Press.

Du Bois, William E.B. (1986) *Writings*, New York: Library of America.

Eden, Kathy (1986) *Poetic and Legal Fiction in the Aristotelian Tradition*, Princeton, NJ: Princeton Univ. Press.

Eil, Philip (2015) 'The Unlikely Reanimation of H.P. Lovecraft,' *The Atlantic*, Aug. 20.

Eliot, Thomas S. (1920) *The Sacred Wood: Essays on Poetry and Criticism*, ed. 1997, London: Faber & Faber.

Everett, Anthony (2013) *The Nonexistent*, Oxford & New York: Oxford Univ. Press.

Farrell, Frank B. (1988) 'Iterability and Meaning: The Searle-Derrida Debate,' *Metaphilosophy*, **19**, 1, pp. 53–64.

Fenster, Mark (2008) *Conspiracy Theories: Secrecy and Power in American Culture*, rev. & updated ed. 1999, Minneapolis, MN: Univ. of Minnesota Press.

Fine, Arthur (1993) 'Fictionalism,' *Midwest Studies in Philosophy*, **18**, pp. 1–18.

Finkelburg, Margalit (2017) 'Diagnosing Fiction: From Plato to Borges,' in Anders Cullhead & Lena Rydholm (eds) *True Lies Worldwide: Fictionality in Global Contexts*, Berlin: de Gruyter, pp. 153–65.

Fletcher, Angus (2021) 'Why Computers Will Never Read (or Write) Literature: A Logical Proof and a Narrative,' *Narrative*, **29**, 1, pp. 1–28.

Fludernik, Monika (1993) *The Fictions of Language and the Languages of Fiction: The Linguistic Representation of Speech and Consciousness*, Abingdon: Routledge.

Fludernik, Monika (2015) 'Blending in Cartoons: The Production of Comedy,' in Lisa Zunshine (ed) *The Oxford Handbook of Cognitive Literary Studies*, Oxford & New York: Oxford Univ. Press, pp. 155–75.

Fludernik, Monika (2018) 'The Fiction of the Rise of Fictionality,' *Poetics Today*, **39**, 1, pp. 67–92.

Fontaine, Matthieu & Shahid Rahman (2010) 'Fiction, Creation and Fictionality: An Overview,' *Methodos: savoirs et textes, Savoirs textes langage*, doi:10.4000/methodos.2343

Frege, Gottlob (1892) 'On Sense and Reference,' in Peter Geach & Max Black (eds) *Translations from the Philosophical Works of Gottlob Frege*, trans. Max Black, Oxford: Blackwell, pp. 56–78.

Friend, Stacie (2011) 'Fiction as a Genre,' *Proceedings of the Aristotelian Society*, **112**, 2, pp. 179–209.

Frigg, Roman (2010) 'Fiction and Scientific Representation,' in Roman Frigg & Matthew C. Hunter (eds) *Beyond Mimesis and Convention*, New York: Springer, pp. 97–138.

Frow, John (2005) *Genre*, Abingdon: Routledge.

Fuentes, Juan Francisco (2013) 'Totalitarian Language: Creating Symbols to Destroy Words,' *Contributions to the History of Concepts*, **8**, 2, pp. 45–66.

Fuller, Lon L. (1930–31) *Legal Fictions*, ed. 1967, Stanford, CA: Stanford Univ. Press.

Furstenau, Marc (2010) 'Introduction,' in Marc Furstenau (ed) *The Film Theory Reader: Debates and Arguments*, Abingdon: Routledge, pp. 1–20.

Gaisser, Julia Haig (2008) *The Fortunes of Apuleius and* The Golden Ass*: A Study in Transmission and Reception*, Princeton, NJ: Princeton Univ. Press.

Galbraith, Patrick W. (2019) *Otaku and the Struggle for Imagination in Japan*, Durham, NC: Duke Univ. Press.

Gallagher, Catherine (1994) *Nobody's Story: The Vanishing Acts of Women Writers in the Marketplace, 1670–1920*, Berkeley, CA: Univ. of California Press.

Gallagher, Catherine (2006) 'The Rise of Fictionality,' in Franco Moretti (ed) *The Novel: History, Geography, and Culture*, Princeton, NJ: Princeton Univ. Press, vol. 1, pp. 336–63.

Gallagher, Catherine (2018) *Telling It Like It Wasn't: The Counterfactual Imagination in History and Fiction*, Chicago, IL: Univ. of Chicago Press.

Gaut, Berys (2010) *A Philosophy of Cinematic Art*, Cambridge: Cambridge Univ. Press.

Gavins, Joanna (2007) *Text World Theory: An Introduction*, Edinburgh: Edinburgh Univ. Press.

Gendler, Tamar Szabó (2000) 'The Puzzle of Imaginative Resistance,' *Journal of Philosophy*, **97**, 2, pp. 55–80.

Genette, Gérard (1980) *Narrative Discourse: An Essay in Method*, trans. Jane E. Lewin, Ithaca, NY: Cornell Univ. Press.

Genette, Gérard (1991) *Fiction and Diction*, trans. Catherine Porter, Ithaca, NY: Cornell Univ. Press, 1993.

Genette, Gérard (1997) *Paratexts: Thresholds of Interpretation*, trans. Jane E. Lewin, New York: Columbia Univ. Press.

Gerrig, Richard J. (1993) *Experiencing Narrative Worlds*, New Haven, CT: Yale Univ. Press.

Gibson, John (2007) *Fiction and the Weave of Life*, Oxford & New York: Oxford Univ. Press.

Gill, Christopher (1993) 'Plato on Falsehood—Not Fiction,' in Christopher Gill & Timothy P. Wiseman (eds) *Lies and Fiction in the Ancient World*, Exeter: Univ. of Exeter Press, pp. 38–87.

Gilmore, Jonathan (2020) *Apt Imaginings: Feelings for Fictions and Other Creatures of the Mind*, Oxford: Oxford Univ. Press.

Gjerlevsen, Simona Zetterberg (2016a) 'Fictionality,' *The Living Handbook of Narratology*, Apr. 5.

Gjerlevsen, Simona Zetterberg (2016b) 'A Novel History of Fictionality,' *Narrative*, **24**, 2, pp. 174–89.

Gjerlevsen, Simona Zetterberg (2019) 'Jokes, Definitions, and Historical Junctures of Fictionality,' *Style*, **53**, 4, pp. 426–30.

Glosson, Sarah (2020) *Performing Jane: A Cultural History of Jane Austen Fandom*, Baton Rouge, LA: Louisiana State Univ. Press.

Goffman, Erving (1959) *The Presentation of Self in Everyday Life*, New York: Doubleday.

Goldstein, Rebecca (2006) 'The Fiction of the Self and the Self of Fiction,' *The Massachusetts Review*, **47**, 2, pp. 293–309.

Goodman, Nelson (1978) *Ways of Worldmaking*, Indianapolis, IN: Hackett.

GPT-2 (2020) 'Extract from Language Models Are Unsupervised Multitask Learners,' in K Allado-McDowell & Ben Vickers (eds) *Atlas of Anomalous AI*, London: Ignota/Ashgate, pp. 191–92.

Green, Dennis H. (2002) *The Beginnings of Medieval Romance: Fact and Fiction, 1150–1220*, Cambridge: Cambridge Univ. Press.

Green, Melanie C. (2004) 'Transportation into Narrative Worlds: The Role of Prior Knowledge and Perceived Realism,' *Discourse Processes*, **38**, 2, pp. 247–66.

Greene, Virginie (2014) *Logical Fictions in Medieval Literature and Philosophy*, Cambridge: Cambridge Univ. Press.

Gronskaya, Natalia E., Valery G. Zusman, & Tatiana S. Batischeva (2012) 'Totalitarian Language: Reflections of Power,' in Paola B. Helszel & Artur J. Katolo (eds) *Autorità e crisi dei potesi*, Padua: Casa Editrice dott. Antonio Milani, pp. 277–89.

Halliwell, Stephen (2002) *The Aesthetics of Mimesis: Ancient Texts and Modern Problems*, Princeton, NJ: Princeton Univ. Press.

Halpern, Mark (2006) 'The Trouble with the Turing Test,' *The New Atlantis*, **11**, pp. 42–63.

Hamburger, Käte (1973) *The Logic of Literature*, trans. Marilynn J. Rose, 2nd rev. ed., Bloomington, IN: Indiana Univ. Press.

Hansen, Per Krogh, & Marianne Wolff Lundholt (2021) '"I Thought Shell Was the Bad Guy": Narrative and Fictionality in Greenpeace's Campaign against the LEGO-Shell Partnership,' *Narrative*, **29**, 1, pp. 29–46.

Harshaw (Hrushkovski), Benjamin (1984) 'Fictionality and Fields of Reference: Remarks on a Theoretical Framework,' *Poetics Today*, **5**, 2, pp. 227–51.

Hatavara, Mari & Jarmila Mildorf (2017) 'Hybrid Fictionality and Vicarious Narrative Experience,' *Narrative*, **25**, 1, pp. 65–82.

Hayot, Eric (2012) *On Fictional Worlds*, Oxford & New York: Oxford Univ. Press.

Heinrich, Joseph, Steven J. Heine, & Ara Norenzayan (2010) 'Most People Are Not WEIRD,' *Nature*, **466** (July 1), p. 29.

Hempfer, Klaus (2004) 'Some Problems Concerning a Theory of Fiction(ality),' *Style*, **38**, 3, pp. 302–24.

Henderson, Dylan (2019) '"The Inability of the Human Mind": Lovecraft, Zunshine, and Theory of Mind,' *Lovecraft Annual*, **13**, pp. 91–101.

Herman, David (2002) *Story Logic: Problems and Possibilities of Narrative*, Lincoln, NE: Univ. of Nebraska Press.

Herman, David (2011) 'Introduction,' in David Herman (ed) *Emergence of Mind: Representations of Consciousness in Narrative Discourse in English*, Lincoln, NE: Univ. of Nebraska Press, pp. 1–42.

Hester, Marcus B. (1966) 'Metaphor and Aspect Seeing,' *Journal of Aesthetics & Art Criticism*, **25**, 2, pp. 205–12.

Hofstadter, Richard (1964) *The Paranoid Style in American Politics*, New York: Vintage, 2012.

Hopkins, Robert (2016) 'Realism in Film (and Other Representations),' in Katherine Thomson-Jones (ed) *Current Controversies in Philosophy of Film*, Abingdon: Routledge, pp. 76–96.

Hylton, Peter (2010) 'Frege and Russell,' in Michael Potter & Tom Ricketts (eds) *The Cambridge Companion to Frege*, Cambridge: Cambridge Univ. Press, pp. 509–49.

Hyman, John, & Katerina Bantinaki (2021) 'Depiction,' *Stanford Encyclopedia of Philosophy* (Fall), https://plato.stanford.edu/archives/fall2021/entries/depiction

Ilie, Cornelia (1998) 'The Ideological Remapping of Semantic Roles in Totalitarian Discourse, or, How to Paint White Roses Red,' *Discourse & Society*, **9**, 1, pp. 57–80.

Ingarden, Roman (1968) *The Cognition of the Literary Work of Art*, trans. Ruth Ann Crowly & Kenneth R. Olson, 1973, Evanston, IL: Northwestern Univ. Press.

Iser, Wolfgang (1993) *The Fictive and the Imaginary: Charting Literary Anthropology*, Baltimore, MD: Johns Hopkins Univ. Press.

James, Erin (2019) 'Nonhuman Characters and the Empathy-Altruism Hypothesis,' *Poetics Today*, **40**, 3, pp. 580–96.

Jauss, Hans Robert (1982) *Toward an Aesthetic of Reception*, trans. Timothy Bahti, Minneapolis, MN: Univ. of Minnesota Press.

Jenkins, Henry (1992) *Textual Poachers: Television Fans and Participatory Culture*, Abingdon: Routledge.

Johnson, Samuel (1984) *The Major Works*, ed. Donald Greene, New York & Oxford: Oxford Univ. Press.

Johnson, Steven (2022) 'A.I. Is Using Language. Should We Trust What It Says?,' *New York Times Magazine*, Apr. 15.

Kantorowicz, Ernst (1957) *The King's Two Bodies: A Study in Medieval Political Theology*, Princeton, NJ: Princeton Univ. Press, 2016.

Keen, Suzanne (2011) 'Readers' Temperaments and Fictional Character,' *New Literary History*, **42**, 2, pp. 295–314.

Kidd, David Comer, & Emanuele Castro (2013) 'Reading Literary Fiction Improves Theory of Mind,' *Science*, **342** (Oct. 18), pp. 377–80.

Kind, Amy (2020) 'Philosophical Perspectives on Imagination in the Western World,' in Anna Abraham (ed) *The Cambridge Handbook of the Imagination*, Cambridge: Cambridge Univ. Press, pp. 64–79.

Kintsch, Walter (1998) *Comprehension: A Paradigm for Cognition*, Cambridge: Cambridge Univ. Press.

Klauk, Tobias, & Tilmann Klöppe (eds) (2014) *Fiktionalität: Ein interdisziplinäres Handbuch*, Berlin: De Gruyter.

Klemperer, Victor (1947) *The Language of the Third Reich: LTI—Lingua Tertii Imperii*, trans. Martin Brady, 2006, London: Continuum.

Koukouri, Maria Danae, & Lambros Malafouris, 'Material Imagination: An Anthropological Perspective,' in Anna Abraham (ed) *The Cambridge Handbook of the Imagination*, Cambridge: Cambridge Univ. Press, pp. 30–46.

Kremer, Michael (2010) 'Sense and Reference,' in Michael Potter & Tom Ricketts (eds) *The Cambridge Companion to Frege*, Cambridge: Cambridge Univ. Press, pp. 220–92.

Kripke, Saul A. (1972) *Naming and Necessity*, Cambridge, MA: Harvard Univ. Press.

Kukkonen, Karin, & Henrik Skov Nielsen (2018) 'Fictionality: Cognition and Exemplarity,' *Poetics Today*, **39**, 3, pp. 473–94.

Kurke, Leslie (2011) *Aesopic Conversations: Popular Tradition, Cultural Dialogue, and the Invention of Greek Prose*, Princeton, NJ: Princeton Univ. Press.

La Caze, Marguerite (2002) *The Analytic Imaginary*, Ithaca, NY: Cornell Univ. Press.

Laird, Andrew (1993) 'Fiction, Bewitchment, and Story Worlds,' in Christopher Gill & Timothy P. Wiseman (eds) *Lies and Fiction in the Ancient World*, Exeter: Univ. of Exeter Press, pp. 147–74.

Lamarque, Peter, & Stein Haugom Olsen (1994) *Truth, Fiction, and Literature: A Philosophical Perspective*, Oxford: Clarendon Press.

Lamarre, Thomas (2018) *The Anime Ecology: A Genealogy of Television, Animation, and Game Media*, Minneapolis, MN: Univ. of Minnesota Press.

Lamb, Jonathan (2011) *The Things Things Say*, Princeton, NJ: Princeton Univ. Press.

Lamb, Patricia Frazer, & Diana I. Veith (1985) 'Romantic Myth, Transcendence, and Star Trek Zines,' in Donald Palumbo (ed) *Erotic Universe: Sexuality and Fantastic Literature*, Santa Barbara, CA: Praeger, pp. 235–55.

LaValle, Victor (2016) *The Ballad of Black Tom*, New York: Tor.

Lavocat, Françoise (2016) *Fait et fiction: Pour une frontière*, Paris: Seuil.

Lea, Richard (2017) 'Fictional Characters Make "Experiential Crossings" into Real Life, Study Finds,' *The Guardian* (UK), Feb. 14.

Leonard, Andrew (2020) 'A Code-Obsessed Novelist Builds a Writing Bot. The Plot Thickens,' *Wired*, Feb. 6.

Levesque, Hector J. (2017) *Common Sense, the Turing Test, and the Quest for Real AI*, Cambridge, MA: MIT Press.

Lewis, David (1978) 'Truth in Fiction,' *American Philosophical Quarterly*, **15**, 1, pp. 37–46.

Lewis, David (1986) *On the Plurality of Worlds*, London: Blackwell.

Liao, Shen-yi, & Tamar Gendler (2020) 'Imagination,' *Stanford Encyclopedia of Philosophy*, https://plato.stanford.edu/archives/sum2020/entries/imagination

Livingston, Paisley (2021) 'History of the Ontology of Art,' *Stanford Encyclopedia of Philosophy* (Fall), https://plato.stanford.edu/archives/fall2021/entries/art-ontology-history

Lobén, Torbjörn (2017) 'Literature as a Vehicle for the Dao: Changing Perspectives of Fiction and Truth in Chinese Literature,' in Anders Cullhed & Lena Rydholm (eds) *True Lies Worldwide: Fictionality in Global Contexts*, Berlin: De Gruyter, pp. 31–49.

Lorenz, Taylor (2021) 'Birds Aren't Real, or Are They? Inside a Gen Z Conspiracy Theory,' *New York Times*, Dec. 9.

Lu, Sheldon Hsiao-Peng (1994) *From Historicity to Fictionality: The Chinese Poetics of Narrative*, Palo Alto, CA: Stanford Univ. Press.

Luetkenhaus, Holly, & Zoe Weinstein (2019) *Austentatious: The Evolving World of Jane Austen Fans*, Iowa City, IA: Univ. of Iowa Press.

Mäkelä, Maria (2019) 'Disagreeing with Fictionality? A Response to Richard Walsh in the Age of Post-Truth Politics and Careless Speech,' *Style*, **53**, 4, pp. 457–63.

Manovich, Lev (2001) 'Digital Cinema and the History of a Moving Image,' in Marc Furstenau (ed) *The Film Theory Reader: Debates and Arguments*, Abingdon: Routledge, 2010, pp. 245–54.

Mar, Raymond A., & Keith Oatley (2008) 'The Function of Fiction Is the Abstraction and Simulation of Social Experience,' *Perspectives on Psychological Science*, **3**, 3 (May), pp. 173–92.

Margolin, Uri (1991) 'Reference, Coreference, Referring, and the Dual Structure of Literary Narrative,' *Poetics Today*, **12**, 3, pp. 517–42.

Martínez-Bonati, Felíx (1960) *Fictive Discourse and the Structures of Literature: A Phenomenological Approach*, trans. Philip W. Silver, 1981, Ithaca, NY: Cornell Univ. Press.

Matravers, Derek (2014) *Fiction and Narrative*, Oxford & New York: Oxford Univ. Press.

McCormick, Peter J. (1988) *Fictions, Philosophies, and the Problems of Poetics*, Ithaca, NY: Cornell Univ. Press.

McHale, Brian (1987) *Postmodernist Fiction*, Abingdon: Routledge.

Meek, James (2020) 'Red Pill, Blue Pill,' *London Review of Books* (Oct. 22), pp. 19–23.

Mehtonen, Päiv M. (2012) 'Speak, Fiction: The Rhetorical Fabrication of Narrative in Geoffrey of Monmouth,' in Panagiotis A. Agapitos & Lars Boje Mortensen (eds) *Medieval Narratives from History to Fiction: From the Centre to the Periphery of Europe, c. 1100–1400*, Copenhagen: Museum Tusculanum/Univ. of Copenhagen, pp. 81–101.

Merrell, Floyd (1983) *Pararealities: The Nature of Our Fictions and How We Know Them*, Amsterdam: John Benjamins.

Michaelian, Kourken, Denis Perrin, & André Sant'Anna (2020) 'Continuities and Discontinuities between Imagination and Memory: The View from Philosophy,' in Anna Abraham (ed) *The Cambridge Handbook of the Imagination*, Cambridge: Cambridge Univ. Press, pp. 293–310.

Miéville, China (2009) *The City and the City*, New York: Macmillan.

Moati, Raoul (2014) *Derrida/Searle: Deconstruction and Ordinary Language*, trans. Timothy Attanucci & Maureen Chun, New York: Columbia Univ. Press.

Mohamed, Premee (2020) *Beneath the Rising*, London: Solaris.

Mohamed, Premee (2021) *A Broken Darkness*, London: Solaris.

Moles, John L. (1993) 'Truth and Untruth in Herodotus and Thucydides,' in Christopher Gill & Timothy P. Wiseman (eds) *Lies and Fiction in the Ancient World*, Exeter: Univ. of Exeter Press, pp. 88–121.

Monk, Patricia (1990) 'The Shared Universe: An Experiment in Speculative Fiction,' *Journal of the Fantastic in the Arts*, **2**, 4, pp. 7–46.

Morgan, Daniel (2006) 'Rethinking Bazin,' in Marc Furstenau (ed) *The Film Theory Reader: Debates and Arguments*, Abingdon: Routledge, 2010, pp. 104–30.

Morgan, John R. (1993) 'Make-Believe and Make Believe,' in Christopher Gill & Timothy P. Wiseman (eds) *Lies and Fiction in the Ancient World*, Exeter: Univ. of Exeter Press, pp. 175–229.

Morris, Michael (2021) *Real Likenesses: Representation in Paintings, Photographs, and Novels*, Princeton, NJ: Princeton Univ. Press.

Morris, Pam (2003) *Realism*, Abingdon: Routledge.

Mullis, Jason (2015) 'Playing Games with the Great Old Ones: Ritual, Play, and Joking within the Cthulhu Fandom,' *Journal of the Fantastic in the Arts*, **26**, 3, pp. 512–30.

Nagel, Thomas (1974) 'What Is It Like to Be a Bat?,' *Philosophical Review*, **83**, 4, pp. 435–50.

Nelson, William (1973) *Fact or Fiction: The Dilemma of the Renaissance Storyteller*, Cambridge, MA: Harvard Univ. Press.

Nichols, Shaun, & Stephen P. Stich (2003) *Mindreading: An Integrated Account of Pretence, Self-Awareness, and Understanding Other Minds*, Oxford: Oxford Univ. Press.

Nielsen, Henrik Skov (2019) 'Response to Richard Walsh,' *Style*, **53**, 4, pp. 444–50.

Nielsen, Henrik Skov, James Phelan, & Richard Walsh (2015) 'Ten Theses about Fictionality,' *Narrative*, **23**, 1, pp. 61–73.

North, Peter (2021) *Bizarre-Privileged Items in the Universe: The Logic of Likeness*, New York: Zone Books.

Ogden, Charles K. (ed) (1932) *Bentham's Theory of Fictions*, Abingdon: Kegan Paul.

Ong, Walter J., S.J. (1982) *Orality and Literacy: The Technologizing of the Word*, New York & London: Routledge.

Paige, Nicholas D. (2011) *Before Fiction: The Ancien Régime of the Novel*, Philadelphia, PA: Univ. of Pennsylvania Press.

Palmer, Alan (2004) *Fictional Minds*, Lincoln, NE: Univ. of Nebraska Press.

Papineau, David (1988) 'Mathematical Fictionalism,' *International Studies in the Philosophy of Science*, **2**, pp. 151–75.

Pavel, Thomas G. (1986) *Fictional Worlds*, Cambridge, MA: Harvard Univ. Press.

Paz, César Guarde (2012) 'Race and War in the Lovecraft Mythos,' *Lovecraft Annual*, **6**, pp. 3–35.

Petroski, Karen (2020) 'Hypothetically Speaking: How to Argue about Meaning,' in Angela Condello (ed), *New Rhetorics for Contemporary Legal Discourse*, Edinburgh: Edinburgh Univ. Press, pp. 119–38.

Phelan, James (1981) *Worlds from Words: A Theory of Language in Fiction*, Chicago, IL: Univ. of Chicago Press.

Phelan, James (2018) 'Fictionality, Audiences, and Character: A Rhetorical Alternative to Catherine Gallagher's "Rise of Fictionality,"' *Poetics Today*, **39**, 1, pp. 113–29.

Phelan, James, & Henrik Skov Nielsen (2017) 'Why There Are No One-to-One Correspondences among Fictionality, Narrative, and Techniques: A Response to Mari Hatavara and Jarmila Mildorf,' *Narrative*, **25**, 1, pp. 83–91.

Phelan, Jon (2021) '"A.I. Richards": Can Artificial Intelligence Appreciate Poetry?,' *Philosophy & Literature*, **45**, 1, pp. 71–87.

Phillips, David P. (1974) 'The Influence of Suggestion on Suicide: Substantive and Theoretical Implications of the Werther Effect,' *American Sociological Review*, **39**, 3, pp. 340–54.

Piper, Andrew (2018) *Enumerations: Data and Literary Study*, Chicago, IL: Univ. of Chicago Press.

Plantinga, Carl (2016) 'Putting Cognition in Its Place: Affect and the Experience of Narrative Film,' in Katherine Thomson-Jones (ed) *Current Controversies in Philosophy of Film*, Abingdon: Routledge, pp. 131–47.

Potolsky, Matthew (2006) *Mimesis*, Abingdon: Routledge.

Pratt, Mary Louise (1977) *Toward a Speech Act Theory of Literary Discourse*, Bloomington, IN: Indiana Univ. Press.

Priest, Graham (2005) *Towards Non-Being: The Logic and Metaphysics of Intentionality*, Cambridge: Cambridge Univ. Press.

Proudfoot, Diane (2006) 'Possible Worlds Semantics and Fiction,' *Journal of Philosophical Logic*, **35**, 1, pp. 9–40.

Quinlan, Joshua A., & Raymond A. Mar (2020) 'How Imagination Supports Narrative Experiences for Textual, Audiovisual, and Interactive Narratives,' in Anna Abraham (ed) *The Cambridge Handbook of the Imagination*, Cambridge: Cambridge Univ. Press, pp. 466–78.

Rader, Ralph W. (2011) *Fact, Fiction, and Form: Selected Essays of Ralph W. Rader*, ed. James Phelan & David H. Richter, Columbus, OH: Ohio State Univ. Press.

Rafetseder, Eva, Renate Cristi-Vargas, & Josef Perner (2010) 'Counterfactual Reasoning: Developing a Sense of "Nearest Possible World,"' *Child Development*, **81**, 1, pp. 376–89.

Raffel, Stanley (2011) 'Understanding Each Other: The Case of the Searle-Derrida Debate,' *Human Studies*, **34**, 3, pp. 277–92.

Rancière, Jacques (2017) *The Edges of Fiction*, trans. Steve Corcoran, 2019, Cambridge & Oxford: Polity.

Rawls, John (1971) *A Theory of Justice*, Cambridge, MA: Belknap Press.

Robbins, Joel, & Alan Rumsey (2008) 'Cultural and Linguistic Anthropology and the Opacity of Other Minds,' *Anthropological Quarterly*, **81**, 2, pp. 407–20.

Roberts, Adam (2006) *Science Fiction*, London: Routledge.

Roberts, Thomas J. (1972) *When Is Something Fiction?* Edwardsville, IL: Southern Illinois Univ. Press.

Rockmore, Tom (2013) *Art and Truth after Plato*, Chicago, IL: Univ. of Chicago Press.

Ronen, Ruth (1994) *Possible Worlds in Literary Theory*, Cambridge: Cambridge Univ. Press.

Routley, Richard, & Valerie Routley (1973) 'Rehabilitating Meinong's Theory of Objects,' *Revue Internationale de Philosophie*, **27**, 104–05(213), pp. 224–254.

Ruff, Matt (2016) *Lovecraft Country*, New York: Harper Perennial.

Russell, Bertrand (1905) 'On Denoting,' *Mind*, **14**, 4, pp. 479–93.

Ryan, Marie-Laure (1991) *Possible Worlds, Artificial Intelligence, and Literary Theory*, Bloomington, IN: Indiana Univ. Press.

Ryan, Marie-Laure (2015) *Narrative as Virtual Reality 2: Revisiting Immersion and Interactivity in Literature and Electronic Media*, Baltimore, MD: Johns Hopkins Univ. Press.

Rydholm, Lena (2017) 'Chinese Theories and Concepts of Fiction and the Issue of Transcultural Theories and Concepts of Fiction,' in Anders Cullhed & Lena Rydholm (eds) *True Lies Worldwide: Fictionality in Global Contexts*, Berlin: De Gruyter, pp. 1–29.

Sainsbury, Richard M. (2009) *Fiction and Fictionalism*, Abingdon: Routledge.

Saler, Michael (2012) *As If: Modern Enchantment and the Literary Prehistory of Virtual Reality*, Oxford & New York: Oxford Univ. Press.

Sartre, Jean-Paul (1940) *The Imaginary: A Phenomenological Psychology of the Imagination*, ed. 2004, Abingdon: Routledge.

Scarry, Elaine (1999) *Dreaming by the Book*, Princeton, NJ: Princeton Univ. Press.

Schachter, Daniel L., & Donna Rose Addis (2020) 'Memory and Imagination: Perspectives on Constructive Episodic Simulation,' in Anna Abraham (ed) *The Cambridge Handbook of the Imagination*, Cambridge: Cambridge Univ. Press, pp. 111–31.

Schaeffer, Jean-Marie (1999) *Why Fiction?*, trans. Dorrit Cohn, 2010, Lincoln, NE: Univ. of Nebraska Press.

Schaub, Michael (2020) 'Alexandra Duncan Withdraws Forthcoming Book,' *Kirkus Reviews*, June 27.

Schiller, Friedrich (1801) *On the Aesthetic Education of Man, In a Series of Letters*, ed. & trans. Elizabeth M. Wilkinson & L.A. Willoughby, 1967, Oxford: Clarendon Press.

Schmitt, Siegfried (1980) 'Fictionality in Literary and Non-Literary Discourse,' *Poetics*, **9**, 5, pp. 525–46.

Sconce, Jeffrey (2004) 'What If?: Charting Television's New Textual Boundaries,' in Lynn Spiegel & Jan Olsson (eds) *Television after TV: Essays on a Medium in Transition*, Durham, NC: Duke Univ. Press, pp. 93–112.

Searle, John (1975) 'The Logical Status of Fictional Discourse,' *New Literary History*, **6**, 2, pp. 319–32.

Searle, John (1977) 'Reiterating the Differences: A Reply to Derrida,' *Glyph*, **1**, pp. 198–208.

Searle, John (1980) 'Minds, Brains and Programs,' *Behavioral & Brain Sciences*, **3**, pp. 417–57.

Seligman, David R. (1976) 'Wittgenstein on Seeing Aspects and Experiencing Meanings,' *Philosophy & Phenomenological Research*, **37**, 2, pp. 205–17.

Sharpe, Christina (2016) *In the Wake: On Blackness and Being*, Durham, NC: Duke Univ. Press.

Shaw, Dan (2016) 'Mirror Neurons and Simulation Theory: A Neurophysiological Foundation for Cinematic Empathy,' in Katherine Thomson-Jones (ed) *Current Controversies in Philosophy of Film*, Abingdon: Routledge, pp. 148–62.

Sidney, Sir Philip (1966) *A Defence of Poetry*, ed. J.A. Van Dorsten, New York & Oxford: Oxford Univ. Press.

Sieber, Tobin (1993) 'The Werther Effect: The Aesthetics of Suicide,' *Mosaic*, **26**, 1, pp. 15–34.

Smith, Barbara Herrnstein (1978) *On the Margins of Discourse: The Relation of Literature to Language*, Chicago, IL: Univ. of Chicago Press.

Smith, David Woodruff (2018) 'Phenomenology,' *Stanford Encyclopedia of Philosophy*, https://plato.stanford.edu/archives/sum2018/entries/phenomenology

Smith, Janet Ferrell (1985) 'The Russell-Meinong Debate,' *Philosophy & Phenomenological Research*, **45**, 3, pp. 305–50.

Smith, Murray (2011) 'On the Twofoldness of Character,' *New Literary History*, **42** pp. 277–94.

Sohn, Stephen Hong (2014) *Racial Asymmetries: Asian American Fictional Worlds*, New York: NYU Press.

Spolsky, Ellen (2016) *The Contracts of Fiction: Cognition, Culture, Community*, Oxford & New York: Oxford Univ. Press.

Starr, Gina Gabrielle (2015) 'Theorizing Imagery, Aesthetics, and Doubly Directed States,' in Lisa Zunshine (ed) *The Oxford Handbook of Cognitive Literary Studies*, Oxford & New York: Oxford Univ. Press.

St. Aubyn, Edward (2015) *The Complete Patrick Melrose Novels*, New York: Picador.

Stecker, Robert (2013) 'Film Narration, Imaginative Seeing and Seeing-In,' *Projections*, **7**, pp. 147–54.

Stein, Robert M. (2006) *Reality Fictions: Romance, History, and Governmental Authority, 1025–1180*, South Bend, IN: Univ. of Notre Dame Press.

Sternberg, Meir (2012) 'Mimesis and Motivation: The Two Faces of Fictional Coherence,' *Poetics Today*, **33**, 3–4, pp. 329–483.

Sterrett, Susan G. (2003) 'Turing's Two Tests for Intelligence,' in James H. Moor (ed) *The Turing Test: The Elusive Standard for Artificial Intelligence*, Dordrecht: Kluwer Academic Publishers, pp. 79–97.

Stock, Kathleen (2017) *Only Imagine: Fiction, Interpretation, and Imagination*, Oxford & New York: Oxford Univ. Press.

Stuart, Michael T., Yiftach Fehige, & James Robert Brown (2018) 'Thought Experiments: State of the Art,' in Michael T. Stuart, Yiftach Fehuge, & James Robert Brown (eds) *The Routledge Companion to Thought Experiments*, Abingdon: Routledge.

Sutton-Smith, Brian (1997) *The Ambiguity of Play*, Cambridge, MA: Harvard Univ. Press.

Tambling, Jeremy (2010) *Allegory*, Abingdon: Routledge.

Tans, Olaf (2014) 'The Imaginary Foundation of Legal Systems: A Mimetic Perspective,' *Law & Literature*, **26**, 2, pp. 127–43.

Tans, Olaf (2016) 'Staging Law's Existence: Using Pretense Theory to Explain the Fiction of Legal Validity,' *Ratio Juris*, **29**, 1, pp. 136–54.

Terrone, Enrico (2021) 'The Standard of Correctness and the Ontology of Depiction,' *American Philosophical Quarterly*, **58**, 4, pp. 399–412.

Teverson, Andrew (2013) *Fairy Tale*, London: Routledge.

Thomasson, Amie (1999) *Fiction and Metaphysics*, Cambridge: Cambridge Univ. Press.

Thompson, Judith Jarvis (1971) 'A Defense of Abortion,' *Philosophy & Public Affairs*, **1**, 1, pp. 47–66.

Thomson-Jones, Katherine (2016) 'Movie Appreciation and the Digital Medium,' in Katherine Thomson-Jones (ed) *Current Controversies in Philosophy of Film*, Abingdon: Routledge, pp. 36–54

Tomasello, Michael (1999) *The Cultural Origins of Human Cognition*, Cambridge, MA: Harvard Univ. Press.

Traiger, Saul (2003) 'Making the Right Identification in the Turing Test,' in James H. Moor (ed) *The Turing Test: The Elusive Standard for Artificial Intelligence*, Dordrecht: Kluwer Academic Publishers, pp. 99–110.

Turing, Alan M. (1950) 'Computing Machinery and Intelligence,' *Mind*, **59**, 236, pp. 433–60.

Urquiza-Haas, Esmeralda, & Kurt Korschal (2015) 'The Mind Behind Anthropomorphic Thinking: Attribution of Mental States to Other Species,' *Animal Behavior*, **109** (Sept.), pp. 167–70.

Utas, Bo (2017) 'Classical Persian Literature: Fiction, Didactics or Intuitive Truth?' in Anders Cullhead & Lena Rydholm (eds) *True Lies Worldwide: Fictionality in Global Contexts*, Berlin: De Gruyter, pp. 167–77.

Vaage, Margrethe Bruun (2015) 'On the Repulsive Rapist and the Difference Between Morality in Fiction and Real Life,' in Lisa Zunshine (ed) *The Oxford Handbook of Cognitive Literary Studies*, Oxford & New York: Oxford Univ. Press, pp. 421–39.

Vaihinger, Hans (1911) *The Philosophy of 'As-If': A System of the Theoretical, Practical, and Religious Fictions of Mankind*, trans. C.K. Ogden, 1925, Eastford, CT: Martino.

vanArendonk, Kathryn (2019) 'Theorizing the Television Episode,' *Narrative*, **27**, 1, pp. 65–82.

Verbaal, Wim (2017) 'How the West Was Won by Fiction: The Appearance of Fictional Narrative and Leisurely Reading in Western Literature (11th and 12th Century),' in Anders Cullhed & Lena Rydholm (eds) *True Lies Worldwide: Fictionality in Global Contexts*, Berlin: De Gruyter, pp. 189–200.

Walker, Sheena Myong (2018) 'Empirical Study of the Application of Double-Consciousness among African-American Men,' *Journal of African American Studies*, **22**, 213 (Sept.), pp. 205–17.

Walsh, Richard (2007) *The Rhetoric of Fictionality: Narrative Theory and the Idea of Fiction*, Columbus, OH: Ohio State Univ. Press.

Walton, Kendall (1978a) 'Fearing Fictions,' *Journal of Philosophy*, **75**, 1, pp. 5–27.

Walton, Kendall (1978b) 'How Remote Are Fictional Worlds from the Real World?,' *Journal of Aesthetics & Art Criticism*, **37**, 1, pp. 11–23.

Walton, Kendall (1984) 'Transparent Pictures: On the Nature of Photographic Realism,' *Critical Inquiry*, **11**, pp. 246–77.

Walton, Kendall (1990) *Mimesis as Make-Believe: On the Foundations of the Representational Arts*, Cambridge, MA: Harvard Univ. Press.

Walton, Kendall (1994) 'Morals in Fiction and Fictional Morality,' *Proceedings of the Aristotelian Society, Supplementary Volume*, **68**, pp. 27–50.

Walton, Kendall (2002) 'Depiction, Perception, and Imagination: Responses to Richard Wollheim,' *Journal of Aesthetics & Art Criticism*, **60**, 1, pp. 27–35.

Watt, Ian (1957) *The Rise of the Novel: Studies in Defoe, Richardson, and Fielding*, London: Chatto & Windus.

Weiner, Joan (1990) *Frege in Perspective*, Ithaca, NY: Cornell Univ. Press.

Weisberg, Deena Skolnick, & Joshua Goodstein (2009) 'What Belongs in a Fictional World?,' *Journal of Cognition & Culture*, **9**, pp. 69–78.

Wellek, René, & Austin Warren (1949) *Theory of Literature*, ed. 1963, New York: Penguin.

Wells, Martha (2017) *The Murderbot Diaries: All Systems Red*, New York: Tor.

Wells, Martha (2018) *The Murderbot Diaries: Artificial Condition*, New York: Tor.

Werth, Paul (1999) *Text Worlds: Representing Conceptual Space in Discourse*, London: Longman.

Wheeler, Gregory (2013) 'Models, Models, Models,' *Metaphilosophy*, **44**, 3, pp. 293–300.

White, Hayden (1978) *Tropics of Discourse: Essays in Cultural Criticism*, Baltimore, MD: Johns Hopkins Univ. Press.

Whitmarsh, Tim (2013) *Beyond the Second Sophistic: Adventures in Greek Postclassicism*, Berkeley, CA: Univ. of California Press.

Wilkerson, Terence E. (1973) 'Seeing-As,' *Mind (New Series)*, **82**, 328, pp. 481–96.

Wilson, George M. (2016) 'Imagined Seeing and Some Varieties of Cinematic Realism,' in Katherine Thomson-Jones (ed) *Current Controversies in Philosophy of Film*, Abingdon: Routledge, pp. 57–75.

Wimmer, Heinz & Josef Perner (1983) 'Beliefs about Beliefs: Representation and Constraining Function of Wrong Beliefs in Young Children's Understanding of Deception,' *Cognition*, **13**, 1, pp. 103–28.

Wimsatt, William K., & Monroe C. Beardsley (1946) 'The Intentional Fallacy,' *The Sewanee Review*, **54**, 3, pp. 468–88.

Wittgenstein, Ludwig (1953) *Philosophical Investigations*, trans. Gertrude E.M. Anscombe, Peter M.S. Hacker, & Joachim Schulte, 4th rev. ed. 2016, Hoboken, NJ: Wiley-Blackwell.

Wollen, Peter (1972) 'The Semiology of the Cinema,' in Marc Furstenau (ed) *The Film Theory Reader: Debates and Arguments*, Abingdon: Routledge, 2010, pp. 179–85.

Wollheim, Richard (1968) *Art and Its Objects*, 2nd ed. 1980, Cambridge: Cambridge Univ. Press.

Wood, Michael (1993) 'Prologue,' in Christopher Gill & T.P. Wiseman (eds) *Lies and Fiction in the Ancient World*, Exeter: Univ. of Exeter Press, pp. xiii–xviii.

Woods, John (1975) *The Logic of Fiction: A Philosophical Sounding of Deviant Logic*, The Hague: Mouton.

Woods, John (2018) *Truth in Fiction: Rethinking Its Logic (The Istanbul Lectures)*, New York: Springer.

Yagisawa, Takashi (2020) 'Possible Objects,' *Stanford Encyclopedia of Philosophy* (Summer), https://plato.stanford.edu/archives/win2022/entries/possible-objects

Yu, Anthony C. (1997) *Rereading the Stone: Desire and the Making of Fiction in* Dream of the Red Chamber, Princeton, NJ: Princeton Univ. Press.

Zdenek, Sean (2003) 'Passing Loebner's Turing Test: A Case of Conflicting Discourse Functions,' in James H. Moor (ed) *The Turing Test: The Elusive Standard of Artificial Intelligence*, Dordrecht: Kluwer Academic Publishers, pp. 121–44.

Zeman, Adam (2020) 'Aphantasia,' in Anna Abraham (ed) *The Cambridge Handbook of the Imagination*, Cambridge: Cambridge Univ. Press, pp. 692–710.

Zittoun, Tania, Vlad Gläveanu, & Hana Hawlina (2020) 'A Sociocultural Perspective on Imagination,' in Anna Abraham (ed) *The Cambridge Handbook of the Imagination*, Cambridge: Cambridge Univ. Press, pp. 143–61.

Žižek, Slavoj (1989) *The Sublime Object of Ideology*, New York & London: Verso.

Zunshine, Lisa (2006) *Why We Read Fiction: Theory of Mind and the Novel*, Columbus, OH: Ohio State Univ. Press.

INDEX

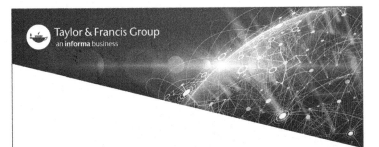

Printed in the United States
by Baker & Taylor Publisher Services